"BENDING THE FUTURE TO THEIR WILL"

"BENDING THE FUTURE TO THEIR WILL"

Civic Women, Social Education, and Democracy

Edited by
Margaret Smith Crocco
and O. L. Davis Jr.

ROWMAN & LITTLEFIELD PUBLISHERS, INC.
Lanham • Boulder • New York • Oxford

ROWMAN & LITTLEFIELD PUBLISHERS, INC.

Published in the United States of America
by Rowman & Littlefield Publishers, Inc.
4720 Boston Way, Lanham, Maryland 20706
http://www.rowmanlittlefield.com

12 Hid's Copse Road, Cumnor Hill, Oxford OX2 9JJ, England

British Library Cataloguing in Publication Information Available

Library of Congress Cataloging-in-Publication Data

"Bending the future to their will" : civic women, social education, and
    democracy / Margaret Smith Crocco, O. L. Davis, Jr., eds.
        p.   cm.
    Includes bibliographical references and index.
    ISBN 0-8476-9111-X (alk. paper). — ISBN 0-8476-9112-8 (pbk. :
alk. paper)
        1. Social sciences—Study and teaching—United States—Philosophy.
    2. Citizenship—Study and teaching—United States—Philosophy.
    3. Multicultural education—United States—Philosophy.   4. Feminism and
    education—United States.   5. Women educators—United States.
    I. Crocco, Margaret.   II. Davis, O. L. (Ozro Luke), 1928–
    LB1584.B453   1999
    70.11'5—DC21   99–14795
                                                                                CIP

Printed in the United States of America

⊖ ™ The paper used in this publication meets the minimum requirements of
American National Standard for Information Sciences—Permanence of Paper
for Printed Library Materials, ANSI/NISO Z39.48–1992.

Contents

Acknowledgments

Mary Ritter Beard's speech is reproduced here with permission of Mount Holyoke College, Archives and Special Collections, South Hadley, Massachusetts.

Margaret Smith Crocco's chapter originally appeared in a slightly modified form under the same title in *Theory and Research in Social Education* 25, no. 1 (Winter 1997): 9–33. Reprinted with permission.

Hazel Hertzberg's "The Challenge of Ethnic Studies" was first published in *Social Education* 36, no. 5 (May 1972): 469–70. Reprinted with permission of the National Council for the Social Studies.

Hilda Taba's "Curriculum Problems," in *Democratic Human Relations: Promising Practices in Intergroup and Intercultural Education in the Social Studies: Sixteenth Yearbook of the National Council for the Social Studies*, ed. Hilda Taba and William Van Til (Washington, D.C., 1945) 60, 61, 62, is reprinted here with permission of the National Council for the Social Studies.

Lucy Maynard Salmon's writings are reproduced here with permission from Vassar College Libraries, Special Collections, Poughkeepsie, New York.

Marion Thompson Wright's dissertation excerpt is reproduced here with permission from Teachers College Press, New York.

Elizabeth Anne Yeager's chapter originally appeared as "Democracy, Social Studies, and Diversity in the Elementary School Classroom: The Progressive Ideas of Alice Miel," in *Theory and Research in Social Education* 26, no. 2 (Spring 1998): 198–226. Reprinted with permission.

The title *"Bending the Future to Their Will"* is taken from an address given by Mary Beard to the biennial convention of the American Association of University Women in 1933. The address was reprinted in the *Journal of the American Association of University Women* 27, no. 1 (October 1933): 11–16. Her statement reads, "Or will American women bend the future to their will as a result of this heritage, and demonstrate an energy of brain as of body, aware of the limits to individualism as well as the shortcomings of sheer *vis inertiae?*"

1

Introduction

Margaret Smith Crocco

This book examines the lives and work of a set of women who forged a distinctive tradition of social education from the late nineteenth to the late twentieth century, one that offered an alternative set of ideas about its means and ends to those propounded by mainstream educational theorists.

In this book we use the term *social education* to suggest that education about democracy and citizenship has occurred in a variety of settings beyond the school. We take social education to mean teaching and learning about how individuals construct and live out their understandings of social, political, and economic relations—past and present—and the implications of these understandings for how citizens are educated in a democracy. In short, social education seeks to address the issue of what skills and knowledge individuals need to live effectively in a democracy, the definition of which we borrow from John Dewey, who considered democracy "a mode of associative living."[1]

By comparison with the concept of social education, *social studies* is a narrower term, one associated almost exclusively with K–12 school settings. The phrase came into currency in 1916 with the National Education Association's (NEA) Committee on Social Studies. In 1921, the National Council for the Social Studies (NCSS) was created, giving the field an institutional life that has often been taken as isomorphic with the larger phenomenon called social education. Undoubtedly, this conflation of the history of the professional organization with social education generally has occurred because NCSS has been quite effective in providing visibility for social studies and guidance to teachers of K–12 social studies. Most recently, the organization has been engaged in much publicized debates over the school curriculum with other disciplines, chiefly history and its professional organizations such as the American Historical Association.

Thus, the concept of social education includes, but is not limited to, social studies. By substituting *social education* for *social studies,* we extend the time line back beyond the NEA's formal introduction of the latter term in 1916 and consider a range of ideas about education, democracy, and citizenship that are in many cases only loosely connected to the schools. The theorizing about social education found here can be distinguished from social studies in several key respects. First, these women's ideas grew out of work not only in schools and universities but also in women's clubs, settlement houses, and activist and professional organizations. Second, several of these women developed their body of work prior to formalization of social studies as a school-based enterprise after 1916. Third, the subjects of this book, with a few exceptions, have not routinely been considered social studies theorists by authors of recent histories of NCSS.[2]

Most of the women discussed in this book have received only superficial treatment within educational history. When mentioned at all, they are portrayed as "colleagues" or "associates"—in other words, as individuals who were present at the creation of social studies but not as creative intellectuals worthy of investigation in their own right. A few have received substantive attention in dissertations, but these studies have generally considered aspects of their lives and work other than their contributions to social education. *"Bending the Future to Their Will"* is the first book to bring these subjects together to review their ideas about social education, to highlight their attention to the implications of individual and group differences for education, and to make a claim for their status as educational theorists.

Several factors explain these subjects' previous invisibility within the history of social education. First, as women, they often worked on the margins of their fields. A number of them—Bessie Louise Pierce and Mary Sheldon Barnes, for example—are virtually invisible within the educational literature. Conversely, while Jane Addams became a prominent, internationally acclaimed figure within the settlement house and peace movements, her work has not typically been identified with mainstream schooling. Furthermore, her views on education have been treated as derivative of John Dewey's. Only recently have scholars begun to explore the original contributions Addams made to Dewey's thinking about education.[3] Likewise, Lucy Sprague Mitchell has been associated with the creation of Bank Street School rather than being considered as an early social studies educator who introduced innovative ideas about geography education.

Second, some of these women's life stories fall within the interstices of other educational histories—the history of social studies as school discipline and of multicultural education. Just as the development of social studies has been treated chiefly from the vantage point of NCSS, recent retrospectives on multicultural education have focused on the groundwork laid by African American scholars and activists working within the tradition of the civil rights movement.[4] Marion Thompson Wright, an African American professor at Howard University who worked with the Association for the Study of Negro Life and History (ASNLH) as well as the National Association for the Advancement of Colored People (NAACP) during the 1940s and 1950s, has received scant attention for her efforts in promoting black history and in the celebrated Supreme Court case *Brown v. Board of Education of Topeka*. Wright's invisibility may reflect the general lack of recognition given women in published accounts of the modern civil rights movement.[5] Likewise, little has been written about the contributions of earlier scholars such as Rachel Davis DuBois and Hilda Taba to what was then called intercultural education.

Finally, the gendered nature of the social sciences and education has positioned women's contributions as low-status "practice" rather than high-status "theory." Jane Addams's legacy is identified with social work rather than sociology.[6] Vassar's administration viewed Lucy Salmon's investigation of domestic service as inappropriate for serious academic inquiry and found her support of woman suffrage unsuitable for a female professor. Mary Beard's lack of doctoral degree and academic affiliation at a time of professionalization and specialization undermined her efforts to speak authoritatively as a historian and gain recognition as a scholar separate from her husband. Some scholars credited the creative impulse behind Alice Miel's investigations into adolescence, suburbia, and education primarily to her male colleagues at Teachers College, Columbia University. Intellectual historians and cultural anthropologists recognize that it is notoriously difficult to determine with any precision the exact origins of many creative ideas and cultural innovations. Where the exchange of ideas in collaborative settings occurs regularly, as in most educational institutions, it seems suspect that women academics are consistently given so little credit as the originators of new ideas and innovative projects.

In this book, we examine a set of women whose careers reflect concerns about the mandate of citizenship education within a democracy coping with rapid social change. These women's responses to such change led them to positions that were more accommodating to individual and group difference, less conformist and assimilationist in orientation, and overall more committed to progressive educational rhetoric in action than those of many progressives, including many of the scholars who founded the field of social studies.[7]

These women were also acutely aware of the effects on their own power, authority, and influence of educational responses to social change that emphasized bureaucratization, professionalization, and hierarchy. As a result of the ascendancy of this platform, women found it increasingly difficult, especially in more established parts of the country like the Northeast, to gain the preparation necessary for leadership. In the new regime credentials rather than experience conferred authority; as women's access to those credentials was limited, their perspectives carried less weight in many academic environments, and institutions such as the normal school lost out to four-year colleges.[8] Several scholars have noted that professionalization within education accelerated in direct relation to educational institutions' perceptions that they were threatened by feminization.[9]

The subjects of *"Bending the Future to Their Will"* looked beyond the platform of standardization and bureaucratization as a blueprint for educational change, believing this approach undermined educators' ability to meet the needs of a diverse student body. Overall, their views reflect various levels of understanding of the role that personal and group differences and social and interpersonal relations play in shaping an individual's experience of education, democracy, and citizenship. Reflecting Dewey's emphasis on the child and his or her setting and needs in shaping education and anticipating what some multicultural theorists call "culturally relevant pedagogy," these women framed their educational theory in terms of the demands of contexts, educational challenges, and specific constituencies.[10]

These women varied, however, in the degree to which they embraced diversity as a pedagogical imperative. Not all of them were "enlightened" in their ideas about race, ethnicity, or even gender. Some of their views are contradictory and tinged with the paternalism so characteristic of progressives; most were silent on the subject of racism. Taken as a whole, however, their work is animated by a particularistic and pluralistic sensitivity to educational means, ends, settings, and audiences that often places them at odds with the ascendant expert knowledge of their day.

Further, the selection of subjects for *"Bending the Future to Their Will"* should not be interpreted as a claim that these women represent the universe of all possibilities nor that they can be considered prototypical of all female educators. We make no pretensions to comprehensiveness or representativeness of the sample included here. The process of inclusion in the book involved nomination by a set of scholars working within social studies of particular women whose work fit the themes of the book. Undoubtedly, we have left out significant figures whose contributions also merit consideration. The process of reclamation in women's history is an ongoing one; we trust others will pick up where this work leaves off.

We are also aware of the narrow range of racial, ethnic, and even geographic backgrounds of those discussed here. Wright is the only nonwhite woman included. Taba, who migrated to the United States in the 1920s from Estonia, is the only true immigrant found in *"Bending the Future to Their Will."* Overall, an "East Coast tilt" in the subjects' institutional affiliations exists, even though several women have roots in the Midwest and Taba spent the greater part of her teaching career at San Francisco State College. Thus, we acknowledge at the outset the limitations and biases represented by this particular collection of women educators.

We argue that the alternative tradition within social education represented by these women's legacy is shaped, at least in part, by the fact that they are women. In saying this, we need to make clear that their different emphases within social education stemmed from women's ambiguous citizenship status. We are not proposing that their views are essentially or naturally female. These women's experiences should be seen as responses to a set of concrete, historical situations shaped by a cultural ideology around gender. Their ideas and actions should be understood as efforts to challenge an order that undermined their ability to create more equitable and inclusive social and educational arrangements. Though each woman made her own accommodation or challenge to this order, their collective critique demands consideration in writing the history of social education in this country.

The specific questions this book seeks to address are: Over the late nineteenth and twentieth centuries, how have (some) women thought about their work in social education, especially, though not exclusively, in regard to citizenship, democracy, and pluralism? What forms does women's theorizing about social education take, and where does evidence exist for this theorizing? In what ways, if any, has this theorizing been different from mainstream ideas? Why might these different perspectives exist?

More broadly, our consideration of the partial nature of past representations of social studies history leads to the following questions: How have we defined social studies and identified its practitioners? How does the field look if we go beyond its institutional embodiment in NCSS and substitute the concept of social education for social studies? Have others besides white women been left out of the picture in histories of the field?

In answering these questions, it is important to note that, unlike prominent male scholars, these women typically did not write lengthy, theoretical tracts. Overall, the evidence we have for their theorizing rests on fragmentary evidence: a few longer published works but mostly short publications, several textbooks, speeches, field research projects, and the evidence that can be culled from the courses they taught, the settings in which they worked, and their political and civic engagements. In short, we find theory both in the publications and in the practice that serves as a legacy of their professional involvements.

The stories told by these women's lives suggest the fluid, contested nature of social education from its outset. Conflicts over the meaning of citizenship in a pluralistic democracy have been a central feature of our nation's history since the birth of the Republic.[11] As the primary vehicle for citizenship education, social education reflects the nation's own gendered and racialized history. Women's relation to social education has largely been a second-class one, with their contributions neither acknowledged by histories of social education nor rewarded by leadership positions in its professional organizations. Examining their views about social education from this vantage point may provide insights into the ways in which other disenfranchised individuals have interpreted citizenship education over the years.

Social Education and Gender

We start from the premise that the construction of academic disciplines has been a social and political as well as an intellectual enterprise. Few would dispute the intellectual dimension. Less widely acknowledged, until quite recently, have been the social and political contexts in which ideas take shape, get codified as disciplinary knowledge, and produce mechanisms for passing this body of knowledge on to subsequent generations. Fledgling academic disciplines gain acceptance within educational institutions through arguments advancing their status as universalistic modes of thinking about the world, significant arenas of human endeavor, and intellectual pursuits susceptible to objective analysis.

"Bending the Future to Their Will" draws on recent scholarship using the lens of gender, itself a social construction, to analyze the development of the social sciences as formalized knowledge domains.[12] From the outset, securing a place for the social sciences in universities and professional organizations has involved contests over power: the power to define, categorize, and legitimize knowledge and ways of attaining knowledge; the power to exclude related academic pursuits from association with these

disciplines; and the power to credentialize agents as authoritative spokespersons for these fields.

What we call the "Western canon," or the knowledge legitimated by schools and institutions of higher education, has been characterized by a resilient hegemony: its paradigms have been presented as universal in scope and its defenders have resisted critiques alleging their partiality in representing human experience.

American institutions of higher learning enshrined the Western canon during the "curriculum ferment" of the late nineteenth century.[13] As schools and colleges moved away from preparation of the clergy towards more secular ends, universities began to include professional preparation in law and medicine and the social and natural sciences, with an emphasis on positivistic research. Departments of economics, political science, and sociology, for example, were created during this period. In response to these innovations, university professors, educational specialists, elementary and secondary school teachers, and administrators launched a series of efforts that led to the creation of the social studies.

Peter Novick describes the transformation of history and the social sciences into the school-based field of the social studies:

> Now it was the educators who were calling the tune, and they were taking a new look at the rationale for history's dominant position. They embraced the "progressive" doctrine of education for "social efficiency." In a report issued in 1916 the National Education Association defined "the cultivation of good citizenship" as the "conscious and constant" purpose of the social studies in the schools.[14]

Shortly thereafter, the National Council for the Social Studies was established in 1921. A number of individuals central to its creation were affiliated with Teachers College, Columbia University.[15] Some of them were associated with the disciplines of history and political science, such as James Harvey Robinson and Charles Beard; others with education, such as Thomas Jesse Jones and John Dewey. While university professors were pivotal in bringing social studies to national attention, leadership passed during the 1920s to educational specialists more closely involved with the schools. Since its inception, problems over the definition of social studies as a federation rather than a fusion of academic disciplines, competing claims for the preeminence of history over the social sciences, and the domination of university faculty over school specialists have plagued the field.[16] Furthermore, social studies experts since 1921 have debated the meaning of citizenship education.[17]

Over its history, social studies came to reflect the same exclusions, partialities, and devaluations that lie at the heart of the Western canon. Gendered and racialized ways of thinking have shaped the field, despite most of its practitioners' modernist faith that the discipline rested on objective and universal foundations. Only quite recently has a systematic critique of social education from the standpoints of gender, race, and class begun to emerge.

Several examples of the kinds of problems endemic to the Western canon in history can be given. Historian Joan Kelly highlights the gendered nature of historical periodization, a fundamental strategy for making sense of the past.[18] She demonstrates that the so-called Renaissance was a time of retraction, rather than expansion, in opportunities and freedoms for women: if a "Renaissance" did exist for women, she argues, it occurred during the Middle Ages, a period in which women's rights and prerogatives were in fuller flower than in the subsequent centuries associated with the label "Renaissance." Similarly, Joan Scott has shown that rubrics such as the "Age of Democratic Revolutions" obscure the ways in which so-called progress, whether in technology, medical science, or politics, has deprived women of autonomy and a sense of community.[19] In short, historical sense-making about the past has often substituted the experiences of men for those of women, claiming its ideas as universal when they have been partial—and thus resting its conclusions about the past on the experiences of only a portion of the human race.

Across the social sciences as well as in history, women's contributions have been ignored, underestimated, or marginalized. Where women appear in the history of the disciplines at all, they typically are featured as followers rather than leaders; their work is associated with practice rather than theory; their ideas are devalued simply because they are propounded by women. Rarely are women portrayed as original thinkers.

In *"Bending the Future to Their Will,"* we argue that struggles over social education occurred within disciplinary and institutional cultures influenced by patriarchal understandings of the genders' proper roles and relationships. Thus, it is not surprising that the women whose work is featured in *"Bending the Future to Their Will"* found their sympathy for alternative and pluralistic approaches to social education suspect within a field emphasizing, as all the disciplines did, monocultural and masculinist modes masquerading as universal ways of thinking, being, and acting.

Moreover, the subjects of this book pursued their activities in social education at a time when women's capacity for such work was considered limited and resistance to women's intellectual leadership was pervasive. Intense mental pursuit was considered "unnatural" for women and at least potentially damaging to women's reproductive organs.

Women college graduates often remained unmarried because many people, male and female, believed intellectual and familial responsibilities for women to be incompatible. All women scholars found their contributions suspect, representatives of a category of persons who existed in an anomalous relation to a natural order in which women's proper sphere was the home.

Thus, women working in social education negotiated, on a daily basis and in countless ways, gendered professional terrain. *"Bending the Future to Their Will"* seeks to use the form of collective biography to explore questions related to these negotiations: What role has gender played in shaping our understandings of what constitutes the curriculum and practice of social education? How have definitions of these matters functioned to include or exclude women? Conversely, how did these women define social education? And, finally, in what ways is their work connected to contemporary concerns in the field?

Women and Citizenship

A certain irony attends the notion of women as civic educators when we recognize that women's own relationship to citizenship has been an ambiguous one. Linda Kerber notes that "Women have been citizens of the United States as long as the republic has existed. Passports were issued to them. They could be naturalized; they could claim the protection of the courts. They were subject to the laws and were obliged to pay taxes. But from the beginning American women's relationship to the state has been different in substantial and important respects from that of men."[20]

At the establishment of the nation, women were defined as dependents of fathers or husbands. While single women had a few prerogatives, married women typically could not own property, make contracts, sue or be sued, sit on juries, or vote (except in New Jersey briefly, between 1776 and 1807).[21] From the middle of the nineteenth century into the early twentieth century, when a woman married a foreigner, she sometimes lost her citizenship.[22] In the eyes of the state, a woman's legal and political status was subsumed under that of the male head of household. Thus, the married woman was labeled "feme covert." In other words, the interests of a woman and her children were "covered over" by those of the male head of household, who represented the family in the public world of law and politics.

Popular ideologies of middle-class men's and women's roles during the nation's early years promoted the notion that the private sphere of home and family was a woman's natural domain. Nevertheless, given the importance of education in undergirding a democratic republic, writers like Thomas Jefferson and Benjamin Rush advocated education for women so that they could serve as "republican mothers" and promoted the concept of free public schools to provide all citizens with the qualities of republican virtue deemed necessary for sustaining democratic institutions. A woman's contributions to democracy, however, were indirect, through moral and educational influence on her sons and through voting by her husband as the head of household.

The contradictions in American views on citizenship have been analyzed by Rogers Smith in his provocative book *Civic Ideals*. Smith finds two competing legacies: One is a tradition that has "officially defined full membership in the American civic community in terms of readiness to embrace egalitarian, liberal, republican political principles."[23] The second, less well recognized tradition has been a more exclusionary approach to American citizenship, or what Smith calls the American "civic hierarchy":

> When restrictions of voting rights, naturalization, and immigration are taken into account, it turns out that for over 80 percent of U.S. history, American laws declared most people in the world legally ineligible to become full U.S. citizens solely because of their race, original nationality, or gender. For at least two-thirds of American history, the majority of the domestic adult population was also ineligible for full citizenship for the same reasons.[24]

During the Jacksonian era, states enacted voting laws that significantly reduced the property qualifications for voting, effectively enfranchising most white men. At the same time, the franchise was denied to women and most blacks. During the mid-nineteenth century, Horace Mann, Catharine Beecher, and others promoted the notion that women's assumption of teaching positions in the growing number of state-sponsored public schools was essential to the future of the democratic republic. Not only would women bring special maternal traits to teaching but also they would accept lower wages, a fact quickly grasped by state and city governments deliberating over the expenses associated with compulsory-education legislation. As a result, the feminization of teaching accelerated throughout the nineteenth and into the twentieth century. Women were seen as suitable for teaching about citizenship education even though they were denied the chief prerogative of citizenship—the vote—in most places across the country until 1920.

Throughout the nineteenth century, married women did see progress in recognition of their property rights in many states. Allowing women to retain their property after marriage came to be seen as helpful to the development of free market and slave economies.[25] During the nineteenth century, women also became the dominant members of church congregations, essential to the churches' activities in social welfare through temperance and benevolence associations; nevertheless, control of these institutions generally remained securely in the hands of an all-male clergy.

After the Civil War, women organized at the national and state levels to demand political and legal rights. In response, both male and female antisuffragists alleged that women's independent status as citizens would undermine the home and the Republic. Some women also demanded the right to attend colleges and universities for professional preparation as doctors, lawyers, or educational administrators; however, they were often denied admission to the institutions of their choice. Again and again, it was argued that women's minds were too feeble, bodies too frail, judgment too dependent on men to give them free access to higher education, economic rights, or the franchise.

Nevertheless, as Elizabeth Cady Stanton and Susan B. Anthony regularly pointed out, women's civic obligation to pay taxes was never questioned by political leaders even as women cried "No taxation without representation." And women's reproductive capacity was deemed of sufficient importance to the nation that the Supreme Court declared in 1908 in *Muller v. Oregon* that it was within the state's interest to limit the hours that women could work: "as healthy mothers are essential to vigorous offspring, the physical well-being of woman becomes an object of public interest and care in order to preserve the strength and vigor of the race."[26]

It was only at the end of the Progressive Era that ratification of the Nineteenth Amendment in 1920 gave women the right to vote, the fullest expression of acceptance as a citizen within the body politic. This achievement came after a century of battle in which women complemented the argument for equality with men with what has been called the "argument from expediency."[27] This justification for women's suffrage emphasized women's differences from, rather than similarities to, men, suggesting that women's moral nature would improve civic life. Both implicitly and explicitly, this argument communicated the notion that the woman's vote could serve as an antidote to the influx of large numbers of immigrants into American society during the first decades of the twentieth century.

Even though women won the franchise, they remained in many respects second-class citizens. Well into the twentieth century, women could not sue abusive husbands for assault and battery, sit on juries in every state, or gain equal wages.[28] As the country finally took a first step towards acknowledging governmental responsibility for its citizens' social welfare, women found that the 1935 Social Security Act excluded all teachers, most librarians, many nurses, and social workers. According to one historian: "The drafters of the original legislation took the position that millions of working women were not really working and therefore were not entitled to Social Security benefits of their own."[29]

It is essential, therefore, for readers to keep in mind the gendered historical context as they encounter the biographies and the primary documents found in *"Bending the Future to Their Will."* The subjects of this book created distinctive approaches to citizenship education and social activism in a democracy to which they were profoundly committed, even though their own status as citizens within it was circumscribed. We must remember that in claiming authority as social educators they violated many of the fundamental axioms of the culture's gender ideology. Their assertions of expertise and intellectual leadership and challenges to established educational practices may seem pallid acts of resistance and rebellion to readers today. The authors of *"Bending the Future to Their Will"* argue, on the contrary, that only by interpreting these women's lives and legacy in a manner alert to the cultural codes at work in their worlds can we fully understand the degree to which these women resisted the impositions of patriarchal ideology and invented their own tradition, more comfortable with alternative possibilities, human particularities, and cultural pluralism.

Civic Women and Social Education

The subjects of this book were variously situated in relation to the developing field of social studies. Mary Sheldon Barnes and Lucy Salmon did most of their work prior to establishment of NCSS in 1921. Only one, Bessie Pierce, rose to a leadership role within this organization. Jane Addams, Mary Beard, and Lucy Sprague Mitchell did not identify themselves with the field of social studies at all; nevertheless, their legacy has influenced later theorists and practitioners within this area. Lucy Salmon was a historian who played a central role in the creation of the new discipline called social studies. Rachel Davis DuBois and Hilda Taba both worked in domains of intercultural education that intersected with the social studies. Alice Miel, Hazel Hertzberg, and Marion Thompson Wright all found themselves more directly connected to social studies through their ties to Teachers College, Columbia University, an institution that played a pivotal role in the establishment and development of the field.

In each of the subsequent chapters, the author analyzes the life and work of the subject, especially in terms of social education, citizenship, and pluralism. Following each discussion, a brief excerpt from the theorist's writing is included to offer a firsthand account of her views. In many of these women's lives, theorizing led to social activism, and the nature of these engagements will also be treated.

Jane Addams has been best known as the founder of Hull House, the settlement house that became her lifework. Petra Munro examines Addams's critique of liberal democracy, commitment to pacifism, and theory of education embodied by the settlement house, a holistic educational and social institution designed to address the needs of the rapidly growing immigrant population around Chicago. Addams's work has relevance to the concerns of contemporary scholars who seek more elastic understandings of educational means and ends than the traditional school generally offers and more pluralistic views of citizenship education.

During the Progressive Era, Mary Sheldon Barnes promulgated teaching methods that relied on the use of artifacts and primary sources to provide students with firsthand, more active experiences of inquiry and learning in the classroom. Frances Monteverde also discusses the influence of Barnes's father, who directed the normal school in Oswego, New York, and introduced his daughter to this "source method." Mary Sheldon Barnes developed her father's method across a variety of fields, eventually bringing these techniques into the emerging discipline of social studies through publication of a number of texts.

Mary Ritter Beard and Marion Thompson Wright both had ties to Teachers College, Columbia University. They shared connections to George Counts, Merle Curti, and John Dewey. Each of these women championed the inclusive curriculum: Beard wrote a number of works about women's history and included this subject in the textbooks she wrote jointly with her husband for the mass market. Wright worked with black teachers and academicians on the inclusion of African American history in the schools. She also served as a research associate in the *Brown* case and fought for recognition of the contributions of black women to the civil rights struggle.

O. L. Davis Jr. examines the life and work of Rachel Davis DuBois. DuBois created the Service Bureau for Education in Human Relations, later known as the Service Bureau for Intercultural Education, in New York City in 1934. At Teachers College, Columbia University, she taught the first courses in intercultural education at the university level in the United States. Under her leadership, the bureau disseminated literature about ethnic and racial groups to schools, universities, and community organizations in an effort to increase self-esteem among students of those groups.

Hazel Hertzberg is perhaps best known as a chronicler of the history of social studies educational reform. Her monograph of that title is a classic in the field. Perhaps less well known is the fact that Hertzberg was a committed activist whose work in the civil rights movement influenced her approach to social education and her understandings of citizenship. By the 1970s, however, Hertzberg found herself fundamentally shaken by the social and political convulsions of this country. Andrew Mullen analyzes Hertzberg's critique of secondary education and her refusal to identify with the women's movement.

For three decades, Alice Miel was a prominent figure in the field of social studies curriculum development for the elementary schools. Elizabeth Yeager examines Miel's advocacy of what she called "democratic social learning" that would extend beyond the formal curriculum. Because Miel developed these ideas during the Cold War and the *Sputnik* crisis, however, her proposals encountered resistance from those seeking to emphasize disciplinary content and structure. Nevertheless, her insistence on a values-based form of social learning prefigures concerns today with character education and ethical learning in the schools.

Lucy Sprague Mitchell, founder of Bank Street College of Education, is more familiar to many readers than the other subjects of this book. Mitchell produced a significant body of work about geography and history for young children. During the Great Depression, Mitchell worked for the Resettlement Administration of the federal government in West Virginia using educational approaches foreshadowing the Foxfire movement. Mitchell believed that children as well as adults should be active constructors of meaning who help re-create the society in which they live in a variety of educational settings not limited to the traditional school. Sherry Field describes her legacy.

Bessie Pierce is the only woman of this group who held a high-level position with NCSS, serving in 1926 as its first female president. Pierce, like Salmon, worked with both the American Historical Association and NCSS to consider the linkages between history, political science, and social studies for the schools. Murry Nelson notes the subtle ways in which Pierce negotiated her status as a woman to move into this leadership position in a male-dominated profession.

Lucy Maynard Salmon was the first professor of history at Vassar College, where she spent her entire career. Chara Bohan describes Salmon's study, *Domestic Service*, for Carroll D. Wright, commissioner of the federal Bureau of Labor and pioneer in the use of statistical methods in labor studies. A lifelong pacifist and suffragist, Lucy Salmon worked with a number of women's groups at the local, national, and international levels. Owing to her outspoken public opposition to World War I, Salmon fought many battles with the Vassar administration and the citizens of Pough-keepsie, New York.

Hilda Taba, like DuBois, was a strong proponent of intercultural/inter-group education. Taba understood curriculum as "the total set of experiences into which schools direct pupils," thus bringing attention to what we call today the "hidden curriculum" and its relationship to citizenship education. Jane Bernard-Powers discusses Taba's background as an immigrant to this country and her suggestion that schools serve as sites for intercultural education.

In the conclusion, Andra Makler addresses themes common to the lives of these women and points of divergence in their beliefs about social education. She connects these women's stories as well to contemporary concerns about the "hidden history" of women as creators of social studies and precursors to contemporary theorists of multicultural education. She considers the following questions: How did these women's concerns about democracy, pluralism, and education shape debate about theory and practice in the field of social education? What do these women's lives and works contribute to our understanding of democracy, pluralism, and the mandate of citizenship education? Her provocative chapter places these women's concerns squarely within the contemporary landscape of social education.

Notes

1. John Dewey, *The Public and Its Problems* (New York, 1927), 148. Benjamin Barber points out in his work *Strong Democracy: Participatory Politics for a New Age* (Berkeley, Calif., 1984) that Dewey thought of democracy in an even stronger way, as the "idea of community life itself" (119).

2. See O. L. Davis Jr., ed., *NCSS in Retrospect* (Washington, D.C., 1996); and the special issue of *Social Education* (vol. 59, no. 7 [November–December 1995]), "A History of NCSS: Seventy-Five Years of Service," edited by Ben A. Smith and J. Jesse Palmer.

3. Charlotte Haddock Seigfried, *Pragmatism and Feminism: Reweaving the Social Fabric* (Chicago, 1996); Margaret Smith Crocco, Petra Munro, and Kathleen Weiler, *Pedagogies of Resistance: Women Educator Activists, 1880–1960* (New York, 1999).

4. See, e.g., James Banks, ed., *Multicultural Education, Transformative Knowledge, and Action* (New York, 1996).

5. Vicki L. Crawford, Jacqueline Anne Rouse, and Barbara Woods, eds., *Women in the Civil Rights Movement: Trailblazers and Torchbearers, 1941–1965* (Bloomington, Ind., 1993).

6. Dorothy Ross, *The Origins of American Social Science* (New York, 1992); Helene Silverberg, *Gender and American Social Science: The Formative Years* (Princeton, N.J., 1998).

7. For a fuller treatment of progressive education's response to minorities, see esp. Paula S. Fass, *Outside In: Minorities and the Transformation of American Education* (New York, 1989).

8. Jürgen Herbst documents the demise of the normal school in *And Sadly Teach: Teacher Education and Professionalization in American Culture* (Madison, Wis., 1989). In *Destined to Rule the Schools: Women and the Superintendency, 1873–1995* (New York, 1998), Jackie M. Blount shows that, despite the impediments, many women did attain leadership positions, even the superintendency, in the first decades of the twentieth century.

9. Charlotte Haddock Seigfried makes this point in *Pragmatism and Feminism*, 70, and cites Rosalind Rosenberg, *Beyond Separate Spheres* (New Haven, Conn., 1982), 48–51.

10. Gloria Ladson-Billings, "Toward a Theory of Culturally Relevant Pedagogy," *American Educational Research Journal* 32 (Fall 1995): 465–91.

11. Smith, *Civic Ideals*; Eric Foner, *The Story of American Freedom* (New York, 1998).

12. Elizabeth Kamarch Minnich, *Transforming Knowledge* (Philadelphia, 1990); Ross, *Origins of American Social Science*; Joan Scott, ed., *Feminism and History* (New York, 1996); Silverberg, *Gender and American Social Science*.

13. Herbert Kliebard, *The Struggle for the American Curriculum, 1893–1958* (New York, 1995).

14. Peter Novick, *That Noble Dream: The "Objectivity Question" and the American Historical Profession* (New York, 1988), 188.

15. Ben A. Smith, J. Jesse Palmer, and Stephen T. Correia, "Social Studies and the Birth of NCSS, 1783–1921," Social Education 59, no. 7 (November–December 1995): 393–99.

16. Hazel Hertzberg, *Social Studies Reform, 1880–1980* (Boulder, Colo., 1981).

17. Stephen J. Thornton, "NCSS: The Early Years," in *NCSS in Retrospect*, ed. Davis, 1–9.

18. Joan Kelly, *Women, History, and Theory: The Essays of Joan Kelly* (Chicago, 1984).

19. Joan Scott, *Gender and the Politics of History* (New York, 1988).

20. Linda K. Kerber, *No Constitutional Right to Be Ladies: Women and the Obligations of Citizenship* (New York, 1998), xx.

21. Neale McGoldrick and Margaret Smith Crocco, *Reclaiming Lost Ground: The Struggle for Woman Suffrage in New Jersey* (Trenton, N.J., 1993).

22. Kerber, *No Constitutional Right*.

23. Smith, *Civic Ideals*, 15.

24. Smith, *Civic Ideals*, 15.

25. Smith, *Civic Ideals*, 230.

26. Quoted in Kerber, *No Constitutional Right*, 72.

27. Aileen Kraditor, *Ideas of the Woman Suffrage Movement, 1890–1920* (New York, 1965).

28. Smith, *Civic Ideals*, 457.

29. Kerber, *No Constitutional Right*, 73.

2

Considering the Source:
Mary Sheldon Barnes

Frances E. Monteverde

Mary Sheldon Barnes
Special Collections of Penfield Library,
State University of New York at Oswego

A frail, dark woman" who provoked lively discussions in her classes at Stanford University from 1892 to 1897,[1] Mary Downing Sheldon Barnes personified the concept of the "invisible woman" in American history.[2] Although she bequeathed a significant legacy to social studies education in the schools—that is, "source method" textbooks and instruction—her achievements have been misunderstood, unheralded, and mainly forgotten by later generations.

In the mid-1870s, she challenged traditional memorization and recitation methods by pioneering an inductive, inquiry approach for precollegiate history classes at Oswego Normal School in New York. Her three landmark texts, published in 1885, 1886, and 1891, provoked "great debate" over primary sources in secondary schools.[3]

The arguments centered on how to use primary, or original, sources. One side contended that they were supplementary, merely illustrative of preestablished conclusions about the past. They caught the student's eye and, like stage props, lent an aura of authenticity to historians' interpretations. In contrast, Mary Sheldon Barnes suggested that students use primary sources inductively as raw material to construct their own knowledge, conclusions, and interpretations of the past. Defenders of her source method believed the process of discovery was as important as, if not more important than, an accumulated body of knowledge.

Latter-day advocates of "inquiry methods" in the 1960s and 1970s could have benefited from fresh scrutiny of Sheldon Barnes's seminal works. If her position in history had been preserved, the "new social studies" movement might have avoided the setbacks experienced in the century before. Reformers of the twenty-first century might similarly benefit from this cautionary tale. Publications in the century after Sheldon Barnes's death, however, demonstrate that the traces of her life and works faded from the collective memory of social studies educators. Key records, which should have related her accomplishments, remained silent.

The purpose here is not to explore the reasons for Barnes's exclusion from the historical record but rather to demonstrate that she merits professional recognition. In the context of her times, she journeyed over an unusual path of intellectual and professional development. Her schoolbooks, while reflecting some cultural values of the period, departed sharply from typical nineteenth-century fare. She attempted to insert critical thinking into the traditional rationale for U.S. civic education.[4]

Learned Invisibility

In their introduction to *Feminisms and Critical Pedagogy* (1992), Carmen Luke and Jennifer Gore review a common predicament. Women educators "stand hip-deep in cultures saturated in phallocentric knowledges, in institutional structures ruled epistemologically and procedurally by men and masculinist signifiers, and in a discipline which despite its historical terrain as 'women's work'—a caring profession—remains [in] the theoretical and administrative custody of men." Metaphorically, Luke and Gore summarized, "We all have learned well the lesson of dutiful daughters in reciting the fathers."[5]

From her study of nineteenth-century textbooks, Ruth Elson discerned a pattern regarding women's status. To gain distinction, women either "died for love or . . . performed great deeds to help husband, parents, or children." Women merited respect but had no ambitions or interests of their own. They submerged their will to others and shunned civic affairs, careers, public speaking, and recognition. They were "regarded as inferior beings whose good [lay] in complete dependence in thought, word, and deed on men." To do otherwise would have subverted the social order.[6]

Cultural Amnesia

Situated in the second half of the nineteenth century, the tale of Mary Sheldon Barnes supports Luke and Gore's analysis, as well as Elson's conclusions. Despite Sheldon Barnes's efforts to plant history in the realm of "neutral" scientific inquiry, dissonant cultural values permeated her work, even her last major project. Starting in 1896, she helped draft and edit the *Autobiography of Edward A. Sheldon*, the history of her father, a pioneer in teacher education.[7]

Read critically, the autobiography all but ignored specific contributions of Mary Sheldon's mother. A brief examination of her father's life provides background information about Mary Sheldon and reveals some unquestioned assumptions imposed by the sociocultural values of her day. Mary's tacit worldview suggests how an invisible cultural web may have blinded her to other paradoxes in her thinking.[8]

Family Background: Unquestioned Silences

Before marrying Mary's mother, Frances A. B. Stiles, in 1849, Edward Sheldon squandered his early adult years in pipe dreams, failed ventures, debts, and broken promises.[9] Two brief passages in the autobiography credit Frances Stiles for his later turnaround.[10] At crucial turning points, however, the mother's specific counsel and activities remain undisclosed.

Frances Stiles Sheldon maintained a cheerful home and bore five children. A former teacher from a prominent Syracuse family, she probably also promoted her husband's career as an educator. Her husband gained appointments as superintendent of schools, first in 1851 in his wife's hometown, then three years later in Oswego.[11] He dictated and monitored the minutest details of curriculum, instruction, and discipline, yet he admitted that his knowledge of education was intuitive. His life had been too active to allow time to read and study or earn an undergraduate degree. Lacking formal education and knowledge, he perhaps relied on his wife's competence to set his standards for the schools.[12] The record is silent.

In 1861, when Mary was a pupil in Oswego public schools, Edward Sheldon initiated a teacher-training school that by 1865 evolved into the nationally acclaimed Oswego State Normal and Training School.[13] A colleague suggested that Edward Sheldon, a master at public relations, was overrated as an innovator.[14] In reality, perhaps Sheldon's wife developed the concept of the Oswego Normal School. The autobiography is silent. In this work, Edward Sheldon does not mention his wife or mother in the list of his "loved ones"—his home, his children, country, nature, and God. They fade into the background, shadows next to his charismatic paternalism.[15] Mary Sheldon Barnes, as editor of his autobiography, seemed to acquiesce to the blurred images of the women in his life. The dutiful daughter had learned her lesson well. Perhaps this acquiescence helps account for her failure to struggle against self-abnegation and the denial of women's causes.

"A Mind's Story": Two Ways of Science

The first of five children in the Sheldon marriage, Mary was born 15 September 1850 in Oswego.[16] In her unpublished manuscript, "A Mind's Story: The Autobiography of a College Girl," she attributed her inquisitive spirit to her mother:

> I remember just the hour when the endless wish to know awoke. . . . I stood in the little dormer window of my room, looking up and out at the clear dome of stars. . . . "The stars are all worlds, are all suns—like our world, like

our sun," said my mother softly. "All those stars?—all worlds?" And through the infinite spaces swept an infinite life . . . in an infinite longing to know the bright worlds, every one.[17]

Her awakening and persistent curiosity thereafter deviated from nine-teenth-century norms, according to Ruth Elson. "The mind of the female [was] to be filled with three subjects: home, duty to family, and religion."[18] If Frances Sheldon recognized her daughter's intellectual gifts and intended to defy the culture's expectations, her lesson endured. Years later, a friend recalled that Mary never ceased to act the role of scholar: "No one ever talked gossip in her presence. . . . Always the conversation was on ideas."[19]

If her mother elevated Mary's drive to know, then her father shaped her beliefs about learning and teaching. Mary's experiences in education up to age twenty-one, including her teacher training and early career as a novice educator, occurred in Oswego. Significantly, the ideas of Swiss educator Johann H. Pestalozzi (1746–1827) dominated the period.

Edward Sheldon introduced Pestalozzian ideas toward the end of the 1850s, when he became dissatisfied with the mechanical tone of Oswego schools. In 1859, he journeyed to Toronto, where he purchased Pestalozz-ian didactic materials for staff development.[20] Mary remembered her delight in exploring those "models, charts, objects, and methods materi-als—including bells, pictures of animals, building blocks, cocoons of silk worms, cotton balls, samples of grain and specimens of pottery and glass-ware—and publications."[21]

During school year 1859–60, Edward Sheldon conducted daily in-ser-vice sessions and Saturday workshops to inculcate Pestalozzi's "object lessons" in the district's teaching staff. With a Swiss-trained consultant, Margaret E. M. Jones, he established in 1861 a training school for local ele-mentary teachers. A model on the horizon of reform, the school soon attracted educators and "pupil-teachers" (student teachers) from other districts, states, and nations. Oswego became an American mecca for Pestalozzian pedagogy.[22] Eventually, the normal school earned Sheldon lasting recognition in U.S. educational history.[23]

Mary Sheldon finished her studies in the Oswego public schools at age sixteen. Then, from 1867 to 1869, she completed a dual program at the nor-mal school. In the interim before entering the University of Michigan in 1871, she taught in the Oswego school system. Thus, her educational life between ages ten and twenty-one was steeped in a nontraditional, Euro-pean pedagogy.[24] Pestalozzian beliefs and practices constituted one of the two pillars that sustained her intellectual and professional development.

Pestalozzian Methodology

Johann Pestalozzi's educational techniques traced their origins to the Enlightenment and the age of science. Rather than repeat meaningless abstractions from books and lectures, his pupils dealt with concrete objects from the environment. Rebelling against dogmatism, the Enlightenment had encouraged Socratic questioning and dialogue, and truth-seeking through sense perceptions rather than authorities and superstition.[25] Pestalozzi stressed the cultivation of observation, reason, and precise speech, as well as the concept of "natural" growth and development. His students actively learned through field trips, manual arts, drawing, outdoor recreation, nature walks, singing, and handicrafts.[26]

Rather than the detachment from society that Enlightenment philosopher Jean-Jacques Rousseau advocated, Pestalozzi emphasized moral education based on Christian caring and reverence for life. Pestalozzi promoted communal values and a love of humanity. He encouraged fulfilling patriotic duties to one's nation and advocated universal public education, especially for the underprivileged and destitute. He believed society could improve through proper education.[27]

"The Object Lesson"

The heart of Pestalozzianism, "the object lesson," centered on three mental functions: perception, conception, and reason. Teachers first honed the children's sensory abilities, especially the powers of discrimination and observation. They focused on ordinary objects—the concrete, the nearby, the known—then moved to the abstract, the remote, the mysterious. The five senses aroused curiosity and inspired investigation. Unquestioned assumptions about nature and culture became visible. Object lessons contrasted sharply with the string of pretentious words that nineteenth-century youngsters read, memorized, and recited from textbooks and classical literature.[28]

The second component required pupils to conceptualize what they had perceived. The teacher elicited discussion, dialogue, descriptions, comparisons, contrasts, and classifications. Pupils made sense of experiences by talking. Color, tone, size, time, weight, and patterns gained significance. Ideally, pupils initiated their own questions and interrogated their physical and social worlds in a lifelong quest for knowledge and meaning.[29]

Ultimately, object lessons sharpened reasoning, judgment, and a sense of justice. Opinions had to be grounded in "real" or tangible evidence, but

Pestalozzi hoped to create compassion as well as critical thought. Lessons with strong moral or spiritual content instilled respect for nature, awe for the divine, and faith in the goodness of creation.[30] Object lessons for both teachers and students required intellect, action, and compassion—the head, hands, and heart.[31]

Mutual affection and respect, rather than tyranny or coercion, characterized the teacher-pupil relationship. Each lesson, which had to be written, had an objective.[32] Ideally, students fashioned their own mental images rather than acquiescing to "truths" imposed by adults. Object lessons unhinged education from vague, abstract language and anchored it in the tangible, observable, moral world of natural law and science.[33]

In 1865 S. S. Greene reported that "object teaching" at Oswego conformed to Pestalozzian principles. Greene also evaluated the normal school, and despite some negative comments, he commended the overall program as sound.[34] Forged from Enlightenment philosophy, these precepts constituted one of the two main intellectual influences in Mary Sheldon's later life.

The Oswego State Normal and Training School

From 1861 to 1865, the Oswego Normal School offered only a pedagogical program in which teacher candidates earned a diploma after just one year of study. Daily, student teachers spent two to three hours on theory and three to five hours in classroom observation and practice. In 1863, when the school joined the New York State educational system, Edward Sheldon added an extensive academic component covering all the subjects that teachers were expected to teach. The levels of preparation were divided into elementary and advanced. In 1867 he added a classical program covering Greek, Latin, and German. By 1881 an additional fourth year focused on professional topics such as school law and ethics.[35]

Different from typical mid-nineteenth-century teacher education programs, Oswego required candidates to work extensively in actual classrooms. Both academic and pedagogical regimens demanded a thorough knowledge of subject matter and superior writing proficiency. Public school teachers played several roles: as models to observe, teachers of theory, and critic-mentors of teaching practice. Teacher-pupils learned to carry out all regular teacher duties.[36]

Only "mature" high school graduates gained admission to the normal school. They tended to be Caucasian women from lower- and lower-middle-class families. They adhered to a strict code of conduct: no dancing, drinking, use of slang, or rebellious behavior. School authorities urged attendance at chapel and prayer meetings. Feminist concerns received little official attention except for the efforts of Dr. Mary V. Lee, a popular professor who rejected fashions that restricted women's freedom of movement and physical comfort, including corsets, bustles, long skirts, and long hair.[37]

Oswego Normal School graduations were gala affairs. They featured teaching demonstrations, orations, and musical performances, as well as religious ceremonies and celebrations. All who completed the courses received diplomas; only the most capable obtained state teaching certificates. In demand throughout the nation, most graduates gained teaching positions immediately; however, women earned about half the men's salary, following a national pattern. Some graduates enrolled in university studies to earn bachelor's degrees, as Mary Sheldon did after two years of teaching.[38]

This era in educational history seemed to offer the promise of more active, humane, and democratic schools. Edward A. Sheldon and Frances Stiles Sheldon immersed their daughter in that world of intellectual curiosity, experimentation, concrete artifacts, dialogue, and debate. When she finished her normal school studies in 1869, at the age of nineteen, Mary Sheldon was a certified teacher with specializations in advanced training and classical studies. Later, she was disposed to follow the lure of science at the University of Michigan. Oswego's interpretation of Pestalozzian principles, which had guided her education from early adolescence, remained with her throughout her intellectual and professional life. As a friend reminisced years later, "With all her warm human interest, she had the mind of a scientist."[39]

"The New Woman" and Scientific Studies

Few women attended college in the early 1870s, according to Ruth Elson.[40] Nevertheless, Mary Sheldon and a handful of others initiated scholarly careers in a new coeducational program at the University of Michigan. As the largest land-grant institution, it attracted a stellar research faculty and prepared the majority of professors for the fledgling women's colleges on the East Coast. Many of these highly educated women became financially independent professionals, or the "New Women," a term Henry James coined for single, expatriate American women living in Europe.[41]

The New Women gave priority to their careers rather than to marriage and motherhood. Traditional in their social values, they seldom volunteered for social welfare work or suffragist causes. "Self-discipline," not "self-sacrifice," seemed to be their slogan. Although Mary Sheldon married later in life, she fit the model, as did her other Michigan colleagues, such as Mary V. Lee, Lucy M. Salmon, and Alice Freeman (Palmer).[42]

Entering the university in 1871 as a sophomore, Mary Sheldon concentrated on the natural sciences, fields considered beyond the intellectual reach of women. She also studied with historian Charles Kendall Adams, a leading proponent of the German "seminar method," or the scientific study of history.[43]

Historians in this camp relied heavily on primary sources to explain the past. Their classes resembled laboratories more than lecture halls. Also known as the "source method," the approach eventually replaced the natural sciences as Mary's passion. It became the second pillar of knowledge that sustained her intellectual and professional life. Her early classroom experiments at Michigan inspired her eventually to compose the first secondary schoolbooks featuring primary sources as suitable material for the study of history.[44]

The Source Method: Science Applied to History

American scholars, such as Mary Sheldon's Professor Adams, flocked to the universities in Germany to learn modern criticism of historical documents and artifacts. Their teaching and scholarship in the United States later reflected the German model. Leopold von Ranke (1795–1886) of the University of Berlin was the most esteemed of these "scientific historians." They believed that firsthand accounts—primary sources—took precedence over secondhand reports and "derived" narratives. Sources closest to historical events would yield the most accurate, plausible explanations of the past.[45]

At the end of *Studies in Historical Method* (1896), Mary Sheldon wrote, "I much regret that I cannot refer to some work of Ranke's on the subject of method, for Ranke is the master of us all." She cited his summary of technique: "All hangs together,—critical study of genuine sources, impartial view, objective description. The end to be aimed at is the representation of the whole truth."[46]

The German source method separated history from its poetic roots and tied it to a simple, scientific writing style, one devoid of flourishes, symbolism, and literary devices. Source-method historians reconstructed an accurate context of past events to avoid "presentist" errors, that is, judgment of the past by contemporary standards. An inductive way of knowing, the source method required an extensive collection of materials and deep analysis of documents to arrive at logical conclusions.[47]

Mary Sheldon readily accepted the source method as an epistemological tool. Similar to object lessons, it rejected memory recitation and gave priority to inquiry, discussion, and reason. The acquisition of information was secondary to the processes of construction, interpretation, and evaluation. Both the object lessons and the source method required careful observation and an inquisitive disposition; both relied on concrete, material evidence or firsthand experiences with objects and artifacts. Both object lessons and the source method urged independent thought and straightforward, unpretentious language to make sense of the past and the present.

In contrast to Pestalozzianism, the source method welcomed print materials (original documents, diaries, myths, sagas, letters, and laws) as well as relics and other artifacts. Source-method units centered around themes and topics, historical problems, and chronological periods, whereas the object lessons often stood alone, lacking cohesiveness with the rest of the curriculum.[48] Sheldon found a comfortable fit in the source method.

Shift in Commitments: Science to Sources

After earning an A.B. degree at the University of Michigan in 1874, Mary Sheldon and her friend Mary V. Lee went to work at Oswego State Normal and Training School. Sheldon taught Latin, Greek, botany, and history instead of chemistry and physics, her preferred assignments. Lee, who had earned a medical degree, taught physiology and physical education. Although Dr. Lee was thirteen years older than Mary Sheldon, they shared a room at the Sheldon home, Shady Shore, from 1874 until Sheldon left to teach at Wellesley College in late 1876.[49]

The period between 1874 and 1876 marked a turning point in Mary Sheldon's career. Her interests definitively shifted from the physical sciences to the scientific study of human history.[50] Tapping many disciplines to construct an understanding of the past, she viewed history as both an inquiry process and a body of knowledge. Prereading questions guided students' analysis of an array of primary sources: maps, diaries, drawings, speeches, tools, letters, inscriptions, myths, poetry, models, and monuments. Homework generated independent judgment, a crucial preliminary to class discussions and debate. Both teachers and learners compared their notes with other narratives and secondary sources.[51]

As evidence of her new commitment, Sheldon declined a chemistry position at Wellesley College in 1876, accepting an offer only when a history post opened later that year. At Wellesley (1876–1879) she used no textbooks and instead reproduced sets of primary source materials for seminar-sized classes.[52] A former student recalled:

[Mary Sheldon] very literally introduced the "laboratory method" into the study of history . . . [and] presented fresh, original and revivifying ways of dealing with historical material. Her references and text-books initiating this method were welcome substitutes for the incredible habit of "learning by rote" prevalent in schools at that time. Reformer, therefore, as well as pioneer, Mrs. Barnes' theory of teaching spread far beyond Wellesley's gates.[53]

Mary Sheldon Barnes synthesized the pedagogy of Johann H. Pestalozzi and the epistemology of Leopold von Ranke. The object lesson and source method drew sustenance from the same paradigmatic well, rationalist and scientific thinking. Her development of inductive methods and materials for teaching secondary school history is a watershed event in the development of U.S. education. The source method is the legacy of her practical and creative vision.

The Itinerant Scholar

Although her Wellesley students may have appreciated her work, administrative conflicts and a decline in health led to her resignation from that college in 1879. Over the next two decades, Mary Sheldon lived in at least ten different places. Despite all her wandering, the last thirteen years of her life witnessed the publication of three landmark history books—*Studies in General History* (1885), *Studies in Greek and Roman History, or Studies in General History from 1000 B.C. to 476 A.D.* (1886), and *Studies in American History* (1891)—and a methods text for teachers, *Studies in Historical Method* (1896).

To transplant inductive methods from college seminars to secondary classrooms implied faith in the intellectual potential of ordinary teachers and pupils to learn the techniques of "modern" history, that is, the source method. Her inference was warranted, for she had worked in both the public schools and teacher education. Introductory notes to her texts repeated her rationale for teaching the source method. Participatory citizenship demanded the same rigorous, inductive search for the truth. Resonating with her Pestalozzian roots, she believed education could be used to improve society.

From Wellesley to Oswego

After leaving Wellesley College in 1879, Mary Sheldon spent the next year in rest and recuperation, then from 1880 to 1882 she traveled to

Europe with her feminist colleague, Mary V. Lee. While in England, Sheldon studied with historian Sir John Seeley at Newnham College of Cambridge University.[54]

When the New Women—Mary Sheldon and Mary Lee—returned to Oswego, Lee resumed her teaching posts in physical education and physiology, while Sheldon taught history and began in earnest to draft her first text, *Studies in General History* (1885). (The first part of the book became *Studies in Greek and Roman History, or Studies in General History from 1000 B.C. to 476 A.D.* [1886], a 255-page volume designed for secondary and normal school students.)[55]

To exacerbate her problems, in 1879 her father, Edward Sheldon, suffered an attack of "nervous prostration," or severe depression. After nearly a decade of waning community support for his schools, he took a three-year leave of absence. Mary's return to Oswego perhaps was partly motivated by this turn of events. Edward Sheldon's autobiography is silent.

By 1883 Edward Sheldon had resumed his leadership and restored confidence in the normal school. Open to new teaching ideas, he accepted Herbartian theories, and after 1887 those new practices displaced the object lessons at Oswego.[56] Her father's willingness to experiment, to adjust to new knowledge, and to rebound after serious setbacks set an example that Mary Sheldon would repeat in her own life.

A Turning Point, Private and Public: 1885

Two events rendered 1885 a watershed date in Mary Sheldon's private and professional life. On 6 August she married her former student, Earl Barnes, a brilliant normal school graduate of the class of 1884. He was eleven years her junior. A month later, on 30 September, her first textbook, *Studies in General History*, was published.[57]

In recognition of her professional achievement, 1885 should be a watershed date in the history of social studies education also.[58] As late as 1896, Mary Sheldon Barnes reported that only one other author introduced primary sources into a school text. A half-century later, Robert E. Keohane, an assistant professor of social sciences at the University of Chicago, judged her first history book as one of the two "better textbooks" of the nineteenth century. In 1958, prominent social studies leaders Edgar B. Wesley and Stanley P. Wronski acknowledged Mary Sheldon Barnes's *Studies in General History* as first in their chronological list of "source method" texts.[59]

Scholars on the Move

Aligned with nineteenth-century customs, Mary Sheldon Barnes's life followed the vicissitudes of her husband's career. He held a teaching post at an academy in Hoboken, New Jersey, from 1884 to 1886. He then returned to the life of a scholar for two years, first at Cornell University, where he studied psychology and history, then at the University of Zurich, where he focused on "pedagogics." From 1889 to 1891 he taught history at Indiana University.[60]

During the same period (1885–1891), Mary Sheldon Barnes dedicated herself to research, writing, and lecturing. She collaborated with historian Andrew Dickson White, who had recently retired as Cornell's president.[61] Her overarching project during the six years was the production of *Studies in American History* (1891), a textbook designed for eighth-grade pupils. (Contrary to the book's title page, unpaginated front matter of the text shows the copyright was hers. Notably, she did not credit Earl Barnes as coauthor of the book in her *Studies in Historical Method* [1896]).[62]

In 1891, her husband, Earl, gained appointment as "Professor of the History and Art of Education at Leland Stanford Junior University."[63] As a teacher of intellectual and educational history, he employed source-method techniques, and as head of the department, he "initiated studies in child development."[64] Mary Sheldon Barnes had to wait until the following year to join the Stanford faculty.

Stanford: Teacher, Researcher, Curricularist

Appointed assistant professor in the history department, Mary Sheldon Barnes in March 1892 became Stanford's first female faculty member. Students accustomed to taking lecture notes found her "give and take discussions . . . disconcerting."[65] She taught nineteenth-century European history and a new course on "Pacific slope history." The latter featured artifacts and documents gathered from Native American settlements, early Spanish or Mexican communities, and the Anglo interlopers who had rushed into the area for gold less than fifty years before. Her collection of more than sixty items included manuscripts, maps, diaries, letters, official papers, chronologies, settlers' memoirs, interview notes, descriptions of Native American handicrafts, mimeographed bibliographies, land titles, and Native American trail maps.[66]

In addition to teaching, she assisted graduate students and teachers in research involving some 1,250 pupils in four California school districts.

She tested assumptions and assertions from her own teaching experiences and beliefs. She and her colleagues investigated such issues as the child's ability to grasp chronology and cause-effect relationships; the value of connecting history to students' interests and experiences; the development of innate curiosity; and the propensity to question, draw inferences, and require evidence. With regard to the source method, she investigated pupils' abilities to distinguish reliable sources and the best ages at which to begin the scientific study of history.[67] Essentially, she questioned the validity of beliefs and practices she had long taken for granted.

On the basis of the research, she devised a guideline for history curriculum that corresponded to three developmental phases. Before age twelve, pupils would focus on richly illustrated biographies, adventure tales, ballads, chronicles, maps, charts, and action stories, as well as vivid pictures, relics, monuments, and portraits. Students aged thirteen to fifteen or sixteen would shift from the explorers and warriors to the projects of statesmen, poets, and thinkers. This second phase required interpretations of more serious documents and literature. Reading between the lines, pupils would search "for the life and thought of the people, and for the standpoint of the narrator[s]." In the third phase, the final year in high school or the early years in college, she suggested in-depth study of one topic. Students would themselves engage in advanced collection, comparison, and criticism of sources, as well as the "most critical interpretation" of content.[68]

Her data suggested that boys and girls were capable of complex thought by age twelve or thirteen; hence, there was no reason to separate the sexes for the study of history. Nevertheless, gender bias entered her work when she recommended epic tales—adventure sagas, stories of heroism, battles, exploration—and the biographies of great men for the early grades.[69] Ruth Elson observed the nineteenth-century tendency: "Schoolbooks were designed for boys" not girls.[70] Great men set the standards. Women, for the most part, were invisible.

The Final Experiment: 1898

Despite their scholarly and teaching successes, the Barneses confronted three major misfortunes in the last decade of the century. Their companion, colleague, mentor, and professor, Mary V. Lee, died in 1892 at age fifty-five.[71] Frances Stiles Sheldon, Mary's mother, died in 1896. The following year, Edward Austin Sheldon, age seventy-four, succumbed also.[72]

In 1897 Mary and her husband resigned their posts at Stanford University; they planned to travel and write in Europe.[73] Shortly before her forty-eighth birthday, in 1898, Mary Sheldon Barnes suffered a recurrence of chronic heart disease. She agreed to a medical procedure although the doctors gave only a one-in-ten probability of success. As one who placed great faith in the tenets of science, she felt obliged to experiment. On 27 August 1898, Mary Sheldon Barnes died in a London hospital as the result of a failed operation. Following her wishes, her husband buried her ashes in the Protestant Cemetery in Rome between the plots of English poets Shelley and Keats.[74]

"Groundbreaking" Publications

Unlike writers of most nineteenth-century textbooks, Mary Sheldon Barnes designed her history books to elicit critical thinking.[75] Arranged as a series of intellectual puzzles, primary sources balanced equal amounts of explanatory narratives. The texts introduced lists of terms and sources, quotations, descriptions—advance organizers for lessons to come.[76]

Within the covers of one book, she collected a panorama of printed extracts: from sacred and secular literature, official documents, oratories, inscriptions, myths, letters, and diaries. Sources or "objects" from many disciplines—science, economics, art, government, military science, sociology, architecture—were integrated with diverse historical topics. Drawings and photographs of relics, monuments, and historic sites transplanted the past into the present. Reproductions of paintings, sculpture, tapestries, mosaics, and buildings linked aesthetics to societal concerns. Maps, charts, lists, and chronologies invoked quick recall of events. Not merely collateral or supplementary, these items served as the indispensable mortar and bricks for inductive, source-method lessons.

Sheldon Barnes's narratives and explanatory passages tended to be concise and lean, whereas the extracts from primary sources contained the rich vocabulary and details of the originals.[77] Ordinary people of various cultures came to life. In *Studies in General History*, for example, passages from Muslim culture described the cultural achievements of historic leaders, Islamic ethical concepts, and common living standards.[78] Through authentic materials, the remote and mysterious came under the learner's close scrutiny.

Critical Thought: Questions and Selections

Nineteenth-century schoolbooks, according to Elson, "made no pretense of neutrality." They avoided critical thinking, pluralism, and comparative religious topics. "Contemporary problems [were] conspicuously absent, and reform movements [were] either ignored or derided."[79]

Sheldon Barnes's books departed radically from those norms. She inserted blocks of questions—clipped, provocative, open-ended—into the selections of original sources. The queries elicited interpretation, reflection, and evaluation. She demanded proof or justification for inferences, judgments, and opinions. Extracts in *Studies in General History* (1885) exposed conflicting views from periods of tumultuous change. The accompanying questions forced students to weigh the merits of arguments, the adequacy of information, and probable causes and effects.[80]

Coverage of current events and controversies extended almost to the books' dates of publication. Sheldon Barnes reported the latest struggles of German and Italian nationalists to establish sovereignty in their territories.[81] Similarly, an updated version of *Studies in American History* (1895 ed.) briefly discussed socioeconomic and political issues confronting the nation, for example, labor relations, the influx of immigrants, Indian affairs, civil service reform, ballot reform, women's suffrage, temperance, free trade, and race relations.[82]

The "Socio-Cultural Filter"

Despite her Pestalozzian and Rankean grounding, her nineteenth-century cultural blinders limited the views presented and the questions posed.[83] She failed to examine some of her own contradictions and unquestioned assumptions, although she expected each student to exercise independent thought and judgment.[84] Her selection of materials and the phrasing of questions would have channeled student answers in predetermined directions—a form of indoctrination, albeit unintended.

Leading questions betrayed a Judeo-Christian perspective. For example, she asked, "How is their [Jewish] morality superior to that of the Assyrians?"[85] A discussion of Islam asked, "How is Christianity superior?"[86] In a nation still struggling for its cultural identity and independence from foreign intrusions, her narrow worldview and cognitive dissonances went unacknowledged and undoubtedly unrecognized as well, even by one who advocated questioning the social milieu. Her questions delimited a small area of acceptable responses, even for one who traveled abroad.

For example, excerpts from the Bible described early Christian communities in the Roman Empire.[87] Her selections supported nineteenth-century mores and values, such as modesty, submissiveness, and domesticity for women; obedience, sobriety, and loyalty for workingmen. The accompanying questions asked, "What virtues did [the Christians] insist upon?" The primary sources that she selected limited the range of possi-ble answers. The question required a tacit assumption that modesty, sub-missiveness, domesticity, obedience, loyalty, and sobriety were virtues.

A four-page extract from the Koran defined a model for women simi-lar to the Christian "virtues."[88] The guide questions asked students to find similarities and differences between Christianity and Islam and to define *"the* essential point of difference" between the two (emphasis added). If the two passages were compared, a religious grounding for women's lower station would have seemed logical, perhaps universal. Ruth Elson declared, in fact, that most nineteenth-century schoolbooks shared a com-mon religious rationale for women's low status in society.[89] A century later, feminists and labor unionists might dispute the labeling of the men-tioned traits as "virtues."

The Source Method for Citizenship

Although her textbooks seem flawed by contemporary criteria, they probably activated student thought more than most schoolbooks in the nineteenth century. The overarching question remained: "Why should students be taught to think?" Her answer: To strengthen the intellectual skills required of citizens in participatory government.[90] In *Studies in Gen-eral History* (1885), she wrote:

> We are called upon every day to judge of laws, of men, of events, of poems and stories, to decide between them, to see what they mean and where they are leading us; and since we are citizens of a republic, we must . . . decide whether these laws shall become the laws of the land, whether these poems and stories shall become popular among us and so come to mark our character, whether we shall make this man or that great and powerful among us.[91]

If people learned "to judge and interpret" what they saw in their own country, they could "make of America . . . the strongest, noblest, finest nation in all the world."[92] Such nationalistic fervor characterized U.S. schoolbooks in the nineteenth century.[93] *Studies in American History* (1891) stated: "[W]hatever else our young people will become, citizens they must be; and the citizen must constantly form judgments of the historical sort. . . . To enable [them] to do this should perhaps be the primary aim of the study of history."[94]

Sheldon Barnes's concept of citizenship related to a "higher form of patriotism" distinguished from blind love of country. Patriotism involved self-government, justice, and fair play. Her purpose was to develop the citizen's independent thought and to preserve the autonomy of the nation-state. She envisioned an undiluted "American type"—with "Aryan blood, English speech, and Christian faith," a distinct national culture.[95] The common school would play a role in guarding American "civilization" from the onslaught of foreign influences.

In contrast to this image of exclusivity, Sheldon Barnes's inclusionary passages recommended the study of immigrants and Native Americans to construct local history and to tie the nation to the wider world. Travel abroad would elevate national standards and life itself. History stretched beyond thinking skills to global concerns. The historian reached to the ancients "to understand and connect with the great peoples of the world."[96]

Her treatments of immigration and pluralism disclosed a blurred, paradoxical set of beliefs. "Immigration after immigration [had] but added to this dominant [American] race excellences derived from long-tested European types, thus producing already a distinct Americo-Saxon."[97] To allay fears of a "cosmopolitan hodge podge," she described "a symposium of highly developed nations, each bringing its own gifts of nature and art." Humanity was a unit, she affirmed. In harmony with natural and social law, the force would propel humankind "toward ends of goodness and happiness by means of conscious human action."[98]

She justified nationalism and patriotism as ingredients for self-governance. As was common in textbooks of that era, hers described inherent national characteristics—a distinct American type.[99] To preserve a strong country, she cautioned, American "blood, speech, and faith" should not mix with "Oriental and African." She referred to the "hated" or "outlandish" foreigners and glorified the "Americo-Saxon race."[100] A century later, her paradoxical remarks perplex and dismay the reader. Was she narrow-minded and ethnocentric or a critical, complex pluralist?

Stuart A. McAninch acknowledged Mary Sheldon Barnes's contributions then criticized her as naive, uninformed, simplistic, unrealistic.[101] He concluded that, under the guise of inquiry methodology, she inculcated her own version of religious, political, and economic truths. She unwittingly restricted or channeled students away from questioning her underlying premises and assumptions. Her questions and choice of materials did not enable students to understand, investigate, or change the realities of pressing social issues. In an extreme accusation, McAninch condemned the Barneses for "legitimating" the racism and classism rampant at the end of the nineteenth century.[102] His critique is flawed by presentist errors; he applies concepts and insights developed over the past century from the social sciences, most of which were embryonic disciplines in the late 1800s.

The conundrum persists, nevertheless. How could she advocate intellectual open-mindedness and a disposition to question yet fail to subject her own contradictions and assumptions to interrogation and healthy debate?

Sheldon Barnes's fear of intrusion by "foreign" powers prevented her from seeing her contradictions.[103] Just as cultural webs blinded her from "seeing" the "invisible women" in her father's history, the ideology of her intellectual and social milieu circumscribed her view of multiple perspectives in society. Foreigners' histories warranted preservation as contributions to the greatness of the whole nation; they merited exclusion as outlandish and unadaptable if they threatened American self-determination.

Earlier commentaries notwithstanding, the last excerpt of the 1903 edition of *Studies in American History* exemplified her source-method approach. After positive and negative reports about both Irish and Chinese immigrants, the text quotes Hannibal Hamlin from an 1894 U.S. Senate report:

> I believe in principles coeval with the foundation of government, that this country is the "home of the free," where the outcast of every nation, where the child of every creed and of every clime could breathe our free air and participate in our free institutions.[104]

She asks the students what can be done to change immigrants into Americans, to trace their own family heritages, and to define what makes an American. Other texts did not raise such questions nor offer a variety of perspectives; they simply told the student what to believe and do.

Sheldon Barnes never intended to make historians of school pupils, as some critics alleged. She acknowledged that source-method lessons required extra instructional time, teachers educated in "scientific" history methods, and abundant artifacts and documents. She never insisted upon primary sources to the exclusion of narrative texts nor claimed to create a final, definitive account of the past. As with science, conclusions in history were tentative. Her approach was an introduction to inquiry learning, not the accumulation of information. The same method required for the study of science and history would apply to autonomous decision making in civic life.[105]

Erasing the Traces

In 1885, Mary Sheldon Barnes's first textbook launched a "great debate" over the use of primary sources in secondary schools.[106] Opposed to the source method, Professor R. H. Dabney, of the University of Virginia, argued that "to teach pupils of any age, condition, and sex to think for themselves and to have opinions of their own on any imaginable subject" should not be the major goal of education. "The main thing is for them . . . to *learn* what is in the book, and to gain from it a keen desire to learn more" (emphasis in original).[107] Primary sources were to stimulate interest in history, to illustrate generalizations, or to supplement an ordinary textbook but not to serve as the "chief object" to train judgment or to create historical narratives. Other opponents, who perhaps agreed with the goals of critical thinking, realistically feared that schools lacked competent teachers, adequate libraries, and sufficient time to implement the program successfully.[108]

Using the Barneses' texts as a basis, in the mid-1890s Professors Fred M. Fling and Howard W. Caldwell successfully initiated a massive in-service program throughout Nebraska to clarify and disseminate source- method teaching. In each county, they created organizations of high school history teachers. Their official journal, the *North-Western Journal of Education*, linked the teachers with Fling and Caldwell. Other historians, such as James Harvey Robinson of Columbia University and George E. Howard of Stanford, joined the cause of the source method in secondary schools.[109]

Clashes of Committees

Both the NEA Committee of Ten report in 1893 and the American Historical Association's Committee of Seven report in 1899 vigorously debated the issue. Charles Kendall Adams, Barnes's history professor at the University of Michigan, led the 1893 NEA Committee of Ten to recommend the inductive use of sources, as Barnes championed. The objective was to cultivate students' intellectual skills, not to create historians of school pupils nor to write history from a limited number of sources. Ultimately, the skills were honed in preparation for active participation in U.S. democracy. The committee's report rekindled passionate discussions over history instruction.[110]

Initial reports in 1897 by the AHA Committee of Seven reflected both sides of the debate: the centrality of sources to teach inquiry, and the adjunct role of sources to illustrate a basic narrative. The final 1899 report of the AHA panel rejected Barnes's approach.[111] In the belief that pupils would arrive at major conclusions with "insufficient basis," the committee recommended "limited contact with a limited body of materials, an examination of which may show the child the nature of the historical process."[112]

The AHA committee, chaired by Andrew C. McLaughlin, rendered historical inquiry subordinate to the acquisition of historical knowledge. Traditional textbook accounts would take precedence over the primary sources. The construction of meaning from sources—a "task that might well have staggered experienced historians," according to Lucy M. Salmon, remained in the hands of authoritative specialists.[113] The memory of Mary Sheldon Barnes, who died the year before the committee's report, was cast aside.

Ignored in Print

The Barnes faction lost the long-term rhetorical war as well as the debate.[114] With only a few exceptions, scholars who should have related to her seminal work neglected her legacy and its importance for U.S. education. Henry Barnard, the first commissioner of the U.S. Bureau of Education, omitted her work from his study of Pestalozzian methods.[115] Nicholas Murray Butler, founder of Teachers College and later president of Columbia University, ridiculed her notion that youngsters were capable of interpreting primary sources.[116] Butler's protégé, Henry Johnson, ignored Sheldon Barnes's significance in his 1915 survey of history teaching, a standard methods text until the 1930s. Erling M. Hunt, Johnson's successor at Teachers College and the first editor of *Social Education,* advocated the use of primary sources as collateral material. Analyst Ruth M. Elson failed to review Barnes's American history text in her study of nineteenth-century elementary-school books. Inquiry innovators of the "new social studies" movement (e.g., Byron Massialis, C. Benjamin Cox, and James Banks) ignored Barnes in their influential texts. Hazel Hertzberg's 1981 account of early social studies education focused on Professors Fling and Caldwell, source method "disciples," instead of Barnes, the originator.[117]

At brief points in the twentieth century, Barnes and the source method resurfaced in the rhetoric. Robert E. Keohane favorably reviewed her work in the late 1940s. In their 1958 methods book, Edgar B. Wesley and Stanley P. Wronski reservedly applauded the use of "sources" and recognized Mary Sheldon Barnes as the first to incorporate primary sources in secondary history books. Toward the end of the 1980s, David W. Saxe and Stuart A. McAninch each reevaluated the importance of her work.[118]

Familiarity with the life and work of Mary Sheldon Barnes might temper today's ahistorical assumptions that original sources, critical thinking, and problem solving are "new" instructional methods. Sheldon Barnes's tale reveals that rote learning and recitation have been considered problematical for at least a century.[119]

Whether in 1890 or 1990, the presentation of "objects" or "original sources" was a mindless exercise if not accompanied by "minds-on" dialogue.[120] A crucial ingredient for reform, the deliberate use of questions to stimulate critical thought shaped the "new" practices of the late nineteenth century. Barnes wove them tightly into her methods and materials. Reformers today, who recommend information technology and other "hands-on" projects to solve educational problems, would benefit from a review of the lessons and rationales that Mary Sheldon Barnes designed more than a century ago.

Revising the Message

The final assessment of individuals seldom yields sharp pictures in black and white. Some snapshots contain clear images of accomplishment. Mary Sheldon Barnes's textbooks, viewed against the backdrop of nineteenth-century U.S. culture, clearly contrasted with the rest of the century's offerings. They deliberately provoked reflection. Their inductive process of constructing knowledge—continuous and imperfect—took precedence over ritual memorization of information. The scrutiny of primary sources—limited yet infinitely imaginative and vast—formed the core activity; the source method was not an illustrative, colorful, peripheral, mnemonic exercise. If her 1885 introduction to the past was inadequate in 1905, Sheldon Barnes invited the student and teacher to revisit the sources and revise the story. Her texts were not the definitive word. The historian's work was never done.

The images within the picture frames, however, are often gray, blurred, and grainy revelations of the cultural contexts in which they were taken. Mary Sheldon Barnes's intellectual precepts claimed to train students to question assumptions and assertions; her history methods required tracing truth claims to original or primary sources. Paradoxically, she herself seemed unable to see past the cultural filter into her own contradictions and limited range of understanding. What, then, was the benefit of the inductive teaching she advocated?

Any selection of sources, primary or secondary, reflects "a point of view" and is thus limited.[121] The social, religious, economic, and political beliefs of Sheldon Barnes's milieu blurred her image as a teacher of critical thought. Tacit, unquestioned cultural values circumscribed her selections of materials and guided her questions. By today's critical standards, her treatments of immigrants, women's status, labor unions, religion, are flawed. Did both she and the source method deserve to be cast aside?

Mary Sheldon Barnes herself punctured the myth of the "unbiased text" in the prefaces of *Studies in General History* (1885) and *Studies in Greek and Roman History* (1886). The historian's observations, judgments, knowledge, and writings—including her own—are not perfect, she said. They "grow out of a peculiar point of view and circumstances of the people enunciating [them]."[122]

That Sheldon Barnes's own published tracts had limitations, contradictions, and biases is undeniable. Her research at Stanford suggests, however, that she had begun to open her pedagogical beliefs and attitudes to cross-examination, experimentation, and revision. Similar to her father when Herbartian pedagogy challenged his Pestalozzian assumptions, she did not stagnate.

She and her method both encouraged ongoing dialogue and search for knowledge. In democratic fashion, she essentially proclaimed to ordinary schoolteachers and students: We need not stagnate in the dogma of the past. These methods are accessible to all, not just elite scholars. You are capable of making sense of the world, of deciding your fate. These exercises in history are practice lessons for democratic citizenship. The historian's and the citizen's work is never done.

Writings of Mary Sheldon Barnes

Mary Sheldon Barnes, *Studies in Historical Method* (Boston, 1896).

The Sources of History

The original materials from which historians work are called sources. *They correspond to fossils in geology, to cases in law, to words in philology; they are the remains of the past, from which all of our knowledge of that past is derived. They consist of the mass of traditions, books, manuscripts, papers, relics, monuments, and institutions in which a generation embodies itself tangibly and visibly. . . .*

In short, the whole embodiment of a generation in descendants, institutions, creeds, and laws, in literature, speech, and set histories, in handiwork and art, is our source for its history, even more than that set and conscious product which it names its history. In this latter the generation is reproduced according to some notion of it formed by itself or others; what seems unnecessary or undesireable is omitted because a history is necessarily written from some one point of view— political, social, or religious. But in the sources, history finds its immortal material for its ever-renewed product. For the content and direction of history changes with every generation. If our ancestors . . . cared for political history and found in political history its needed pabulum, we who need a social history need not despair . . . for the sources still are ours. . . . These sources are the mothers of history on which all historical narratives and judgments must rest, and to which all historical narratives and judgments must appeal. (Pp. 7–8)

The Study of Contemporary History

It will readily be seen that if any one wishes to study history from the sources, he must either have recourse to collections ready made, or to the field of local and contemporary history. In fact, away from great libraries, these are the only possible openings for original historical work. Contemporary history has the great advantage of being living history, involving the question of the day; its sources are those on which the adult citizen must continually construct his own judgments—judgments which underlie the history of the future. The newspaper, the magazine, the living man and woman, the growing connection of events—all these are our own constant sources of information; and if the teacher himself has had a good training in history, it is a part of his work to train his students as far as he can to weigh this contemporary evidence, estimate its comparative values, learn to judge of character, recognize the causes and forms of personal bias, and form independent and thoughtful judgments, or, what is sometimes more to the purpose, learn to suspend his judgment altogether for want of sufficient evidence. In such a course, too, the student should learn how to help himself in a great library to the material which bears on the most recent questions. He should learn the use of encyclopedias, atlases, catalogues, [indexes to periodical literature], the Statesman's Year Book, *and similar aids. (Pp. 12–13)*

Principles of the Historical Method

The materials of history are peoples, their environment, and their products; and since books are the great treasure-house in which peoples have stored the records of their past, the library becomes the chief laboratory and workshop of the historian. But, after all, the student must remember that even books are but second-hand records, ill understood without living contact with men and things. For men and things are records, too, and the truest record of the progress of humanity. We can neither understand the man of the past without knowing the man of to-day, nor the man of to-day without knowing the man of the past.

Since sources are the material from which historical judgments are formed, since their value depends solely on their nature as evidence, and since no historical judgments are permanent or complete, but only relative to circumstance and knowledge, we should not only work with sources as much as possible, but train ourselves as carefully as possible to a critical consideration of their nature as evi-

dence, as well as to a critical estimate of judgments based upon them. . . .

History is not much longer destined to sleep while little books and dogmatic teachers tell weary souls what history was and did. Presently she will wake and enter into life. Then shall we see that the past lives in the present, and only there; that into the present we must look, and look again, until we can discern the forms, ideas, institutions, of the past in their vital connections with the present. And as science has pushed her way out of the narrow text-book and the common school-room, with its dogmatic teacher into the world of phenomena, and into special laboratories fitted with work-tables, collections, and apparatus, with specialist-students always at hand to assist and direct, so history is destined to push its way out of that same narrow text-book and common schoolroom, with its dogmatic teacher, into the world of human nature, and into special seminaries, fitted with maps, pictures, and books, with a work-table for every student, *the whole presided over by a specialist who can guide the student to his sources, and show him how to interpret them truly and critically. The college will realize this first; but in time the seminary is as surely destined as the laboratory to work its way in modified forms into every place where history is taught. One aim will take us surely to this ideal end; namely, the endeavor to see, to feel, the real thing. (Pp. 43–45)*

Notes

1. Robert E. Keohane, "Barnes, Mary Downing Sheldon," in *Notable American Women, 1607–1950: A Biographical Dictionary,* ed. Edward T. James (Cambridge, Mass., 1971), 92–93.

2. Maxine Greene, "Gender, Multiplicity, and Voice," in *Ninety-Second Yearbook of the Society for the Study of Education,* part 1, *Gender and Education,* ed. Sari Knopp Biklen and Diane Pollard (Chicago, 1993), 245; Ruth Miller Elson, *Guardians of Tradition: American Schoolbooks of the Nineteenth Century* (Lincoln, Neb., 1964), vii; Margaret Smith Crocco, "Making Time for Women's History When Your Survey Course Is Already Filled to Overflowing," *Social Education* 61, no. 1 (January 1997): 32–37.

3. Robert E. Keohane, "The Great Debate over the Source Method," *Social Education* 13, no. 5 (May 1949): 212–18.

4. Hazel Whitman Hertzberg, "Social Studies—Meanings and Beginnings," in *Social Studies Reform, 1880–1980,* ed. Hazel Hertzberg (Boulder, Colo., 1981), 1–24.

5. Carmen Luke and Jennifer Gore, *Feminisms and Critical Pedagogy* (New York, 1992), 2–3.

6. Elson, *Guardians,* 301–12.

7. See Charles R. Skinner, "Life and Character of Dr. Sheldon: Memorial Address before National Education Association at Washington, D.C., July 7, 1898," reprinted in Edward Austin Sheldon, *Autobiography of Edward A. Sheldon,* ed. Mary Sheldon Barnes (New York, 1911), 237–43.

8.   Patricia A. Alexander, Diane L. Schallert, and Victoria C. Hare, "Coming to Terms: How Researchers in Learning and Literacy Talk about Knowledge," *Review of Educational Research* 61, no. 3 (Fall 1991): 315–43.

9.   Sheldon, *Autobiography*, chaps. 5, 8–13.

10.   Sheldon, *Autobiography*, 85–88, 206–15.

11.   Sheldon, *Autobiography*, chap. 5; 62–64; chaps. 15 and 16

12.   Sheldon, *Autobiography*, 62–64, 79, 100–115, 124, 133–34, 218–19.

13.   Sheldon, *Autobiography*, 217; S. S. Green, "Objective Teaching: Its General Principles and the Oswego System," Report of the Committee of National Teachers' Association in the Annual Meeting, 1865, (n.p., n.d.), in *Pestalozzi and His Educational System*, ed. Henry Barnard (Syracuse, N.Y., [1906?]), 443–68.

14.   Dorothy Rogers, *Oswego, Fountainhead of Teacher Education: A Century in the Sheldon Tradition* (New York, 1961), 43. For examples of his gift for public relations, see Sheldon's *Autobiography*, 93, 101–3, 104–7, 133, 140–44, and chaps. 25, 34.

15.   Rogers, *Oswego*, 43, 70–72. Letters by his teaching staff illustrate the paternalistic image; see Sheldon, *Autobiography*, chaps. 34 and 35, and 200–203.

16.   Keohane, "Barnes," 92.

17.   Cited in Rogers, *Oswego*, 51–52.

18.   Elson, *Guardians*, 309.

19.   Cited in Rogers, *Oswego*, 52.

20.   Rogers, *Oswego*, 5–6; Sheldon, *Autobiography*, 116–18.

21.   Sheldon, *Autobiography*, 216.

22.   Sheldon, *Autobiography*, map in unpaginated photographic insert between pp. 150 and 151, as well as chaps. 18–21, 23, and 37; Rogers, *Oswego*, 6–8 and chap. 2.

23.   See William C. Schubert, *Curriculum, Perspective, Paradigm, and Possibility* (New York, 1986), 70.

24.   Keohane, "Barnes," 92–93; Albert Picket and John Picket, eds., two untitled reports, *Academician*, 1819, reprinted in *Pestalozzi and His Educational System*, ed. Barnard, 397.

25.   F. Busse, "Object Teaching: Principles and Methods," in *Pestalozzi and His Educational System*, ed. Barnard, 189.

26.   Carl von Raumer, "The Life and Educational System of Pestalozzi," in *Pestalozzi and His Educational System*, ed. Barnard, 50–126; Sheldon, *Autobiography*, chaps. 20, 24.

27.   Von Raumer, "Life and Educational System," 50–126; "Primary Instruction by Object Lessons: Report of National Teachers Association Committee on the Primary Schools of the City of Oswego in New York," in *Pestalozzi and His Educational System*, ed. Barnard, 405–28; Picket and Picket, *Academician*, 395–99.

28.   Elson, *Guardians*, viii, chap. 1; Busse, "Object Teaching," 185–203; von Raumer, "Life and Educational System," 50–126; Sheldon, *Autobiography*, chaps. 20, 24.

29.   Busse, "Object Teaching," 190–91; von Raumer, "Life and Educational System," 75–77; Sheldon, *Autobiography*, chaps. 20, 24.

30.   Busse, "Object Teaching," 189–203; Sheldon, *Autobiography*, chaps. 20, 24.

31. "Primary Instruction by Object Lessons," 405, 407.

32. Busse, "Object Teaching," 193–203.

33. "Primary Instruction by Object Lesson," 407–8; Sheldon, *Autobiography,* chaps. 24, 25, 29. Records show that both Pestalozzi and Sheldon suffered lapses into "abstract verbiage." See Mary Sheldon Barnes, ed., "Review and Reminiscence," in *Autobiography,* by Sheldon, 221–24; Rogers, *Oswego,* 21, 79–80.

34. Sheldon, *Autobiography,* 164; Greene, "Objective Teaching."

35. Rogers, *Oswego,* chap. 2; Keohane, "Barnes," 92–93.

36. Rogers, *Oswego,* chap. 4; Greene, "Objective Teaching," 443–68; Sheldon, *Autobiography,* chap. 29.

37. Rogers, *Oswego,* 22–23, 41–42, 48–50, and chap. 4.

38. Rogers, *Oswego,* chaps. 2, 4; Keohane, "Barnes," 92.

39. Cited in Rogers, *Oswego,* 52.

40. Elson, *Guardians,* 309–10.

41. Ruth Bordin, "The New Woman," in *Alice Freeman Palmer: The Evolution of a New Woman,* June 1995. <http://www.press.umich.edu/bookhome/bordin/ch1, html #NT1.1> [accessed 9 February 1998].

42. Bordin, "New Woman"; Rogers, *Oswego,* 48–50; Sheldon, *Autobiography,* 131.

43. Elson, *Guardians,* 306–8, 310; Keohane, "Barnes," 92–93; Hertzberg, "Social Studies," 7.

44. Edgar B. Wesley and Stanley P. Wronski, *Teaching Social Studies in High Schools,* 4th ed. (Boston, 1958), 376; Keohane, "Great Debate," 212–18; Mary Sheldon Barnes, *Studies in Historical Method* (Boston, 1896), 10, hereafter cited as Barnes, *SiHM.*

45. Richard J. Evans, *In Defense of History* (London, 1997), 18.

46. Cited in Barnes, *SiHM,* 144.

47. Evans, *In Defense of History,* 16–22 and chap. 4.

48. Keohane, "Barnes," 92–93; Keohane, "Great Debate," 212–18; Stuart A. McAninch, "The Educational Theory of Mary Sheldon Barnes: Inquiry Learning as Indoctrination in History Education," *Educational Theory* 40, no. 1 (Winter 1990): 45–52; Wesley and Wronski, *Teaching Social Studies,* 370–77; Mary Sheldon Barnes, *Studies in General History* (Boston, 1885), v–vii, hereafter cited as Barnes, *SiGH;* Mary Sheldon Barnes and Earl Barnes, *Studies in American History* (Boston, 1891), iii–iv, hereafter cited as Barnes and Barnes, *SiAH.*

49. Rogers, *Oswego,* 48–50; Sheldon, *Autobiography,* 131.

50. Keohane, "Barnes," 92. Rogers (p. 50) claimed that Barnes taught chemistry at Wellesley College from 1876 to 1878, an account that differs from Keohane's report and the title pages of each textbook attributed to Sheldon Barnes.

51. Barnes, *SiGH,* v–vii; Fling and Caldwell, *European and American History,* 9–32; Keohane, "Great Debate," 213.

52. Keohane, "Barnes," 92–93.

53. Mary B. Jenkins, "Michigan Women at Wellesley," *Wellesley Alumnae Magazine,* December 1924, 57–59.

54. Keohane, "Barnes," 93; Rogers, *Oswego,* 48, 50.

55. Sheldon, *Autobiography*, 172; Keohane, "Barnes," 93; Barnes, *Studies in Greek and Roman History* (1897 ed.), 255. Hereafter cited as Barnes, *SiGRH*.

56. Sheldon, *Autobiography*, chaps. 34, 37; Keohane, "Barnes," 92–93; Rogers, *Oswego*, 12–13.

57. Keohane, "Barnes," 93; Rogers, *Oswego*, 50–52. See unpaginated front matter of Barnes, *SiGH*.

58. Rogers, *Oswego*, 50–52; Keohane, "Great Battle," 212–18; Keohane, "Barnes," 93.

59. Barnes, *SiHM*, 10; Keohane, "Great Debate," 212; Wesley and Wronski, *Teaching Social Studies*, 376.

60. Keohane, "Barnes," 93.

61. Keohane, "Barnes," 93.

62. Barnes, *SiHM*, 10.

63. Barnes and Barnes, *SiAH*, title page.

64. Keohane, "Barnes," 93.

65. A recollection of Henry D. Sheldon, cited in Keohane, "Barnes," 93.

66. Patricia White, encoder, "Guide to the Mary Sheldon Barnes Pacific Slope Collection, 1769–1898: Collection number M0067" in online catalog (Stanford, Calif.: Department of Special Collections, Green Library, Stanford University Libraries, 1997) [accessed 10 February 1998]; Rogers, *Oswego*, 50–52; Keohane, "Barnes," 93.

67. Barnes, *SiHM*, 23–29, 57–105.

68. Barnes, *SiHM*, 104–5.

69. Barnes, *SiHM*, 102–3.

70. Elson, *Guardians*, 302.

71. Rogers, *Oswego*, 48–50.

72. Sheldon, *Autobiography*, 183.

73. Keohane, "Barnes," 93.

74. Keohane, "Barnes," 93; Rogers, *Oswego*, 51.

76. See author's note in Keohane, "Great Debate," 212. Compare Elson, *Guardians*, viii, and the prefaces to Barnes, *SiGH*; *SiGRH*; *SiHM*; and Barnes and Barnes, *SiAH*.

77. See, e.g., "The Defense and Death of Socrates," in Barnes, *SiGH*, 107–10.

78. Barnes, *SiGH*, 280–85, 315–18.

79. Elson, *Guardians*, 338–40.

80. See, in Barnes, *SiGH*, the treatments of the Renaissance–Reformation, 396–438; the ancien régime, 459–74; the French Revolution, 474–86; and various strands of socialist thought, 534–39.

81. Barnes, *SiGH*, 491–533.

82. Barnes and Barnes, *SiAH* (1903 ed.), 390–404.

84. Barnes, *SiHM*, 37.

85. Barnes, *SiGH*, 28–29.

86. Barnes, *SiGH*, 281.

87. Barnes, *SiGH*, 219–21.

88. Barnes, *SiGH*, 276–79.

89. Elson, *Guardians*, 303.

90. Barnes, *SiHM*, 32.

91. Barnes, *SiGH*, vii.

92. Barnes, *SiGH*, viii.

93. Elson, *Guardians*, 338.

94. Barnes and Barnes, *SiAH*, iii.

95. Barnes, *SiHM*, 110, 116. 119.

96. Barnes, *SiHM*, 17–23, 30–31, 107.

97. Barnes, *SiHM*, 117.

98. Barnes, *SiHM*, 128–29.

99. Elson, *Guardians*, 337–40; Barnes, *SiHM*, 106–21.

100. Barnes, *SiHM*, 111, 117–20.

101. McAninch, "Educational Theory," 45–52.

102. McAninch, "Educational Theory," 50.

103. Barnes, *SiHM*, 120. Also see Elson, *Guardians*, 339–42.

104. Barnes and Barnes, *SiAH*, 403.

105. Barnes, *SiHM*, 132–37; Keohane, "Great Debate," 212–18.

106. Keohane, "Great Debate," 212–18.

108. Cited in Keohane, "Great Debate," 213.

109. Keohane, "Great Debate," 213–14.

107. Keohane, "Great Debate," 213; Fred Morrow Fling and Howard W. Caldwell, *Studies in European and American History: An Introduction to the Source Study Method in History* (Lincoln, Neb., 1897), 9–32.

110. Keohane, "Great Debate," 213–14; Hertzberg, "Social Studies," 8–12.

111. Keohane, "Great Debate," 215–16; Hertzberg, "Social Studies," 16.

112. Cited in Keohane, "Great Debate," 216.

113. Salmon is cited in Keohane, "Great Debate," 217.

114. Keohane, "Great Debate," 218; Hertzberg, "Social Studies," 3–16.

115. Barnard, *Pestalozzi and His Educational System*.

116. Keohane, "Great Battle," 216. See also Nicholas Murray Butler, introduction to *Teaching of History in Elementary and Secondary Schools*, by Henry Johnson (New York, 1917).

117. Johnson, *Teaching of History*, vii–xi, 360–61, chaps. 11, 12; Erling Messer Hunt, interview by George L. Mehaffy, 2 April 1977, in Norwich, Vermont, untranscribed tapes 1, 2, 3, 5, Oral History in Education Collection, College of Education, University of Texas at Austin; Elson, *Guardians*; Byron G. Massialas and C. Benjamin Cox, *Inquiry in Social Studies* (New York, 1966); James A. Banks, *Teaching Strategies for the Social Studies: Inquiry, Valuing, and Decision–Making*, 4th ed. (New York, 1990); Hertzberg, "Social Studies," 1–24.

118. Keohane, "Great Debate," 212–18; Wesley and Wronski, *Teaching Social Studies*, 376–77; David Warren Saxe, "Mary Sheldon Barnes and the Introduction of Social Sciences in Public Schools," *Social Studies* 80 (September/October 1989): 199–202; McAninch, "Educational Theory," 45–52.

119. As an example of such current beliefs, see Elizabeth K. Wilson and George E. Marsh II, "Social Studies and the Internet Revolution," *Social Education* 59, no. 4 (April/May 1995): 198–202.

120.   O. L. Davis Jr., "Beyond Beginnings: From 'Hands–on' to 'Minds-on,'" *Journal of Curriculum and Supervision* 13, no. 2 (Winter 1998): 119–22.

121.   Barnes, *SiHM*, 7.

122.   Barnes, *SiHM*, 127.

3

Lucy Maynard Salmon:
Progressive Historian, Teacher, and Democrat

Chara Hauessler Bohan

Lucy Maynard Salmon
Special Collections, Vassar College Libraries,
Poughkeepsie, New York

L ucy Maynard Salmon (1853–1927) possessed a distinctive vision of education in America that was progressive, democratic, and pluralistic. Undoubtedly, this vision was shaped by her status as a woman in a time when few women were educated and most were disenfranchised. Aware of her own exceptional educational background and standing in academia, Salmon assiduously worked to improve education. A noted historian at Vassar College, Salmon not only developed innovative teaching methods for her classroom but also lectured and wrote about such practices, thereby earning national recognition as an educator. Although she experienced many successes in advancing knowledge about teaching and history in general, she also encountered sharp professional criticism. For example, her work on the American Historical Association's Committee of Seven, which examined the secondary history curriculum nationwide, helped expand and standardize secondary course offerings in history; yet Salmon's first major historical work on domestic service, if not derided, met with unenthusiastic reception by the community of historians.

Salmon's recommendations for the teaching of school history were progressive. Rejecting the transmission model of learning, Salmon favored instructional methods that encouraged independent thinking and judgment. She encouraged students to embrace history in a pluralistic sense, as a subject that encompassed all aspects of human endeavors rather than one limited only to military and political events. In her own scholarship, she wrote about the history of ordinary elements of life, such as domestic service and the newspaper. Such nontraditional subjects often were dismissed as insignificant by leading historians in the late nineteenth and early twentieth centuries.

Moreover, Lucy Salmon advocated and implemented innovative methods of teaching history. She believed that students should learn history, not only through texts, but also by experiencing and examining their own communities. Although she promoted a balanced approach to teaching secondary school history that included textbooks, source documents, lectures, and independent research, she especially encouraged students' use of source documents in the classroom because she believed that this approach was neglected routinely in history courses. Indeed, her legacy at Vassar is as the professor who urged her students "to go to the sources."[1] Furthermore, Salmon urged students to become involved in community endeavors; she practiced these beliefs herself. Active in the civic community at national and local levels, Salmon held leadership roles in suffrage organizations, historical associations, and community improvement groups.

Salmon's work and career, however, have been marginalized and largely forgotten. Perhaps her ideas were too innovative and democratic for a society that had not fully realized participatory democracy and that in practice did not support equal education for all of its citizenry, specifically women. Indeed, many people with whom she worked and communicated opposed women's education, suffrage, and women's professional pursuits. A century later, Salmon's work suggests ways in which social studies education, citizenship education, and history education can be reconceptualized to encompass a pluralistic and democratic society for the education of all Americans.

A Glimpse at a Life

Salmon was born on 27 July 1853, in Fulton, New York. In this period before the American Civil War, rural living was typical.[2] She lived her formative years in the latter half of the nineteenth century, and her childhood memories include spending much time sewing clothes, a chore that Salmon grew to dislike.[3] Her preference to play outdoors conflicted with Victorian-era customs for girls. Although outwardly shy, she was bold enough to break with some social conventions, in a pattern that eventually became familiar. In her later years, for example, she created a stir at Vassar by riding her bicycle around the campus. At the time, such physical exertion was deemed inappropriate for ladies.

Salmon was born to a family of English and French descent.[4] Salmon's mother, Maria Maynard Salmon, had studied under Mary Lyon at Ipswich Seminary and later became the principal of Fulton Female Seminary. Because Salmon's mother was an extremely well educated woman for this period, Lucy Salmon's decision to pursue a university education, although unusual for a woman in the mid-1870s, was possible because of family support. Lucy Salmon attended Fulton for two years and continued her education at Ann Arbor High School in Michigan, close to relatives, to obtain the necessary preparation to enter the University of Michigan.

In 1876 the University of Michigan conferred on Salmon an A.B. in history. She studied under Charles Kendall Adams, the prominent professor of history who later became president of Cornell University and the University of Wisconsin.[5] Immediately after taking her degree, Salmon became principal of McGregor High School in Iowa.[6] After a successful five-year tenure as principal, Salmon returned to the University of Michigan and in 1883 earned a master's degree, concentrating her studies on European history and English and American constitutional history. Subsequently, she served for three years as an instructor at the Indiana State Normal School at Terre Haute.

In 1885 she was one of the first women to join the American Historical Association (AHA), having been recommended for membership by her mentor at Michigan, Charles Kendall Adams.[7] When the chance for her to become a fellow in American history at Bryn Mawr College arose in 1886, Salmon accepted the opportunity to study under a young professor named Woodrow Wilson.[8] Bryn Mawr was only in its second year of operation when Salmon matriculated.

After completing her year as a fellow in history in 1887, Salmon was appointed an associate professor of history at Vassar College, a school for women, which had been established in 1865. Initially, Salmon was the only history professor at the college, but the department quickly expanded. Lucy Salmon went on to a long and distinguished career as the chair of the history department at Vassar (1887–1927). She became an authority on domestic service and the role of the newspaper in historical studies. She published comprehensive books on these topics: *Domestic Service* (1897), *Progress in the Household* (1906), *The Newspaper and the Historian* (1923), and *The Newspaper and Authority* (1923). Her teaching and writings also focused on general history and history education.[9]

In addition to her research contributions, Salmon led a distinguished career as a teacher and member of national history and education associations. She served as a member of the Executive Council of the American Historical Association and several prominent AHA committees and founded the Association of History Teachers of the Middle States and Maryland, the oldest extant council devoted to history education. In addition, she held leadership positions in the national suffrage movement and was active in local community organizations. Salmon's involvement in these and other prominent organizations earned her national recognition.

Developing Awareness of Gender and Its Influences on Salmon's Career

Issues of gender shaped Salmon's career and work in many ways throughout her life. When she chose to attend college, few options were available for women in higher education. In 1870, two years before Salmon entered the University of Michigan, 60 percent of the colleges in the United States offered degrees exclusively to men, and 12 percent of all colleges were for women only. At the remaining coeducational institutions men overwhelmingly outnumbered women.[10] Among the general population, few Americans entered college, and fewer than 1 percent of women aged eighteen to twenty-one attended college.[11]

Once at college, women still faced many difficulties. For example, not all professors at institutions of higher learning favored women's education. Indeed, Woodrow Wilson, Salmon's mentor at Bryn Mawr, was distinctly unhappy teaching women, confiding to his wife during his third year at the college:

> When I think of you, my little wife, I love this "College for Women," because *you* are a woman: but when I think only of myself, I hate the place very cordially: for you are the *only* woman hereabouts of your genuine, perfect sort—the only woman anywhere of your perfect title to be worshipped by men.[12]

As for Salmon, Wilson wrote that she "needed only constant encouragement—but that amounted to carrying her on my shoulders. I'm *tired* of carrying female Fellows on my shoulders!"[13] Clearly, Wilson had little regard for women's academic potential. Because of such attitudes, professional opportunities for women were limited throughout higher education during the 1870s, and earning a degree was quite a challenge for women.

Early female graduates of colleges believed they must choose between marriage and a career. For many of these women, especially those from the upper classes, the choice of paid work brought social disapproval. However, higher education provided many women with a heightened sense of independence, and teaching became the most common field of employment for these women. Like other women of the time, Salmon chose teaching as her profession and never married. She believed, however, that women should not enter teaching unless they had a true sense of vocation.[14] Salmon, who taught at Vassar for forty years, believed that teaching was her calling. The field in which she chose to teach, however, was dominated by males. Indeed, most of her colleagues in the American Historical Association were men.

Significantly, Salmon was one of a small number of women in the AHA and certainly the most influential female member of the organization during its early years. In 1885, Salmon joined the AHA with 10 other women. Three others had joined the previous year, the first year of the AHA's existence. At the time Salmon became affiliated with the AHA, membership totaled 375.[15] Without a doubt, Salmon's participation in some of the association's activities was difficult. Although the AHA accepted women members, many of the early council dinners occurred in all-male clubs such as New York's Metropolitan and Century Clubs.[16]

Furthermore, the association only slowly recognized women for leadership roles. By 1920, for example, approximately 19 percent of the AHA members were women; nevertheless, before 1933, only 5 women were among the 96 members who had served on the association's executive council.[17] Salmon was one of those 5 early female leaders.

Upon Salmon's nomination to the council, Louise Fargo Brown, a colleague and then dean at the University of Nevada, wrote that she was glad to see Salmon receive the recognition she had so long deserved.[18] In 1915, AHA members elected Salmon to the executive council along with Eugene C. Barker, Guy Stanton Ford, Charles H. Haskins, Ulrich B. Philips, and Samuel B. Harding.[19] She served on the council from 1915 to 1919.

In all her AHA leadership roles, Salmon endured gender discrimination. As early as 1897, Salmon accepted an invitation to join the AHA's Committee of Seven, to consider the teaching of history in secondary schools, and to make recommendations for college entrance examinations. When Salmon suggested the addition of another woman to the Committee of Seven, she was rebuffed. In a letter to George Burton Adams dismissing Salmon's request, Herbert Baxter Adams, a fellow committee member, wrote, "I am inclined to think that one woman is enough!"[20]

Undeterred, Salmon continued her quest to increase female leadership. Although some men on the executive council acted surprised that Salmon did not attend more dinners or say more at the meetings, in the face of discrimination and rejection, Salmon's ability to participate and to influence others was limited.[21] Yet she continued subtly to insist that women should be considered for AHA positions. For example, in a letter to Edvarts B. Greene, Salmon wrote, "I do not wish to seem to press the names of women for membership on any of these committees; and yet, as I think I have written more than once before, I can but feel that the Association has by self-denying ordinance been deprived of the services of a good many able women."[22]

She advanced women for higher positions in other groups as well. For example, when the presidency of Vassar College became vacant in 1913, Salmon endorsed two women candidates. She also wrote to the Vassar trustees to ask if the faculty could self-govern until the appointment of a new president.[23] Although the trustees did not choose either of Salmon's candidates, Henry Noble MacCracken, who became the fifth president of Vassar, was ideologically and educationally progressive. Throughout Salmon's career, she promoted many women and especially supported former female students in their professional careers. Salmon's skillful advancement of women was characteristic of a myriad of endeavors that she pursued.

Salmon paved the way for more females to participate in leadership roles not only in the AHA but also in the political arena. In the early 1900s,

Salmon accepted leadership positions in the burgeoning suffrage movement and assisted with the cause to enfranchise women throughout the country. She not only headed the suffrage movement at Vassar, but she also became an officer of the National College Equal Suffrage League, an auxiliary of the National American Woman Suffrage Association (NAWSA), and she served on the Executive Advisory Council of the Congressional Union for Woman Suffrage led by Alice Paul. Undoubtedly, Salmon's work for suffrage was not only an extension of her efforts to promote women but also part of her broad vision of a truly democratic society in which all citizens contributed to the civic community and weaved its history.

Indeed, her commitment to the women's suffrage movement ultimately contributed to a controversy with Vassar president James Monroe Taylor. In the early 1900s, Taylor attempted to prohibit suffrage movement activities on the Vassar campus.[24] In fact, Salmon wrote to Frances Davenport in 1906 that suffrage "has always been a tabooed question here,—has never been debated in the college since I have been here as far as I know, but there seems to be some interest in the subject now."[25]

Salmon and other faculty members who participated in the suffrage movement were forced to go off campus for their activities. In 1906, she spoke at the Thirty-Eighth Annual Convention of the National American Woman Suffrage Association in Baltimore that honored the eighty-sixth birthday of Susan B. Anthony. In Salmon's address, she recalled having attended in 1863, at the tender age of ten, her first suffrage meeting and one at which Anthony spoke.[26] Salmon grew up in the Finger Lakes region of New York, near Seneca Falls. Still, Salmon confessed that many years passed before she became interested in the fight for suffrage.

By 1911, Salmon was committed to suffrage activities not only in New York but also at the national level. Despite the continuing prohibition of suffrage activities on the Vassar campus, Salmon was elected vice president of the National College Equal Suffrage League. That same year, as "presiding officer" of the Vassar suffrage movement, she entertained the Reverend Anna Howard Shaw, president of NAWSA, at her Poughkeepsie home before Shaw gave a public lecture.[27]

Ideologically, Salmon tended to align herself with Shaw and the more conservative wing of the suffrage movement, despite Salmon's long acquaintance with Harriot Stanton Blatch, Vassar College class of 1878, the daughter of Elizabeth Cady Stanton, who headed the more radical New York suffrage movement.[28] Both Blatch and Alice Paul, who led the Congressional Union for Woman Suffrage (later known as the National Women's Party), had been influenced by the confrontational activities of the English Pankhursts. The Congressional Union attracted much public attention by staging suffrage parades, and many Americans generally considered their political tactics to be shocking. Although Salmon attended the first meeting of the Congressional Union's Advisory Council at Alice Paul's personal invitation, she must have been an apprehensive participant. After two and one-half years, Salmon requested that her name be removed from the files of the New York Congressional Union's Advisory Council.[29] Salmon agreed to the Reverend Shaw's request that she devote all of her efforts to NAWSA.

At the local level, in no small measure due to Salmon's efforts, the suffrage movement gained popularity among Vassar students. Salmon helped recruit members to the student suffrage organization. In addition, she invited prominent suffragists, such as Charlotte Perkins Gilman, Anna Howard Shaw, and Harriot Stanton Blatch, to come to Vassar to speak about the movement. In order to avoid the campus ban, one meeting was held in the cemetery across the street from Vassar. Several New York newspapers featured reports of the event.[30]

President Taylor clearly became upset about the publicity generated by this "graveyard rally," but suffrage activities at Vassar continued despite his disapproval. Indeed, a year later, a debate about suffrage was held on campus. When Taylor learned that faculty participated in the debate, he criticized them for violating his policy against discussion of controversial subjects on campus.[31] Salmon and other affected faculty members believed that his policy limited their academic freedom of speech. Consequently, they objected not only to the policy but also to Taylor's exclusion of the faculty in matters of governance. Salmon's stated beliefs and actions in the midst of this controversy reflected her continued commitment to democracy at the local and national levels. In the wake of such criticism, Taylor decided that, at age sixty-five, he should retire from the Vassar presidency.

During the subsequent interim period, while the board of trustees searched for a replacement, Salmon and other prominent faculty members began to implement changes in the system of governance at Vassar to give faculty members a greater role in making policy. Once again, Salmon pressed to implement her vision of a more democratic society. She offered several suggestions for the choice of president, stressing the need for reorganization of the administration.[32] In addition, Salmon described several candidates that she favored, two of whom were women graduates of Vassar College. Clearly, she never stopped her crusade to help women obtain leadership roles and viewed colleges for women as central to such possibilities. In fact, ten years earlier, she had written to a former student, "The discouraging feature is the indifference of the public to needs of the woman's college, while pouring out with lavish hand for the man's college. But perhaps we shall come into our own in time."[33]

Issues of gender certainly affected Salmon's professional and personal life. That she taught at a college for women was not coincidental; faculty positions for women generally were scarce in the 1880s. Although colleagues in history throughout the country were predominantly male, the proportion of male and female faculty at Vassar was more balanced, and, of course, all of the students were female. When Salmon came to Vassar, female faculty members were expected to live with the students. These faculty members acted as house mothers to assist the women students, who were perceived as needing supervision. Salmon disliked living in the dormitories with students because she had no privacy. After a two-year leave of absence from 1898 to 1900, during which time she traveled in Europe, studied, and attempted to recover from exhaustion and depression, Salmon returned to Vassar. Shortly after her return, Salmon and Adelaide Underhill, a close friend and former student who later became the Vassar librarian, decided to share a house on Mill Street in Poughkeepsie. They lived together throughout the remainder of their lives, and neither woman married.[34] Each grew to rely on the other for professional and emotional support.[35]

Lucy Salmon's sexual orientation has been debated, although little evidence exists about this aspect of her life.[36] Clearly, she had close female friends. However, the customs of the Victorian era must serve as a context to shape understanding of Salmon's relationships. Carroll Smith-Rosenberg argues that nineteenth-century American society did not place taboos on female relationships; the societal structure, in which women routinely formed friendships separate from male relations, encouraged "homosocial ties."[37] Indeed, Smith-Rosenberg found in her study that the notoriously repressive Victorian sexual ethos may have been more flexible than societal conventions in the twentieth century. Furthermore, at colleges for women, such as Vassar, most relationships, both public and private, necessarily were between women. Former history department chair Evalyn Clark recalls that there was a closeness in the community because faculty lived, dined, and worked together. Most women, she explains, remained unmarried, because at that time a married woman would have been viewed as not being dedicated to her profession.[38] In other words, living with other women, choosing not to marry, and engaging in scholarly pursuits were the norm for women faculty at Vassar. Despite Salmon's success in the male-dominated historical profession, women were her primary focus throughout her professional and personal life at Vassar.

Although close relationships between women were quite common at Vassar, Salmon clearly was particularly committed to Underhill both professionally and emotionally. The two women lived together for nearly thirty years, and only death ended their relationship. In her will, Salmon provided Underhill a life estate, which upon Underhill's death was transferred to Vassar.[39] In writing to Salmon, friends frequently sent regards to Miss Underhill; likewise, Salmon mentioned her housemate in letters to others.[40] Whenever the two women were separated, they corresponded extensively with one another. In their letters, both expressed love for one another. For example, in one letter Salmon wrote to Underhill, "Meantime remember that blue or not blue, I always have a heart full of love for you."[41] On a professional level, the two collaborated on increasing the acquisitions of the Vassar library. In most respects, Salmon and Underhill's relationship grew to be mutually supportive.

Salmon's Conception of History

Salmon's distinctive vision of education was influenced by issues of gender and was reflected in her writing and teaching of history. As a student, Salmon wrote political history, but as a faculty member she decided to write about nontraditional historical topics. Early in her career, she investigated domestic service, primarily in the United States. Toward the end of her career, Salmon researched the history of the newspaper. Examination of domestic help enabled Salmon to explore the history of ordinary people, both employees and employers, whereas her newspaper inquiry allowed her to study a medium widely available to all people and which she believed reflected society as a whole.

Salmon chose innovative methods such as surveys and statistics to collect data for her research for *Domestic Service*. Although these methods were uncommon forms of historical inquiry at the turn of the twentieth century, they were typical of the work of the new professional social scientists like Florence Kelly, Jane Addams, Carroll Wright, and later Mary Beard, who increasingly discussed ideas and methods with one another.[42] In fact, Wright, the first commissioner of the U.S. Bureau of Labor and later the president of Clark College, assisted Lucy Salmon in obtaining and calculating census and statistical data for *Domestic Service*. These scholars claimed modern scientific knowledge as the basis of their authority.[43]

Salmon's work on domestic service, however, received negative criticism in journals such as *New England Magazine*, which saw it as a work "beneath the dignity of a historian."[44] Indeed, Salmon was aware of the poor reception her book received and complained in a letter to Underhill: "I spent $1500 on [*Domestic Service*] and nobody has cared specially about it—it passed unnoticed at the college except a word from Miss Wood and Dr. Taylor. *The Nation* said the work wasn't worth doing, the American publishers say it is not a financial success, the English publishers that no amount of advertising would ever sell the book, the history people say I have wasted my time on it, the economic people that I don't know about economics—and so it goes."[45]

Still, Salmon's research on domestic service was a seminal work in an emerging "new" field of study, the art and science of homemaking, alternatively called home economics, domestic science, and home arts.[46] By the turn of the century this field became an organized effort in the feminization of women's education. Home economics was both traditional and feminist. It included a number of topics related to the "women question," such as the situation in which females destined for employment as domestic servants were thought by many Americans to need proper training.[47] No previous scholarship had focused on this ancient and predominantly female field of employment. Unwilling to dismiss or ignore this area of study, Salmon presented her continued work on domestic service in a more readable and popular format in *Progress in the Household*.[48]

Salmon's selection of domestic service signified her commitment to broadening established conceptions of suitable topics for historical study. Certainly, she was not alone in this endeavor. Other prominent historians, including James Harvey Robinson, Frederick Jackson Turner, Charles Beard, and Woodrow Wilson, also advocated a "new social history." Rather than confining history to military and political figures and events, these historians sought to broaden the base upon which history was written. Salmon, in writing about domestic service, created a new social history and also revealed her burgeoning democratic sentiments. She believed that all people contributed to history and that their stories needed to be told. Salmon's pluralistic approach was unique, however, in that she wrote about a predominantly female occupation comprising primarily immigrants and minorities of low socioeconomic status. Significantly, not only did Salmon write about a neglected class of people, but she also implemented democratic principles by widening the audiences for whom she wrote.

Although Salmon's work on domestic service was not well received, she won more acclaim for her research and writing about the newspaper and the teaching of history. During a sabbatical in 1921, Salmon worked on her manuscript on the newspaper before returning to a more general book on historical material over which she had labored sporadically for years.[49] Indeed, the newspaper material proved to be so vast that Salmon decided to divide the subject into two separate books, *The Newspaper and Authority* (1923) and *The Newspaper and the Historian* (1923). For nearly three decades at Vassar College, Salmon taught an advanced elective course on historical material in which students learned about numerous forms of historical evidence, such as the newspaper.[50] Indeed, Salmon's course had been so well liked by one former student, Anna Justice, that when Justice died, her life was honored through money donated specifically in memory of Salmon's course. Vassar president Henry Noble Mac-Cracken acknowledged this distinction in a letter to Salmon.[51]

Clearly, the newspaper held tremendous interest for Salmon because of its increasing importance during her lifetime as a source of information. Indeed, newspapers were the preeminent form of mass communication in an era that predated radio, television, and film. During the Civil War, American newspapers first established the practice of printing special Sunday editions with war news,[52] and they remained an important source of war information during World War I. Even though Salmon witnessed the birth of new forms of communication in the early twentieth century, the newspaper remained a dominant source of information during her lifetime. Readership continued its impressive growth. For example, in 1842 one in twenty-six New Yorkers bought a Sunday paper, but by 1899 that figure had increased to one in two.[53] Salmon's investigation of the newspaper revealed another aspect of her belief in democratic principles, for the newspaper was widely available and widely read.

In *The Newspaper and Authority* and *The Newspaper and the Historian* Salmon explored a wealth of issues relating to the newspaper, such as freedom of the press, regulation and taxation of the press, the law of libel, sources and bias of the news, the writing of editorials, the influence of the newspaper on public opinion, and the value and danger of the newspaper as a source of historical information. Salmon's stated purpose in writing *The Newspaper and Authority* was to consider "how far the restrictions placed on the newspaper press by external authority have limited its serviceableness for the historian in his attempt to reconstruct the past."[54]

Whereas contemporary historians understand the value of newspapers to their research, their use was not part of accepted practice during Salmon's lifetime. In fact, she argued, "the belief that the press can not be used to reconstruct the past because of its manifold inaccuracies, is not well founded."[55] Despite the yellow journalism of the 1890s, Salmon contended that the press generally strove for accuracy. Nonetheless, she acknowledged that some mistakes were inevitable. Salmon believed, however, that the newspaper was useful for historians, not as a tool to portray information accurately, but as a means through which the historian could interpret the time period under investigation:

> In spite of its name, the chief function of the newspaper is not to give the news, it is not even exclusively to reflect public opinion,—important as that is,—but it is to record all contemporaneous human interests, activities, and conditions and thus to serve the future. What the historian wishes from the newspaper is not news,—that always ultimately comes to him from other sources,—but a picture of contemporary life.[56]

Salmon further claimed that editorials, illustrations, and advertisements were of most immediate service to the historian in their reconstructions of the past. For example, she explained that illustrations revealed how women's lives had changed in the early twentieth century. Earlier papers did not portray women outside of fashion magazines or society scenes. However, in the 1910s and 1920s, newspaper illustrations depicted women in all sorts of activities, such as professions, businesses, industry, and even athletics.[57] In her claim that the newspaper was useful for its reflections of society, Salmon advanced the new social history. Rather than examining the newspaper for information on political or military history, Salmon argued for its use in the portraiture of contemporary times. Yet, Salmon did not entirely negate the newspaper's usefulness in depicting the topics of traditional history. Indeed, advertisements and illustrations revealed "the very real sufferings and privations entailed by war."[58] Salmon believed that the press ultimately was the most important source available to the historian for portrayals of life during the past three hundred years. Yet, the manner in which she advocated portraying life was very different from the conventional history of the day. Moreover, her vision was more democratic. The newspaper could be used to reflect society as a whole—to show ordinary people engaged in popular activities.

Salmon's two exhaustive works on the newspaper were generally well received by the academic community. The *American Historical Review* offered a highly favorable critique, stating that the two volumes were "the most thoroughgoing analysis of newspaper values that has ever been undertaken."[59] Preserved Smith, another reviewer, wrote that, "Outside her own college and beyond the memory of the present generation, Miss Salmon's fame will rest on her two volumes on the newspaper."[60] Former student Mary Ross most aptly wrote:

> The most important contribution of *The Newspaper and the Historian* still is the underlying thesis which Miss Salmon's class first illumined to me—that history must be written "in the round," that to be true it must picture the

things all sorts of men and women wanted to do, and tried to do, as well as those which the "great men" actually did.[61]

Salmon's Instructional Procedures

As previously noted, Salmon became one of the early advocates of the new social history. She recognized the tendency of early American historians to emphasize military and political affairs and to ignore other phenomena of society. Salmon believed that appropriate application of scientific methods to the study of history could be useful but should not be overemphasized.[62] The use of scientific processes could advance knowledge and aid in quests for truth, although she did not think historical truth could be ascertained with complete certainty. Salmon also reasoned that scientific principles could be applied to the study and teaching of history and therefore could assist in improving education. The methods of teaching history that she advanced were both innovative and progressive.

In *The First Yearbook of the National Society for the Scientific Study of Education,* Salmon further developed her ideas about the teaching of history.[63] She noted that the object of the study of history differed for readers, students, and historians.[64] When selecting materials for the study of history, therefore, teachers must consider not only the variety of history offered but also the stages of mental development of students at different ages. Furthermore, Salmon claimed that the study of history had the dual purpose of enhancing reasoning skills and providing direct information.

Salmon explained that in its infancy, history instruction was conducted simply by the memorization method, where the textbook was viewed as "infallible and the chief educational purpose served by the teaching of history was that of training the verbal memory."[65] Salmon thought that memorization was a poor method of teaching history, but she also disliked the "source method" in which textbooks were sometimes discarded completely and students taught to reconstruct history from original documents. She argued that such a method placed too great a demand on immature students. Rather, at the secondary level, Salmon favored a balanced approach, similar to the method of teaching history advanced by the Committee of Seven. In this process, teachers supplemented the textbook with illustrative material and original source documents. Salmon did not favor any one method exclusively. Indeed, she rarely advanced extreme measures in educational endeavors. Instead, she believed that reading textbooks, listening to lectures, and going to the sources were all integral components of the process of learning history. However, she ardently emphasized the use of sources because she understood that their use in learning history was most often neglected. At the university level, in fact, Salmon achieved deserved prominence for her advocacy of the use of sources in teaching history.

Salmon's prominence in the teaching of history earned her an invitation to join the AHA's Committee of Seven in 1896.[66] In order to foster more uniformity in secondary school history, the AHA appointed the Committee of Seven to consider this burgeoning subject and to make recommendations for college entrance requirements in history.[67] After conducting a comprehensive, nationwide survey of the teaching of history in the nation's schools and examining the data, the committee recommended a four-year sequence of courses that consisted of four blocks or periods.[68] The Committee of Seven's recommendations significantly affected the development of the history curriculum in the nation's schools.[69] The success of the committee's work in bringing approximate uniformity to the history curriculum was widely acknowledged.[70] Indeed, the resultant standardization met the appeals of many college entrance officials.

Salmon's influence on the Committee of Seven's work was seen in its recommendation that courses employ original sources to enhance students' historical study. In fact, the committee stated, "The use of sources in secondary work is now a matter of so much importance, that it seems to demand special and distinct treatment."[71] The committee noted that if memorization as an instructional method continued to strengthen, retention of history in the curriculum would be jeopardized. The committee averred, instead, that students should be taught how to read history books, how to think about historical facts, and how to analyze the relationships between evidence and historical statement.

Indeed, many of the Committee of Seven's recommendations related to central tenets of Salmon's beliefs about how history should be taught. She also contributed to the committee's work by spending the summer of 1897 studying methods of historical instruction in German and Swiss-German schools. Salmon presented the findings of this inquiry in an AHA paper, "History in the German Gymnasia," which became one of the appendices of the Committee of Seven report. This report revealed pedagogical methods of historical instruction foreign to the United States. The committee believed that German practices offered particularly valuable lessons for American schools because, of those studied, German history teachers were the most thoroughly prepared in both historical content and instructional pedagogy.

Salmon's research in Europe was not always easy to conduct. She wrote, for example, that one of the directors of a German school "grunted and said in effect that he didn't want any women in his school, but since he apparently had to give permission he would do it," and although other schoolmasters were polite, "they usually say that a woman in a gymnasium is an unheard of thing."[72] Despite difficulties, Salmon persevered. Indeed, the Committee of Seven recommendations were followed in American secondary schools for more than thirty years.[73] Vestiges of her recommendations remain evident in the secondary social studies curriculum today. They include her emphasis on the use of primary source documents and her expansive notion of social history.

At the university level, the ultimate goal of history instruction, according to Salmon, was to encourage students to undertake independent work by providing them with original source material.[74] Her advocacy of the use of historical sources by students became the cornerstone of her life's work and was a remarkably progressive method of teaching history in the late 1800s and early 1900s. Indeed, she planned for her "magnum opus" a book on the subject of historical material.[75] Although it was never completed during her lifetime, her Vassar colleagues and friends published her unfinished manuscript in 1933 as *Historical Material*.

Salmon was attracted to progressive methods of history instruction for several reasons. Primarily, she concluded that students' independent research and use of source materials enhanced their critical thinking skills and was a more stimulating method of learning history than rote memorization. Furthermore, she determined that sources of historical information were available everywhere, even in one's backyard. In fact, she published a pamphlet entitled "History in a Back Yard."[76] Such a perspective reflected her democratic philosophy that individuals could undertake historical study about a wide range of topics and that history could appeal to an audience larger than a select group of academicians. In fact, she attempted to garner support for a new AHA magazine devoted to literary history that would appeal to general readers, but her effort was rebuffed by several colleagues, including William Roscoe Thayer and Frederick Jackson Turner.[77] Turner dismissed Salmon's interest in such a new journal by responding that he did not think that the association could fund such an endeavor but that a solution might be "a department of the present *Review* [*American Historical Review*] . . . devoted to papers more interesting to general readers of the *Review*."[78] Salmon believed that "literary history," with its attention to prose, was more interestingly written than "traditional or academic history" and would appeal to a wider audience. Once again, her democratic principles were apparent, and her interest presaged by some forty years the commercial success of *American Heritage* magazine.[79]

Salmon's innovative methods of teaching history were also reflected in the work of her college students. For example, in a study of unwritten historical material, Salmon encouraged students to research the question, "What may be learned of the history of Poughkeepsie from a study of Main Street?" Salmon's pupil G. L. Chase (Fletcher) noted that history was revealed on a trolley ride along the main street where the architecture of the buildings reflected Dutch and colonial influence, the signs and symbols were traditions handed down from times when the public was generally illiterate, and the names of the shops and residents revealed the influence of immigrants of German, Dutch, Chinese, Italian, French, Irish, and Jewish descent.[80] Not only did the history Salmon conveyed to her class reflect an interest in material culture and the built environment, but also it demonstrated her conviction that historical material and study were accessible everywhere. Main streets existed all across America; therefore, most Americans could study history in their own backyard.

Salmon's teaching also reflected concern for diversity and pluralism. In one of Salmon's courses, History R, "Ethnic Elements in American History," one student examined the contributions of immigrants to American music. In this course, students considered "the part taken by different national elements in the development of America . . . and of [their] contribution to the discovery, exploration and settlement of the country and to its political, social, literary and industrial development."[81] Other student research topics included traditional military and political events as well as more unusual topics such as the indentured servant in the Middle Colonies; the farming frontier in Massachusetts; and a comparison of the politics, fashion, transportation, and fads in 1897 and 1907 through an examination of *Life* magazine in both years.[82] Clearly, Salmon encouraged her students not only to study and research both traditional and unusual topics but also to use innovative methods for gathering historical information.

Salmon's Legacy

Salmon remained throughout her career an advocate of a history curriculum that was educationally progressive. She dismissed the notion that memorization by itself was of primary value, and she objected to the notion of studying history solely for patriotic purposes. She believed that historical studies should include a broad range of topics and that critical thinking skills and independent research should be encouraged for mature students. Her interest in the newspaper reflected not only its usefulness to the historian but also its appeal as a source of information about all people.

She understood that a newspaper reflected the society in which it was produced. Furthermore, Salmon's historical investigation of domestic service demonstrated her concern for women's issues and contributed to the legitimation of an entirely new field of study, home economics.

Salmon firmly believed that the principal value to be derived from studying history was to "practice the understanding in pronouncing judgments."[83] Her position attracted ample support from advocates of the new social history. Still, Salmon's methodology and ideology highlighted the division that existed among historians in the late nineteenth and early twentieth centuries about the nature of their discipline.[84] The first professional historians turned to science in order to search for laws of historical development. They believed that the past could be reconstructed in a strictly factual manner. Lucy Salmon and other advocates of the new social history challenged a strictly scientific approach to history and instead encouraged an interpretive history that emphasized all aspects of human development (such as domestic service or the newspaper), embraced methods employed by the social sciences (e.g., surveys), and accentuated the relationship between the past and the present.

Salmon's viewpoint was distinctive, however, in the depth of her commitment to democratic ideals. She included attention to people typically overlooked, particularly women and immigrant groups; still, her tone was never strident. She included women in the pages of her written history, worked for suffrage, and promoted women for leadership positions. Notably, she herself advanced to leadership roles within the male-dominated historical profession and received acclaim for her work on the newspaper and the teaching of history. She founded the Association of History Teachers of the Middle States and Maryland (which later became the Middle States Council for the Social Studies), an organization that brought together historians and history teachers and worked to improve education for all. Salmon's ideas continue to be debated today, although without attribution. Discussion over methods and purpose in studying history persists.

Salmon's legacy is complex but relevant in many ways. In her leadership in the historical profession and in the suffrage movement, she paved the way for women who followed. These women benefited from increased opportunities and fewer closed doors. No longer would female history professors, for example, teach about "The Appointing Power of the President" without having the right to vote. In other ways, her advocacy of the new social history opened entirely new fields of research. Prior to Salmon's inquiry, no scholar had examined the history of domestic service, because historians viewed it as ordinary and lacking scholarly merit.

Salmon, on the other hand, thought the ordinary, everyday aspects of life merited examination. To Salmon, the newspaper, main streets, and backyards typified the pageantry of contemporary life. Thus, she advanced them as useful and valid sources for historical study. Finally, many of her recommendations for history instruction remain timeless, yet basic, such as her familiar advice to students, "Go to the sources." Despite the dominance of the textbook, particularly at the secondary school level, Salmon's methodology has been advocated for more than a hundred years.

Salmon's work in the suffrage movement, her fields of research and innovative methods of teaching history reflected her commitment to democratic principles that included civic education for Americans regardless of gender or social status. Throughout her career, however, Salmon made teaching her first priority. The extensive correspondence she maintained with former pupils and their accolades to her teaching testify to her remarkable abilities.[85] The Vassar community lauded her accomplishments. In 1923, becoming seventy years of age in the summer, she faced the prospect of mandatory retirement. Vassar president Henry MacCracken wrote that he hoped to find a way that she could stay, for he thought she was a remarkable teacher.[86] Happily, he later reported to her that the board of trustees had voted to suspend the college's retirement requirement, "as a cordial recognition of the completion of your recent works of research and your continued success as a teacher, and of the position which you hold in the Faculty of Vassar College and in the world of American scholarship."[87]

In 1926, friends and former students established the Lucy M. Salmon Fund in the hope that the money from the endowment would enable her to pursue research on historical material while she continued to teach a course on the topic.[88] Salmon taught and wrote until her death, of a stroke, on 14 February 1927. Perhaps the most significant tribute was the 1943 publication of a biography of Salmon by her former colleague Louise Fargo Brown, entitled *Apostle of Democracy*.[89] Salmon pursued democratic principles with conviction in all her teaching and civic actions.

Writings of Lucy Maynard Salmon

Lucy Maynard Salmon, "What is Patriotism?" *Teachers College Bulletin*, December 1896, 9–16.

What is patriotism? The question comes with half a sneer from the cynic who sees how many crimes are committed in its name. . . . It comes from the politician whose every act makes it synonymous with selfishness and greed. It comes from earnest men and women who sometimes doubt whether its possession be a virtue or a vice.

Not only is there doubt as to the adequacy of former conceptions of patriotism to meet the views held to-day in regard to its nature, there is a somewhat wide-spread conviction that patriotism itself is dying out. The press and legislative bodies are teeming with regrets over the decline of patriotism and with plans for resuscitating it. . . . There is everywhere the feeling that ideas of a country, like its products, need to be protected from foreign competition. In all of these regrets and suggestions it is clearly evident that the kind of patriotism whose decay is lament-ed, is that which consists in a glorification of the past, a magnifying of the histo-ry of heroic achievement of the worthiness of a country. It is this tendency to magnify the past of one's country, that leads to the belief that knowledge, as it increases, tends by widening the horizon, to decrease patriotism. . . .

One cannot indeed lament the decline of patriotism of this variety, nor is it to be believed that its revival would be materially facilitated by learning patriotic songs, saluting the flag and studying the Constitution, all of which have been proposed as means of curing the evil. . . .

Undoubtedly a part of that fear that patriotism is declining, comes from anx-iety lest cosmopolitanism supplant it. The fear is not an unreasonable one, for a certain so-called cosmopolitanism has its dangers. It sometimes implies a total lack of interest in the affairs of one's own country, a carping, destructive criticism that finds nothing admirable in our political, social, industrial or educational sys-tems. . . .

True patriotism and true cosmopolitanism carry with them breadth of view, noble ambitions and high ideals. Both are ever on the quest for all that is best in every land in order that that native land, through the assimilation of new ideas, may attain its highest, broadest and fullest development. . . .

No teacher can do efficient work who does not strike his roots deep down into the soil where his lot is cast. The teacher is indeed a teacher, but he is first of all an individual, then a citizen, a member of the community in which he lives, with all the dignities, honors, emoluments and responsibilities belonging to the posi-tion. He is a citizen with a certain occupation, but that occupation should not absorb him to the exclusion of all other interests. He is a citizen with the same duties and with as many duties as have his fellow citizens. If he does not take root in the state and in the community, he is like the grain that falls on stony places and withers away because it has no deepness of earth. Action is equal to reaction, and the teacher who does best his own individual work, is he who has the largest and broadest interests that take him outside of that work.

But for far higher and deeper reasons than for the influence it has on himself and his work, should the teacher feel this responsibility to the state. . . . [E]very citizen owes a debt of gratitude to his country. It is a debt that has come from long and arduous service on the part of those who have built up the nation, a service that hundreds of thousands gladly have rendered. . . . It is a debt that can be paid only as each citizen does what lies within his power to give the state higher and nobler ideals and helping it attain them. It is a debt that the teacher is peculiarly well able to discharge, since opportunities of education have come to him in richer measure than to many others. . . .

The teacher, too, is waking from his political lethargy. He goes abroad and returns with his eyes open to the possibility of improvement in American civic life, he joins a Good Government Club, he becomes a member of a board of charity, an inspector of streets, an almshouse commissioner, sometimes an alderman. He is becoming more of a man and less of a machine as he enriches his life with these interests outside of his routine work. . . .

But does patriotism end with the acknowledgment that it has its civic as well as its martial side? Does it end with the recognition by the state of the service that can be rendered it by able educators, as by other citizens, in helping it reach its highest development? Does it end in a realization by the teacher as by other citizens, of the responsibility of citizenship?

This would seem to be all, if the meaning of patriotism in its narrow and restricted sense is accepted. Yet to an American it ought to mean far more. The Americans are the only people in the history of the world who have given their lives for so subtle and intangible an object as the maintenance of the supremacy of a written instrument—they ought to be capable of the truest, loftiest, most unselfish patriotism. The American nation . . . ought . . . to realize that patriotism and cosmopolitanism are but different terms for the same idea, that patriotism is not limited by national boundaries, and that cosmopolitanism is not like the sluggish stream that empties itself into the ocean, leaving no trace of its point of union with the sea. Americans, more than any other nation, ought to have a clear vision of the fact that on the one hand they cannot maintain as a nation a separate, isolated existence, and that on the other hand every other nation has a sacred right to its own industrial and political existence. America should be foremost in realizing that to attain its own highest development and to assist other nations to attain theirs, it must recognize the brotherhood of nations as well as of man.

Notes

1. Nancy MacKechnie, Vassar College archivist, interview by author, 23 October 1997, Poughkeepsie, New York.
2. Standard Certificate of Death for Lucy Maynard Salmon, Register of Deaths in the City of Poughkeepsie, County of Dutchess, State of New York.

3. Louise Fargo Brown, *Apostle of Democracy* (New York, 1943), 19–20.

4. Brown, *Apostle of Democracy*, 3.

5. Transcripts of Lucy Maynard Salmon, University of Michigan, A.M. 1883, A.B. 1876, Office of the Registrar, Ann Arbor, Michigan; "Charles Kendall Adams,"in *Webster's New Biographical Dictionary*, ed. Robert McHenry and Frank Calvillo (Springfield, Mass., 1983), 11.

6. Lucy Maynard Salmon Papers, *Finding Aid*, Special Collections, Vassar College Libraries, Poughkeepsie, New York, p. 3. Hereafter cited as Salmon Papers.

7. Murry Nelson, "Lucy Maynard Salmon (1853–1927): Pioneering Views in Teaching History," *Social Studies* 87 (January/February 1996): 8.

8. "Lucy Maynard Salmon," in *Dictionary of American Biography*, ed. Dumas Malone (New York, 1963), 8: 312.

9. See, e.g., *What Is Modern History?* 1917; *Why Is History Rewritten?* (New York, 1929), published posthumously; *Historical Material* (New York, 1933), published posthumously; "Some Principles in the Teaching of History," in *National Society for the Scientific Study of Education*, ed. Charles A. McMurry (Chicago, 1908), 11–61; "History in Elementary Schools," *Education Review* 1 (January–May, 1891): 439–52; and "Does the College Curriculum Promote Scholarship?" *Addresses and Proceedings of the Sixtieth Annual Meeting of the National Education Association* (3–8 July 1922): 737–45.

10. Barbara Solomon, *In the Company of Educated Women* (New Haven, 1985), 44.

11. Solomon, *Company of Educated Women*, 62.

12. Woodrow Wilson to Ellen Axson Wilson, 4 October 1887, in *The Papers of Woodrow Wilson*, ed. Arthur Link (Princeton, N.J., 1976), 5: 605.

13. Woodrow Wilson to Ellen Axson Wilson, 5: 605.

14. Solomon, *Company of Educated Women*, 128; Lucy Salmon to Emily Balch, in *Improper Bostonian: Emily Greene Balch, Nobel Peace Laureate*, by Mercedes Randall (New York, 1964).

15. Nelson, "Lucy Maynard Salmon," 8.

16. David Van Tassel, "From Learned Society to Professional Organization: The American Historical Association, 1884–1900," *American Historical Review* 89 (October 1984): 952.

17. Arthur Link, "The American Historical Association, 1884–1984: Retrospect and Prospect," *American Historical Review* 90 (February 1985): 5.

18. Louise Fargo Brown to Salmon, 20 December 1915, Salmon Papers, box 6, folder 1.

19. Ray Allen Billington, "Tempest in Clio's Teapot: The American Historical Rebellion of 1915," *American Historical Review* 78 (April 1973): 368–69. The printed ballots for this election are in the Frederick Jackson Turner Papers, Henry E. Huntington Library and Art Gallery, TU box 59.

20. Herbert B. Adams to George B. Adams, 7 January 1897, George Burton Adams Papers, Manuscripts and Archives, Yale University Library.

21. Brown to Salmon, 19 November 1917, Salmon Papers, box 6, folder 2. Louise Fargo Brown was working with J. Franklin Jameson in Washington, D.C.,

in 1917 and conveyed sentiments about Salmon that Jameson had expressed to her.

22. Lucy Salmon to Edvarts B. Greene, 25 November 1919, American Historical Association Records, Library of Congress, series A, box 9.

23. Elizabeth Daniels, *Bridges to the World: Henry Noble MacCracken and Vassar College* (Clinton Corners, N.Y., 1994), 78.

24. Debbie Cottrell, *Pioneer Woman Educator: The Progressive Spirit of Annie Webb Blanton* (College Station, Texas, 1993), 52; Daniels, *Bridges to the World,* 65.

25. Lucy Salmon to Frances Davenport, 18 November 1906, Salmon Papers, box 3, folder 2.

26. "Address by Professor Lucy M. Salmon" (speech given at the Thirty-Eighth Annual Convention of the National American Suffrage Association, 7–13 February 1906, Baltimore), Salmon Papers, box 56.

27. Anna Howard Shaw to Lucy Salmon, 14 September 1911, Salmon Papers, box 51, folder 9; "The Suffrage Meeting," *Eagle,* 8 September 1911, Salmon Papers, box 51, folder 9.

28. See Harriot Stanton Blatch to Lucy Salmon, 20 April n.d., 17 March 1897, 22 March 1897, 25 October n.d., 22 January 1925, Salmon Papers, box 47, folder 14; Margaret Smith Crocco, "The Road to the Vote: Women, Suffrage, and the Public Sphere," *Social Education* 59 (September 1995): 257–64.

29. Alice Paul to Lucy Salmon, 3 August 1914; Mary Blackford to Lucy Salmon, 15 December 1916, 10 January 1917; Mrs. Henry Wade Rogers to Lucy Salmon, 28 December 1916, 8 January 1917, Salmon Papers, box 51, folder 9.

30. "To Punish Girl Suffragists," *New York Herald,* 10 June 1908; "Vassar Meets in Graveyard," *New York Sun,* 9 June 1908. Clippings in the James M. Taylor Papers, Special Collections, Vassar College Libraries, Poughkeepsie, New York, box 1, folder 15.

31. Daniels, *Bridges to the World,* 67; and Cottrell, *Pioneer Woman Educator,* 52.

32. Lucy Salmon to Alumnae Council, 28 September 1914, Salmon Papers, box 3, folder 1.

33. Lucy Salmon to Edith Rickert (Vassar class of 1891), 26 June 1906, Salmon Papers, box 4, folder 1.

34. Brown, *Apostle of Democracy,* 140–41, 181.

35. See, e.g., Cottrell, *Pioneer Woman Educator;* Susan Ware, *Partner and I: Molly Dewson, Feminism, and New Deal Politics* (New Haven, Conn., 1987); Nelson, "Lucy Maynard Salmon."

36. Nelson, "Lucy Maynard Salmon," 12.

37. Carroll Smith-Rosenberg, "The Female World of Love and Ritual: Relations between Women in Nineteenth-Century America," *Signs* 1 (Autumn 1975): 27; and Carroll Smith-Rosenberg, review of *Independent Women: Work and Community for Single Women, 1850–1920,* by Martha Vicinus, *Signs* 13 (Spring 1988): 648.

38. Evalyn Clark, former history department chair, Vassar College, oral history interview by author, 23 October 1997. Tape deposited at the Oral History in Education Collection, College of Education, University of Texas at Austin.

39. Will of Lucy Maynard Salmon, Salmon Papers, Hollinger box 47, folder 9.

40. See Louise Fargo Brown to Lucy Salmon, 29 July 1915, Salmon Papers, box

6, folder 1; Louise Fargo Brown to Lucy Salmon, 19 November 1917, Salmon Papers, box 6, folder 2; Lucy Salmon to Edith Rickert, 29 July 1907 and 8 June 1909, Salmon Papers, box 4, folder 2; Lucy Salmon, "Remember the Library," *Vassar Quarterly* 8 (November 1922): 55.

41. Lucy Salmon to Adelaide Underhill, 17 May 1894, Salmon Papers, Hollinger box 45, folder 13.

42. Dorothy Ross, *The Origins of American Social Science* (Cambridge, England, 1991), 158.

43. Ross, *Origins of American Social Science*, 62.

44. *New England Magazine* 8 (1893): 175–84.

45. Lucy Salmon to Adelaide Underhill, 11 November 1898, Salmon Papers, Hollinger box 45, folder 13.

46. Jane Bernard-Powers, *The 'Girl Question' in Education: Vocational Education for Young Women in the Progressive Era* (London, 1992), 12.

47. See, for a current example, Arlie Russell Hochschild, *The Time Bind: When Work Becomes Home and Home Becomes Work* (New York, 1997); Ruth Schwartz Cowan, *Household Technology from the Open Hearth to the Microwave* (New York, 1983).

48. Lucy Salmon, *Progress in the Household* (New York, 1906).

49. Brown, *Apostle of Democracy*, 244.

50. Vassar College catalogues, 1900–1927.

51. Henry Noble MacCracken to Lucy Salmon, 7 June 1918, Salmon Papers, box 7, folder 10.

52. Michael Schudson, *Discovering the News: A Social History of American Newspapers* (New York, 1978), 99.

53. Schudson, *Discovering the News*, 99.

54. Lucy Salmon, *The Newspaper and Authority* (New York, 1923), v; for contemporary discussion of the nature of the state and its legitimate functions and justifications, see Robert Nozick, *Anarchy, State, and Utopia* (New York, 1974).

55. Lucy Salmon, *The Newspaper and the Historian* (New York, 1923), 469.

56. Salmon, *The Newspaper and the Historian*, 470.

57. Salmon, *The Newspaper and the Historian*, 475.

58. Salmon, *The Newspaper and the Historian*, 482.

59. *American Historical Review* 30 (October 1925): 146–47.

60. Brown, *Apostle of Democracy*, 245.

61. Mary Ross, review of *The Newspaper and the Historian*, by Lucy Salmon, *Vassar Quarterly* 9 (November 1923): 244.

62. Lucy Salmon, "The Teaching of History in Academies and Colleges," *Academy* 5 (September 1890): 285.

63. Salmon, "Some Principles," 1–61.

64. Salmon, "Some Principles," 31.

65. Salmon, "Some Principles," 48.

66. Nelson, "Lucy Maynard Salmon," 8.

67. American Historical Association, *The Study of History in Schools: Report to the*

American Historical Association by The Committee of Seven (New York, 1899), v. Hereafter cited as Committee of Seven.

68. Committee of Seven, 34–35.

69. Howard Boozer, "The American Historical Association and the Schools, 1884–1956" (Ph.D. diss., Washington University, 1960), 62–66.

70. James Sullivan, "Suggested Changes in Course of Study in History," *History Teacher's Magazine* 2 (January 1911): 103.

71. Committee of Seven, 101.

72. Lucy Salmon to Adelaide Underhill, 15 August 1897, Salmon Papers, Hollinger box 45, folder 13.

73. Van Tassel, "From Learned Society," 952; Boozer, "American Historical Association," 62–66; Michael Whelan, "History as the Core of Social Studies Curriculum," in *The Social Studies Curriculum: Purposes, Problems, and Possibilities*, ed. E. Wayne Ross (Albany, N.Y., 1997), 28; Glenn Kinzie, "Historians and the Social Studies: A History and Interpretation of the Activities of the American Historical Association in the Secondary School Social Studies, 1884–1964" (Ph.D. diss., University of Nebrasaka, 1965), 40–47.

74. Salmon, "Teaching of History," 289.

75. Lucy Salmon to Frances Davenport, 9 September 1909, Salmon Papers, box 3, folder 2.

76. Lucy Salmon, "History in a Back Yard," reprinted in *Historical Material*, 143–57.

77. William R. Thayer to Lucy Salmon, 1 January 1918, Salmon Papers, Hollinger box 47, folder 13; and Frederick Jackson Turner to Lucy Salmon, 11 November 1910, Salmon Papers, Hollinger box 47, folder 13.

78. Turner to Salmon, 11 November 1910.

79. *American Heritage* began publication in 1954 and was begun by former editors at *Life* who were "fired with the conviction that history belongs to the people and not just to scholars." Information on *American Heritage* found on its home page on the Web at <www.americanheritage.com> [accessed 2 November 1998].

80. Vassar College Student Collection, Student Notecards, box 77, folder G. L. Chase (Fletcher) 1911, Special Collections, Vassar College Libraries, Poughkeepsie, New York.

81. Vassar College catalogue, 1910–1911, "Courses of Instruction: History, Course R. Ethnic Elements in American History," 47.

82. Vassar College Student Collection, Student Notecards, box 76, folder Helen C. Cole (VC 1926); box 76, Folder Anne Goodrich (Swann) (VC 1917); and box 77, G. L. Chase (Fletcher) 1911.

83. Lucy Salmon, "The Teaching of History in the Elementary Schools," *Educational Review* 1 (January–May, 1891): 443.

84. Carol Gruber, *Mars and Minerva: World War I and the Uses of the Higher Learning in America* (Baton Rouge, La., 1975), 37–41.

85. Salmon Papers, *Finding Aid*, 19–24.

86. Henry Noble MacCracken to Lucy Salmon, 17 February 1923, Salmon Papers, box 7, folder 13.

87. Henry Noble MacCracken to Lucy Salmon, 13 March 1923, Salmon Papers, box 7, folder 14.

88. Henry Noble MacCracken to Lucy Salmon, 26 June 1926, Salmon Papers, box 7, folder 14.

89. Brown, *Apostle of Democracy.*

4

"Widening the Circle": Jane Addams, Gender, and the Re/Definition of Democracy

Petra Munro

Jane Addams
University of Illinois Library,
Jane Addams Memorial Collection

This chapter situates Jane Addams as a social philosopher whose gender, race, and class analyses provided a radical critique of the fundamental assumptions of classical liberal democracy. The phrase "widening the circle" is taken from an article written by Addams entitled "Widening the Circle of Enlightenment: Hull House and Adult Education."[1] Addams used the term to make the point that the focus of education should be enlarged to include adults, mothers, immigrants, and laborers, as well as new fields of study such as vocational (as opposed to industrial) education. Addams not only used Hull House to expand the opportunities for education to a larger segment of the population but also challenged the very assumptions of public education that emerged in what has been termed the Progressive Era.

Addams's vision of "social democracy" challenged dominant discourses of political thought by exposing the deeply gendered categories of political theory that conceptualized rights as universal, individual, natural, and inalienable. Addams was engaged in revising conceptions of politics and power by viewing them through the lens of gender. She articulated the ways in which the political sphere was demarcated as public/private, how concepts such as citizenship appeared to be gender neutral, and how liberal political discourse excluded the experiences of immigrants and women, especially the experiences of women's collective action. In widening the circle, I hope to recuperate Addams not only as a central figure in the history of social studies education but also as an astute social critic and theorist who anticipated many of the critiques of contemporary feminist political theorists.[2]

For Addams, democracy would not be achieved until women's values had full expression in society. Rejecting a universalistic or equality-oriented view of democracy as devaluing of women, Addams maintained that recognizing difference, not minimizing it, was essential to democracy. For Addams, as for many contemporary feminists, gender "equality" ultimately meant the assimilation of women to men under the guise of a gender "neutral" politics.[3] In this way, the concept of equality functions as oppressive rather than liberatory by keeping women subject to male-defined values and institutions masquerading as universal.

Like late-twentieth-century social theorists grappling with the shifting meanings of democracy in a post–Cold War, postmodern, multicultural, and global society, Addams confronted complex questions:[4] Does democracy require a recognition of difference? What role does social equality play in democracy? How should we frame a political theory based on "multiple intersecting differences"?[5] Can this be accomplished without either the loss of political agency or the balkanization of identity politics?

I will focus on Addams's critique of the fundamental assumptions of classical liberal democracy. For Addams, the concept of universal, individual rights and its corollary concepts of natural man and inalienable rights ultimately functioned to obscure difference and thus neglected the experiences of women and immigrants. Liberal democracy's focus on inalienable rights assumed a static view of the political process and threatened to impose a conformity of political behavior. For Addams, who saw democracy as a living, breathing social organism, liberal democracy failed to provide the flexibility to respond to social change. In addition, Addams critiqued the focus of classical democracy on political rights at the expense of the social and economic dimensions of democracy. Classical liberal democracy would be insufficient to address the social problems of the day because it was incapable of creating social equality. The alleviation of economic inequalities was a prerequisite for the social interaction that was democracy. Democracy was a collective, not an individual, act.

Democracy as a Social Organism

> To attain individual morality in an age demanding social morality, to pride one's self on the results of personal effort when the time demands social adjustment, is utterly to fail to apprehend the situation.
>
> —Jane Addams, *Democracy and Social Ethics*

Addams's focus on social adjustment, rather than individual accommodation, as a remedy for social ills compels me to nominate her as a neglected social critic of bourgeois individualism and liberal democracy. Influenced by John Stuart Mill's view of individual morality as part of a "social organism," Addams rejected the notion of universal, individual, natural rights as antithetical to the very foundations of democracy.[6] She argued that much of the "ethical maladjustment in social affairs arises from the fact that we are acting upon a code of ethics adapted to individual relationships but not the larger social relationships."[7] Classical democracy, based on the concepts of natural man and the doctrine of inalienable rights, reinforced political participation as individual and thus actively undermined the social interaction on which democracy was predicated. This focus on the individual as foundational to democracy hindered the very social relations that Jane Addams saw as central to developing the sense of social responsibility necessary to democracy.

No progressive reformer, according to Lois Rudnick, understood better than Jane Addams the cognitive dissonance Americans experienced as they applied nineteenth-century rural values and standards of behavior to twentieth-century urban, industrialized society.[8] In *Newer Ideals of Peace*, Addams critiqued the doctrines of liberal democracy as framed by the "founding fathers," especially Thomas Jefferson.[9] For Addams, these philosophies were no longer viable. She maintains that although these

> men were strongly under the influence of peace ideals which were earnest-ly advocated . . . their idealism, after all, was founded upon theories con-cerning "the natural man," a creature of the sympathetic imagination.
>
> Because their idealism was of the type that is afraid of experience, these founders refused to look at the difficulties and blunders which a self-governing people were sure to encounter, and insisted that, if only the peo-ple had freedom they would walk continuously in the paths of justice and righteousness. It was inevitable, therefore, that they should have remained quite untouched by that worldly wisdom which counsels us to know life as it is, by that very modern belief that if the world is ever to go right at all, it must go right in its own way.[10]

A political system in which the founders of the Republic talked of "nat-ural man" but conceptualized citizens as abstract, disembodied beings would be incapable of "substituting a machine of newer invention and greater capacity."[11] Consequently, democracy as envisioned by the found-ing fathers would no longer suffice to meet the conditions of turn-of-the-century American society.

In *Democracy and Social Ethics*, Addams maintained that the emerging democratic nation-states of the eighteenth century were dependent on "penalties, coercion, compulsion, [and] remnants of military codes." The very concepts of natural rights and inalienable rights were rooted in the relation "between sovereign and subject, between lawmaker and those whom the law restrains, which has traditionally concerned itself more with the guarding of prerogative and with the rights of property than with the spontaneous life of the people."[12] In other words, classical liber-al democracy was based on a mistrust of the masses. The democratic nation-state, with its rhetoric of natural rights, was based not on a true belief in equality but on suspicion and the interests of the upper classes. For Addams, these inherent foundational premises made liberal democ-racy an unacceptable form of government.

According to Addams, the concepts of inalienable and natural rights were inherently problematic because they ignored the reality that "rights are not 'inalienable,' but are hard-won in the tragic processes of experience."[13] If the experiences of women and immigrants were to count as political, the notions of natural and inalienable rights needed to be reconceptualized as socially produced, not static, and as historically and contextually situated, not as God given. The static view of rights embedded in liberal notions of democracy threatened to impose a conformity of political behavior that restricted the flexibility of democracy to respond to social change and oppression. Like contemporary feminists, Addams was also concerned that the concepts of universal and natural rights, on which notions of the political, especially citizenship, were founded, made invisible gendered and ethnic experiences.[14] As Iris Marion Young maintains, the "discourse of liberal individualism denies the reality of groups . . . and in fact obscures oppression."[15] For Addams, the experiences of women and immigrants as a site for theorizing the political were obscured by the discourses of liberal democracy.

If democracy was to function as a living, breathing, social organism, then radical changes in its very premises were needed. Addams's critique of liberal democracy as obscuring the experiences of women and immigrants through the discourse of universal natural rights is exemplified in two major social issues of the day—the so-called immigrant problem and women's suffrage.

Democracy as "Diversified Human Experience"

A central focus of Addams's theorizing about democracy emerged out of her experiences living at Hull House, in the heart of Chicago's immigrant community. The exploitation, oppression, and manipulation of immigrants by industry, the educational system, and politicians reinforced for Addams the limitations of liberal democracy. The roots of civic corruption that plagued turn-of-the-century cities could be traced to the belief "that our early democracy was a moral romanticism, rather than a well-grounded belief in social capacity and in the efficiency of the popular will."[16]

Ironically, the discourse of universal experience embedded in liberal democracy legitimated the "othering" and marginalization of immigrants. This mistrust of immigrant culture and experience was manifested in dominant ideologies of assimilation and Americanization that emerged in response to immigration. Ignoring a critique of the capitalist/industrial order, many Americans focused on racial and ethnic differences as the cause of social turbulence and moral decay. A proponent of Americanization, Stanford professor Ellwood P. Cubberly, described the southern and eastern European immigrant:

> illiterate, docile, lacking in self-reliance and initiative and not possessing the Anglo-Teutonic conceptions of law, order and government, their coming has served to dilute tremendously our national stock and to corrupt our civic life.[17]

For Cubberly, the first task was to break up ghettos and assimilate immigrants by divesting them of their ethnic character.

This ideology of Americanization reached its peak during World War I and in the early 1920s, when nationalist and xenophobic sentiments were extremely strong. At the height of the Red scare, Hull House provided a safe house for immigrants accused of "radical" and "un-American thinking." During the 1920s, Addams opposed immigration quotas, thereby adopting another controversial stance. She was critical of the narrowness of Americans:

> As Spain in the sixteenth century was obsessed by the necessity of achieving national unity, above the variety of religions, so Twentieth Century America is obsessed by the need of national unity above all else.[18]

She was unwavering in her stance against the nativism expressed in the war fever prior to, during, and immediately following World War I.

Addams staunchly rejected Americanization and assimilation. Instead, her conception of democracy was grounded in the necessity of recognizing the "social capacity and efficiency of the popular will," particularly that of immigrants, women, and the working poor. Rather than corrupt American culture and society, immigrants could, according to Addams, teach Americans a great deal. In contrast to the dominant ideologies arguing that immigrants were responsible for the decay of the moral fiber of America, Addams maintained that it was the immigrant who could regenerate a decaying America.[19] Democracy should be a flexible and expansive form of government that could grow and be enriched by immigrant culture. In fact, democracy was the product of "diversified human experience and its resultant sympathy."[20] For Addams, social democracy embraced immigrants by bringing their values into the community, not by erasing their ethnic culture and lifestyle. Thus, she stated that "the identification with the common lot, which is the essential idea of democracy, becomes the source and expression of social ethics."[21] Her belief that the "common man" had something to teach Americans was evident in the following statement:

It is no easy task to detect and to follow the tiny paths of progress which the unencumbered proletarian, with nothing but his life and capacity for labor, is pointing out for us. These paths lead to a type of government founded upon peace and fellowship as contrasted with restraint and defense. They can never be discovered with the eyes of the doctrinaire. From the nature of the cases, he who would walk these paths must walk with the poor and oppressed, and can only approach them through affection and understanding. The ideas of militarism would forever shut him out from this new fellowship.[22]

Despite her naive idealization and romanticization of the immigrants, Addams again reinforces the notion that democracy must be flexible enough to take into account the experiences of others rather than be locked into a system of universal, natural rights. Difference, not equality, becomes the basis for a true democracy.

To reduce Addams's motivations to maternalism or "noblesse oblige," as has often been done, is to simplify and decontextualize her complex relationship with the local communities in which she lived. In fact, rather than having a condescending view of immigrants, she saw them as playing a central role in shaping democracy. She states in *Democracy and Ethics:*

We know instinctively that if we grow contemptuous of our fellows, and consciously limit our intercourse to certain kinds of people whom we have previously decided to respect, we not only tremendously circumscribe our range of life, but limit the scope of our ethics.[23]

It was her belief that "to know all sorts of men, in an indefinite way, is preparation for better social adjustment—for the remedying of social ills."[24] This outlook was the basis for her work at Hull House.

Her vision of radical democracy as a social organism took seriously the experiences of immigrants and African Americans as a site for theorizing the political. Embracing difference through acknowledging collective experience, not universal, abstract individualism, was paramount if democracy was to avoid the supposed neutrality and objectivity that cloaked the experiences of specific groups like immigrants and women. Addams's analysis of gender, as manifested in her views on suffrage, reflects parallel lines of thinking.

Women's Suffrage as "Means to an End"

Addams's critique of universal natural rights was seen most readily in her belief that women's suffrage was not a goal in and of itself but part of a larger vision of social change. While active in the work of the National American Woman Suffrage Association (NAWSA) and serving as its first vice president, Addams nonetheless recognized the limitations of suffrage in bringing about radical change in social relations.[25] The full realization of democratic ideas would require more than granting suffrage to all citizens. In effect, focusing on suffrage reinforced the notions of natural rights and democracy as public and individual. As Alasdair MacIntyre suggests, the doctrine of rights is "tradition bound, not a discovery of something universal."[26] An understanding of citizenship as public and individual not only obscures the political nature of the everyday work of women (such as teaching, mothering, housework, and community and union activities) but also negates alternative epistemological foundations of citizenship based in women's experiences.

For Addams, democracy entailed not only the recognition of women as citizens but also a redefinition of citizenship. Historically, women could not be full citizens. Carol Pateman reminds us that "women, our bodies and distinctive capacities, represented all that citizenship and equality are not. Citizenship has gained its meaning through the exclusion of women, that is to say (sexual) difference."[27] The very concept of citizenship was dependent on subordination. The exclusion of women from citizenship did not, however, mean that women had no political duties. The eighteenth-century doctrine of "republican motherhood" maintained that women's political duty (not right) was to bear children (sons) and rear them as virtuous citizens. Demanding that women's role as mothers not be seen as subordinate to citizenship, Mary Wollstonecraft, in *Vindication of the Rights of Women*, and Olympe de Gouges, in *Declaration of the Rights of Woman and the Female Citizen*, both argued that female difference, especially motherhood, should be the basis of equal citizenship. To claim the special role of women as mothers as the rationale for citizenship is, as Pateman asserts, to "demand the impossible; such difference is precisely what patriarchal citizenship excludes."[28] And in fact fuller citizenship for women, when it did come in the form of voting rights, was justified ultimately on the basis of difference, even though writers like Elizabeth Cady Stanton had argued for suffrage from the standpoint of equality. In the end, women's claim to higher moral ground was more compelling to legislators than the claim to the vote based on equity. Alice Paul's frustrations during the 1920s in building a base of support for the Equal Rights Amendment on the victory of the Nineteenth Amendment indicated just how tenuous public support was for women's claims to equality with men.

Addams used the notion of gender difference as manifested in the ideology of separate spheres to argue for women's role in the public sphere.

However, she broadened the conception of women's experience beyond mothering and housekeeping. Elevating suffrage as the symbol of citizenship in a democracy reified masculinist conceptions of "politics," thereby obscuring the ways in which women saw themselves as political actors, particularly the work of women's collective action.[29] She included women's collective action and women's pacifism as sites from which to redefine the political. Although Addams has been critiqued as essentializing women's innate moral nature, Victoria Brown maintains that Addams's conception of the differences in the political values of men and women were attributable to women's experiences, not innate habits or instincts.[30] In fact, for middle-class and upper-middle-class women the rhetoric of women's innate feminine altruism and motherly charity was embraced as the cloak under which even the most forceful social and political actions were advanced.[31] Brown maintains that Addams's focus on women's collective duty to reform was a "function of the very particular emphasis Addams placed on economic democracy, [rather] than an accommodation to conservative nostalgia for selfless womanhood."[32]

Addams's vision of "radical democracy" conceptualized citizenship, not as private and individual, but as an ongoing determining of "ideals by our daily actions and decisions not only for ourselves, but largely for each other."[33] In this sense, Addams did not put the classical liberal emphasis on women's individual right to the vote. If democracy was to function as "social organism," citizenship needed to be reconceptualized as a collective act not an individual one. Citizenship that focused on the right to vote functioned to define the political as public and individual. This thrust of classical democracy towards political rights alone reinforced abstract individualism and failed to develop a notion of individual rights as product of collective life. It was the social responsibility to the collective, not the individual, that characterized Addams's vision of radical democracy as a social organism. Her commitment to honoring difference, not equality, as central to democracy has yet to be taken seriously as a site for rethinking the political.

Social Democracy

According to Addams, liberal democracy, with its roots in a preindustrial agrarian society, had not been designed for the needs and conditions of an emerging industrial society. The radical changes brought on by industrialization required a reenvisioning of democracy in which "changes could be considered as belonging to the community as a whole."[34] For Addams, democracy was dependent on social interaction in which diversity was seen as a strength. Yet social interaction was hampered by a class system that created large gaps in economic conditions. Without economic equality, democracy could not flourish. Addams maintained that until class and gender barriers were removed, the social interactions that were the heart of democracy could not occur. In fact, the reduction of democracy to securing the "rights of man" obscured the "duties to humanity," in particular duties to the working classes.[35] In formulating a philosophy of social justice based on economic equality, Addams drew from a variety of social theories, including socialism, Marxism, Fabianism, and cultural feminism. Influenced by Marx, Tolstoy, Ruskin, Ward, Perkins, and others, Addams's pragmatism incorporated a critique of capitalism and gender relations. According to Jill Ker Conway, Addams's social critique "was free from the usual progressive concern with institutionalizing middle-class values. It was future oriented, ready to accept radical change and optimistic about the potential of the American city to become a genuinely creative, pluralistic community."[36]

A Peaceful Working-Class Revolution

Addams had an abiding faith in the working classes. In the Pullman strike of 1894, in which she acted as an arbitrator, her sympathies clearly were with the workers, as evidenced by her comments in her publication *A Modern Lear:*

> We are all practically agreed that the social passion of the age is directed toward the emancipation of the wage-worker; that a great accumulation of moral force is overmastering men and making for this emancipation as in another time it has made for the emancipation of the slave; that nothing will satisfy the aroused conscience of men short of the complete participation of the working classes in the spiritual, intellectual and material inheritance of the human race.[37]

Social democracy was predicated on the recognition and valuing of the experiences of the working classes. The reform of society through democratic decision making necessitated that experiences of all groups be validated. According to Kathryn Kish Sklar: "At the core of Addams' considerable genius lay a Darwinian belief in the vitality of the human species as expressed in working-class people and a determination to join these people, whatever the cost."[38] Sklar characterizes well the absolute belief Addams invested in the working class. However, despite Addams's support of the working poor and labor unions, as well as strikes, her commitment to nonviolence resulted in equating class struggle with war. Class struggle, as articulated in Marxist-socialist thought, was, for Addams, a form of militarism that ultimately undermined the building of community and thus hindered democracy.

A social theory like Marxism that described society as composed of monolithic groups like "proletariat" and "bourgeoisie" threatened to solidify differences; it failed to recognize the communitarian threads that connected groups. Addams rejected the Marxist assumption that class antagonism was the impelling force leading to social revolution. For Addams, the struggle for economic, political, and social advantages was not rooted solely in material needs and limited by the modes of production. Rather, it was rooted in the militarism inherent in notions of "struggle" and "revolution," to which Addams objected on the grounds that military values were "destructive, masculine, and inferior to the more socially advanced feminine values of cooperation and pacifism."[39]

At the same time, Addams shared with Marxist analysis a firm belief in economic equality.[40] Her ongoing struggle with Marxist thought is recalled in *Twenty Years at Hull House,* in which she reflects that she "longed for the comfort of a social creed, which should afford at one and the same time an explanation of the social chaos and the logical steps towards its better understandings."[41] And yet Addams was suspicious of totalizing social theories. In the case of Marxist-socialist thought, Addams critiqued the theory of class conflict as solidifying a monolithic, static view of class that oversimplified and obscured the differences among the working poor with whom Addams interacted on a daily basis at Hull House. She also rejected the notion of false consciousness of the working classes. The idea that members of the working class were ignorant of their oppression and its causes reinforced conceptions of the working class as disempowered and thus ultimately reproduced the very hierarchies that Addams was contesting.

Despite her criticism of Marxism, Addams supported the work of labor unions, although she continually sought nonviolent methods of resolution. In the 1895 publication *Hull House Maps and Papers,* Addams discussed her commitment to laborers and support of their efforts to break the cycle of poverty. Addams was especially interested in supporting trade unions for women. Women's labor unions in Chicago were organized primarily through Hull House and included the Cloakmakers' Union, the Shirtmakers' Union, and the Chicago Women's Trade Union League. Mary Kenney, a union organizer, accepted Addams's invitation that the Bookbinders Union meet at Hull House. Kenney eventually formed the Jane Club, a rented residence for self-supporting working women. Addams advocated the workers' goals of a shorter workday, increased wages, better industrial and general education, and worker protection in the marketplace. Ultimately, though, Addams was committed to a trade union movement oriented toward large-scale social change, not the limited economic benefits of a short-term contract. In fact, she believed labor unions were ultimately a tool of capitalists because they reduced negotiations to single industry issues rather than systematic change.

Addams's unwavering commitment to a cooperative society was deeply embedded in her belief that a social analysis based on a conflict model of society reinforced the conflict process.[42] In this sense, the "radical" nature of her thought, in which social change was dependent on cooperation and peace rather than conflict and aggression, clearly delineated her from other progressives and pragmatists. Addams's rejection of a conflict model as a basis for understanding society and social change and her adoption of a "cooperative-democratic" model of criticism and analysis differed radically from Marxist analysis.[43] Social change for a democratic society was contingent on a rejection of militarism in all its forms, including class struggle. Her understanding of democracy was predicated on cooperation and pacifism, approaches that Addams saw as specifically linked to women's nature and values that were denied expression in a patriarchal society.

Cultural Feminism, Pacifism, and Democracy

Addams's problem with socialist thought stemmed not only from its militarism but also from its rigid orthodoxy and truncated analysis of women's status and values. She believed that social theories predicated on militarism necessarily excluded women. As a consequence, "there was no place for woman and her possible contribution in international affairs under the old diplomacy."[44] Until women's values had full expression, society could not be democratic. Like contemporaries Charlotte Perkins Gilman and Mary Ritter Beard, Addams based her analysis of social relations on women's subjugation as the primary form of oppression. Furthermore, she argued that the oppression of women retarded all human progress.

As a cultural feminist, Addams believed in the superiority of women's values, worldviews, and behavior. This view was not out of line with the dominant ideology of separate spheres in which women were seen as morally superior to men, providing them with "specialized feminine perceptions of social injustice . . . [coming] from women's innate passivity and from women's ability to empathize with the weak and dependent."[45] For Addams this ideology could not be carried to its logical extreme because women were denied full expression in a patriarchal society. Addams carried the ideology of separate spheres to the point where she held that the exploiters of society were masculine and that women shared the true vision of a democratic society.[46] Rather than interpret this as complicity with gender ideologies, I would argue that Addams's standpoint functioned as a form of strategic essentialism.[47] Embracing dominant gender ideologies, she simultaneously disrupted them. This was perhaps nowhere more apparent than in her staunch belief in the natural humanitarian and pacifist traits of women.

Drawn to the cooperative philosophies of Tolstoy and Kropotkin, Addams embraced the concepts of nonresistance and pacifism as central to defining and changing class exploitation.[48] Although Addams eventually criticized Tolstoy as being too utopian and individualistic, she was drawn to his vision of "bread labor," which positioned a simple life connected to the soil as central to a philosophy of nonresistance.[49] This concept appealed to Addams because of the positive connotations associated with making and creating food, traditionally the work of women. The connection between food production and pacifism provided Addams a conceptual framework for using women's experiences as central to shaping public policy and international affairs.

Addams's commitment to nonviolence and pacifism was evidenced in her staunch opposition to World War I. Addams traced this opposition to the early fall of 1914 when a small group of social workers held a series of meetings at the Henry Street Settlement in New York with the goal of formulating a reaction to war. From these meetings, several organizations emerged, including the Union Against Militarism and the Women's Peace Party, in which Addams served as chairman. Three thousand people attended the first convention of the Women's Peace Party in January 1915. Among other demands for limiting arms production and the substitution of economic pressure for warfare, the platform called for education of youth in the ideals of peace, the further humanizing of governments by the extension of suffrage to women, and the investigation of the economic causes of war. The articulation of the connections between education, economics, and gender in addressing militarism as a form of oppression reflected the gendered analysis of change that was undertheorized in traditional Marxist-socialist thought. Most important, her vision of democracy extended the notion of equality to incorporate not only political equality but also social and economic equality. Without economic equality, political and social democracy could not be achieved. In this regard, Addams provided a radical critique of liberal classical democracy with its emphasis on political rights.

For Addams, social democracy would not be realized until women's culture had full expression. Hull House became the realization of women's culture and the manifestation of Addams's ideals of social democracy. Addams's concept of "widening the circle" speaks directly to the issue of how to envision a form of democracy that recognized difference while also maintaining a standpoint politics. Addams was ultimately committed to a separatist standpoint, one that rejected liberal, mainstream, heterosexist assumptions regarding social relations. Although men also lived there, Hull House was a woman's collective established to contest the nuclear, patriarchal family, which Addams saw as inherently undemocratic.[50] True democracy would entail a radical restructuring of social relations that honored a multiplicity of modes of association. Hull House thus became the embodiment of Addams's intention to provide an alternative to the male success myth by creating a "paradigm of national character and culture that is predominately female and includes previously excluded racial and ethnic groups."[51] According to Anne Firor Scott, settlement houses not only were "miniature republics" in which women learned about politics but also were in themselves institutions that contested politics as usual.[52] Hull House thus provided a radical reenvisioning of political culture in which community networks, not individual rights, were the foundation of democracy.

Conclusion

Addams's contribution to social education is her redefinition of citizenship and democracy. For Addams, citizenship was a collective act, not an individual, private act that culminated in the vote. At the heart of her critique of democracy was her rejection of the concept of universal, natural, individual rights, which she ultimately viewed as being assimilationist and obscuring difference. Pluralism was viewed by Addams as enhancing democracy. Yet, in order for citizens to benefit from diversity through interactions across lines of gender, race, class, and ethnicity, there needed to be social and economic equality. Without this, democracy could not come to full fruition. Democracy, as understood by Addams, was a process, a way of life, that necessitated interaction between people. This process required cooperation and pacifism but ultimately resulted in increased empathy and understanding. Violence of any kind, including class struggle, hindered the relationships between people that were a prerequisite for democracy.

Addams's critique of liberal democracy challenges social studies educators to rethink notions of citizenship and democracy. What might a civics curriculum look like that defined citizenship as a collective, cooperative act rather than as merely the duty to vote? How would we teach democracy if we envisioned it as a living, breathing organism—as a way of life? What would it mean to question the taken-for-granted assumptions inherent in the concepts of individual, universal rights? How might we teach democracy as situated, equivalent rights rather than as static, equal rights? In a time when diversity is constructed as a threat to democracy, perhaps leading to our collective demise as a civic polity, I believe that Addams's social theorizing can point towards a renewed vision of the possibilities and necessity of embracing diversity as central to the project of truly achieving American democracy.

Writings of Jane Addams

Jane Addams, *Democracy and Social Ethics* (New York, 1902), 6–12.

We are learning that a standard of social ethics is not attained by traveling a sequestered byway, but by mixing on the thronged and common road where all must turn out for one another, and at least see the size of one another's burdens. To follow the path of social morality results perforce in the temper if not the practice of the democratic spirit, for it implies that diversified human experience and resultant sympathy which are the foundation and guarantee of Democracy.

There are many indications that this conception of Democracy is growing among us. We have come to have an enormous interest in human life as such, accompanied by confidence in its essential soundness. We do not believe that genuine experience can lead us astray any more than scientific data can.

We realize, too, that social perspectives and sanity of judgment come only from contact with social experience; that such contact is the surest corrective of opinions concerning the social order, and concerning efforts, however humble, for its improvement. Indeed, it is a consciousness of the illuminating and dynamic value of this wider and more thorough human experience which explains in no small degree that new curiosity regarding human life which has more of a moral basis than an intellectual one.

The newspapers, in a frank reflection of popular demand, exhibit an omnivorous curiosity equally insistent upon the trivial and the important. They are perhaps the most obvious manifestations of that desire to know, that "What is this?" and "Why do you do that?" of the child. The first dawn of the social consciousness takes this form, as the dawning intelligence of the child takes the form of constant question and insatiate curiosity.

Literature, too, portrays an equally absorbing though better adjusted desire to know all kinds of life. The popular books are the novels, dealing with life under all possible conditions, and they are widely read not only because they are entertaining, but also because they in a measure satisfy an unformulated belief that to see farther, to know all sorts of men, in an indefinite way, is a preparation for better social adjustment—for the remedying of social ills.

Doubtless one under the conviction of sin in regard to social ills finds a vague consolation in reading about the lives of the poor, and derives a sense of complicity in doing good. He likes to feel that he knows about social wrongs even if he does not remedy them, and in a very genuine sense there is a foundation for this belief.

Partly through this wide reading of human life, we find in ourselves a new affinity for all men, which probably never existed in the world before. Evil itself does not shock us as it once did, and we count only that man merciful in whom we recognize an understanding of the criminal. We have learned as common knowledge that much of the insensibility and hardness of the world is due to the lack of imagination which prevents a realization of the experiences of other people. Already there is a conviction that we are under a moral obligation in choosing our experiences, since the result of those experiences must ultimately determine our understanding of life. We know instinctively that if we grow contemptuous of our fellows, and consciously limit our intercourse to certain kinds of people whom we have previously decided to respect, we not only tremendously circumscribe our range of life, but limit the scope of our ethics.

We can recall among the selfish people of our acquaintance at least one common characteristic—the conviction that they are different from other men and women, that they need peculiar consideration because they are more sensitive or more refined. Such people "refuse to be bound by any relation save the personally luxurious ones of love and admiration, or the identity of political opinion, or religious creed." We have learned to recognize them as selfish, although we blame them not for the will which chooses to be selfish, but for a narrowness of interest which deliberately selects its experience within a limited sphere, and we say that they illustrate the danger of concentrating the mind on narrow and unprogressive issues.

We know, at last, that we can only discover truth by a rational and democratic interest in life, and to give truth complete social expression is the endeavor upon which we are entering. Thus the identification with the common lot which is the essential idea of Democracy becomes the source and expression of social ethics. It is as though we thirsted to drink at the great wells of human experience, because we knew that a daintier or less potent draught would not carry us to the end of the journey, going forward as we must in the heat and jostle of the crowd.

Notes

1. J. Addams, "Widening the Circle of Enlightenment: Hull House and Adult Education," *Journal of Adult Education* 2 (Fall/Winter 1930): 276–79.

2. G. Bock and S. James, eds., *Beyond Equality and Difference: Citizenship, Feminist Politics, and Female Subjectivity* (London, 1992); Z. R. Eisenstein, *The Color of Gender: Reimaging Democracy* (Berkeley, Calif., 1994); B. Laslett, J. Brenner, and Y. Arat, *Rethinking the Political: Gender, Resistance, and the State* (Chicago, 1995).

3. L. Bloom, "The Politics of Difference and Multicultural Feminism: Reconceptualizing Education for Democracy," *Theory and Research in Social Education* 26 (Winter 1998): 30–49; C. Pateman, "Equality, Difference, Subordination: The Politics of Motherhood and Women's Citizenship," in *Beyond Equality and Difference*, ed. G. Bock and S. James (London, 1992).

4. N. Fraser, "Equality, Difference, and Radical Democracy," in *Radical Democracy: Identity, Citizenship, and the State*, ed. D. Trend (New York, 1996); C. Mouffe, "Feminism, Citizenship, and Radical Democratic Politics," in *Social Postmodernism: Beyond Identity Politics*, ed. L. Nicholson and S. Seidman (Cambridge, N.Y., 1995); A. Whitson and W. Stanley, "'Re-minding' Education for Democracy," in *Educating the Democratic Mind*, ed. W. Parker (Albany, N.Y., 1996).

5. Fraser, "Equality, Difference, and Radical Democracy."

6. J. Addams, *Democracy and Social Ethics* (New York, 1902), 268.

7. Addams, *Democracy and Social Ethics*, 221.

8. L. Rudnick, "A Feminist American Success Myth: Jane Addams' *Twenty Years at Hull House*," in *Tradition and Talents in Women*, ed. F. Howe (Urbana, Ill., 1991), 145–67.

9. J. Addams, *Newer Ideals of Peace* (New York, 1911).

10. Addams, *Newer Ideals of Peace*, 31–32.

11. Addams, *Newer Ideals of Peace*, 34.

12. Addams, *Democracy and Social Ethics*, 33.

13. Addams, *Democracy and Social Ethics*, 32–33.

14. Eisenstein, "The Color of Gender"; L. Stone, "Feminist Political Theory: Contributions to a Conception of Citizenship," *Theory and Research in Social Education* 24 (Winter 1996): 36–53; I. Young, "Gender as Seriality: Thinking about Women as a Social Collective," in *Rethinking the Political: Gender, Resistance, and the State*, ed. B. Laslett, J. Brenner, and Y. Arat (Chicago 1995), 99–124.

15. Young (in "Gender as Seriality," 104) suggests that without conceptualizing women as a group in some sense, it is not possible to conceptualize oppression as a systematic, structured, institutional process.

16. Addams, *Newer Ideals of Peace*, 34.

17. E. Cubberly, *Changing Conceptions of Education* (Boston, 1909), 15–16.

18. J. Addams, *The Second Twenty Years at Hull House* (New York, 1930), 296.

19. Rudnick, "Feminist American Success Myth," 151.

20. Addams, *Democracy and Social Ethics*, 12.

21. Addams, *Democracy and Social Ethics*, 11.

22. Addams, *Newer Ideals of Peace*, 30.

23. Addams, *Democracy and Social Ethics*, 10.

24. Addams, *Democracy and Social Ethics*, 8.

25. Charlotte Perkins Gilman rejected suffrage, believing that equal relations between the sexes would emerge only when economic inequalities, such as women's use as domestic slaves, were redressed. Mary Ritter Beard, although an ardent suffragist, also questioned investing energy in a political reform that left the foundations of American society untouched and brought women into a political culture defined by men for men. Simple-minded slogans calling for equality, she insisted, denied the power and force of the moral community of women. The militant call for absolute equality, Beard believed, denied the existence and value of female culture.

26. Alasdair MacIntyre, *After Virtue: A Study in Moral Theory* (Notre Dame, Ind., 1984), quoted in Nel Noddings, "Social Studies and Feminism," *Theory and Research in Social Education* 20 (Fall 1992), 230–41. Noddings suggests that if "the different voice of women were to speak in the social studies," a different emphasis would emerge in curriculum. Citizenship, the chief rationale for social studies education, does not include much of what is considered private, such as family membership or homeworking, thus embedding gender bias at the very root of social studies education.

27. Pateman, "Equality, Difference, Subordination," 19.

28. Pateman, "Equality, Difference, Subordination," 20.

29. Gerda Lerner suggests that the "historiographic emphasis on the organized women's movement reflects traditional interest in organized political activity in the public realm." See G. Lerner, *The Creation of Feminist Consciousness* (New York, 1993), 13.

30. V. Brown, "Jane Addams, Progressivism, and Woman Suffrage," in *One Woman, One Vote: Rediscovering the Woman Suffrage Movement*, ed. M. Wheeler (Oregon, 1995), 179–202.

31. M. Ryan, *Womanhood in America* (New York, 1979).

32. V. Brown, "Addams, Progressivism, and Suffrage," 183.

33. Addams, *Twenty Years at Hull House*, 256.

34. Addams, *Newer Ideals of Peace*, 124.

35. Addams, *Newer Ideals of Peace*, 29.

36. J. Conway, "Women Reformers and American Culture, 1870–1930," *Journal of Social History* 5 (Spring 1971–72): 164–77.

37. J. Addams, *A Modern Lear: Jane Addams' Response to the Pullman Strike of 1894* (Chicago, 1994), 20. The original response appeared in *Survey* 29 (2 November 1912): 131–37.

38. K. Sklar, *Florence Kelley and the Nation's Work: The Rise of Women's Political Culture, 1830–1900* (New Haven, Conn., 1995), 176.

39. M. Deegan, *Jane Addams and the Men of the Chicago School, 1892–1918* (New Brunswick, N.J., 1990), 226.

40. Addams's sympathy with Marxist thought was evident in her support of the Russian Revolution. This support resulted in her labeling by the United States government as the "most dangerous woman" in America, as noted in Deegan, *Addams and the Chicago School*, 7.

41. Addams, *Twenty Years at Hull House*, 187.

42. In this regard, Addams differed dramatically from her contemporaries at the University of Chicago who relied on a "social-technological" analysis of social relations; see Deegan, *Addams and the Chicago School.*

43. Deegan, *Addams and the Chicago School,* 256.

44. Addams, *Democracy and Social Ethics,* 81.

43. Jill Ker Conway suggests that the failure to see women's activism for what it is, a real departure from women's domesticity, indicates the controlling power of the stereotypes of the female temperament. These stereotypes continued, according to Conway, unaltered from the 1870s to the 1930s; see Conway, "Women Reformers," 166.

46. Conway, "Women Reformers," 171.

47. G. Spivak, *The Postcolonial Critique: Interviews, Strategies, Dialogues* (New York, 1990).

48. Deegan, *Addams and the Chicago School,* 275.

49. Tolstoy was a continuing influence throughout Addams's life, as evidenced by her ongoing study of him through the 1930s, when she compared his ideas with those of Gandhi.

50. Sklar, *Kelley and the Nation's Work,* 130.

51. Rudnick, "Feminist American Success Myth," 146.

52. A. Scott, *Natural Allies: Women's Associations in American History* (Urbana, Ill., 1993).

5

Shaping Inclusive Social Education:
Mary Ritter Beard and Marion Thompson Wright

Margaret Smith Crocco

Mary Ritter Beard
Permission by Schlesinger Library,
Radcliffe College. Photo by Underwood &
Underwood, Washington, D.C.

Marion Thompson Wright
Reprinted by permission of Giles R. Wright.

In 1996 the seventy-fifth anniversary of the founding of the National Council for the Social Studies (NCSS) was marked by the publication of a number of valuable retrospectives concerning the field's origins and evolution.[1] These studies focused chiefly on the organizational embodiment of the social studies movement through NCSS. As such, they represent only partial explanations for the contemporary character of social education, especially its development in settings beyond official professional channels. Because these retrospectives take the history of the field as that of the organization, they fail to consider a tradition of concern with issues of diversity that was developed outside the boundaries of NCSS. Over the last several decades, research by Hazel Hertzberg, Murry Nelson, Oliver Keels, and others indicates that a broader, less institutionally oriented approach to defining the origins of social studies also exists.[2] This chapter is situated in that latter tradition, relying on a foundational rather than an organizational perspective in analyzing the field's history. More concretely, by substituting the concept of social education for that of social studies, consideration can be given to two women who advocated treatment of diversity at an early stage in social studies' development as a field but who had only weak ties to institutional channels within the emergent discipline.

Just as writing the history of a field can be considered a political act, determining whose story gets told in state-sponsored curricula has become highly contested terrain.[3] Knowledge production by academic researchers continues to expand the scope of material with at least potential relevance to social studies education, while multicultural educators have heightened demands that each group's history be reflected in school curriculum. Even if such demands were to abate, the pressures on social studies emanating from the trickle-down force of a university-fed knowledge explosion in areas like women's history and black history will surely continue. As a result, social studies will undoubtedly grapple with the matter of inclusive curriculum for many years to come. Clarifying social educators' past attention to diversity is important to a comprehensive understanding of the growth and development of social studies as well as instructive for future consideration of these issues.

Mary Ritter Beard and Marion Thompson Wright had only indirect ties to the emerging structures within social studies education. Between 1910 and 1960, the period in which these women worked, social studies was, of course, less defined in its contours than it is today. Although Beard and Wright in many respects worked on the margins of social studies education, their pioneering efforts have proved significant in defining the field, even if they are less widely acknowledged than those of other social studies progenitors like Charles Beard and George Counts.

As regards the organizational level, Linda Levstik has commented that

> NCSS was the product of two social phenomena. The first was the move toward professionalism among historians and a concomitant interest in how history was taught in the schools. The second was a growing interest among social scientists and social welfare advocates in an integrated field—often called "social studies"—aimed at social improvement and civic responsibility.[4]

The work of Beard and Wright developed within the intellectual milieu of "the new social history," which overlapped significantly with both groups Levstik describes. Beard's and Wright's contributions extended new social history into an interdisciplinary consideration of gender and race with the explicit aim of bringing this knowledge into the schools. Like that of scholars in both groups Levstik identifies, Beard's and Wright's research was motivated by contemporary concerns and the desire to ameliorate social inequalities. Their lack of connection to official organizations within social studies can be explained by a number of factors, including race and gender, but has undoubtedly contributed to their invisibility within mainstream histories of the field.

While the terms *multiculturalism* and *multicultural education* have gained prominence in the last ten years, the roots of these approaches to social studies can be traced back beyond the 1960s, despite Garcia and Buendia's discovery of the almost total absence of articles on diversity in the NCSS publication *Social Education* prior to this date.[5] Looking beyond the pages of this journal is necessary, therefore, in identifying the origins of an inclusive approach to social studies curriculum. Between 1910 and 1950, Beard wrote numerous books and articles on women's history and education and promoted her views through speeches, course syllabi, and textbooks written with her husband, Charles Austin Beard.[6] Wright served as scholar, counselor, and teacher educator between 1940 and 1962 at Howard University, helping to bring African American history into the schools through vehicles such as the *Negro History Bulletin* and Negro History Month.

In 1996 the president of the American Studies Association, Elaine Tyler May, gave a speech that offers a model for the kind of approach I have adopted in this chapter. May's address, "The Radical Roots of American Studies," suggests that academic creation stories tend to be oedipal tales, revolving around "killing off the alleged fathers to create a new, oppositional scholarship."[7] The founders of American studies shared many social reconstructionist traits: political engagement, recognition of the ill effects of industrial capitalism, and profound sensitivity to the class divisions within the United States. Merle Curti, Wright's dissertation sponsor at Teachers College, Columbia University, was involved in both movements. May's address invites scholars to a fresh round of mythmaking concerning the origins of American studies. "With canon bashing the rage in so many fields of late, it is time that we bash our own canon, too," she concludes, "to see what's really in there and to add a few more voices to the canon fodder."[8]

While it is not my intention here to bash the "creation canon" in social studies, I do wish to suggest the partiality of past examinations focusing on institutional arrangements. Only by looking beyond the centerpiece of the recent retrospectives, NCSS and its organ, *Social Education*, can we gain an understanding of the paths by which other voices contributed to social studies curriculum development for the schools.

The Intellectual Context

In her examination of the origins of social science in the United States, Dorothy Ross asserts that "Dewey's pragmatism, like the characteristic doctrines of Progressive social science, emerged directly from the Gilded Age crisis of American exceptionalism and revised the exceptionalist heritage to embody the new liberal and historicist awareness of change."[9] Defining history as the study of social change prompted James Harvey Robinson and Charles A. Beard to reconsider whether the promises of democracy had been met for all America's constituent groups. Keenly aware that only by excluding the stories of the disenfranchised and underprivileged could the claim to exceptionalism be sustained, they looked toward education to close the gap between ideal and real.

As Hazel Hertzberg has shown, "It was the advocates of the social studies, forwarding a vision of history advocated by Robinson, who stepped forward to bridge the gap between the academic study of the past and the modern concern for the production of good citizens."[10] Social studies reformers in the early years of this century found much inspiration in Dewey's work, especially his advocacy of closer links between school and society.[11] Dewey's orientation to social science made him sympathetic to the "new social history," which Hertzberg defines as "progressivism manifest in the historical profession."[12] He and his followers were deeply involved in many of the progressive initiatives of the day, such as the settlement-house and women's rights movements, causes to which Mary Beard and Marion Wright also subscribed.

Robinson and Charles Beard were colleagues and close friends of

Dewey's, and the three ate lunch regularly together during their years at Columbia.[13] This trio, along with Arthur Schlesinger at Harvard University and a number of other scholars, collaborated with representatives of elementary and secondary schools, normal schools, and teacher education colleges to promote a curriculum designed for social efficiency and good citizenship. In 1920 a group of professors in education and social studies subjects from Teachers College, Columbia University suggested the formation of an organization to address issues related to articulation of the nature of the emerging field and its practice in the schools. As Stephen J. Thornton reports, as a result of this overture, a meeting was held in 1921 in Atlantic City, New Jersey, at which NCSS was founded.[14]

About the same time, Carter G. Woodson, a student of Schlesinger's at Harvard, built on the foundation laid by W. E. B. Du Bois and others in scholarship on African American history. In 1915 Woodson published *The Education of the Negro prior to 1861*, and in 1933, *The Mis-education of the Negro*. Because mainstream publishers would not consider their work, over the next two decades Woodson and his colleague, Charles Wesley, created the Association for the Study of Negro Life and History (ASNLH) as a means of directly disseminating their research to the public. Encouraged by white historians such as Albert Bushnell Hart of Harvard, a central figure in the social studies movement,[15] Woodson and Wesley pioneered the production and dissemination of knowledge about African American history to teachers, scholars, and the general public.[16] They shared a belief that this new knowledge would enhance black self-esteem and improve white attitudes toward African Americans.[17]

The Beards' shared goal was "to convert the present into a more decent future."[18] Education, broadly conceived, was the means they adopted for promoting social change. The first civics textbook they wrote in 1914 criticized other textbooks for holding the view that civic life was static rather than dynamic and progressive.[19] This book was written at Mary Beard's suggestion in order to include women in the idea of citizenship, since by this time they constituted the majority of high school students.[20] She returned to her idea of women as citizens the following year in *Women's Work in Municipalities*.[21]

One of the Beards' closest friends was Merle Curti. Curti received his Ph.D. at Harvard, where he was a student of Frederick Jackson Turner's. After Turner's retirement, Curti worked with Schlesinger. Curti taught briefly at Beloit and Smith Colleges before coming to Teachers College, Columbia University, in 1938. His years at Teachers College were limited to four; he spent the remainder of his career in the Department of History at the University of Wisconsin.[22]

During the 1930s, Curti was associated with George Counts, Charles Beard, and John Dewey in the publication of *The Social Frontier*. Counts recruited Curti into the Department of History and Social Studies at Teachers College. At that time, the department offered degrees in history, educational sociology, geography, and social studies. A pacifist and socialist, Curti shared many of the Beards' social concerns: women's rights, the plight of the average workingman, and racial discrimination. During his education at Harvard, he became a friend of Charles A. Wesley, Carter Woodson's colleague at ASNLH. According to Meier and Rudwick's history of the development of the black historical profession, during the 1930s and 1940s, Curti "would journey periodically to Washington to meet with Woodson, and he was the first in the guild to seek seriously to integrate the history of blacks into his monographs on the American past."[23]

While at Teachers College, Curti guided the development of Wright's powerful work on Negro education in New Jersey, more accurately described as a full history of African Americans in the state. During the 1950s, Wright served as research assistant for the National Association for the Advancement of Colored People (NAACP), "compiling evidence for the public school desegregation cases" that would be decided in *Brown v. Board of Education* in 1954: "The methods of research she used to gather data on New Jersey were applied to a study of the United States as a whole, showing injurious patterns of discrimination throughout the nation."[24]

In 1932, Charles Beard wrote *A Charter for the Social Sciences in the Schools*, characterizing the goal of social studies as "inquiry rather than indoctrination."[25] This book was part of a series; both Counts and Curti contributed volumes.[26] Curti's *Social Ideas of American Educators* became the basis for several of the courses he offered at Teachers College. A subsequent volume, *Growth of American Thought*, won the Pulitzer Prize.[27] This book drew heavily on the research of the ASNLH on antebellum black thought and included an entire chapter on Booker T. Washington, an "unprecedented" step, according to Meier and Rudwick.[28] Curti also wrote *Control of Social Studies Textbooks* for NCSS and the National Education Association (NEA);[29] this book reflected his concurrence with Charles Beard that social studies ought to be inquiry oriented.[30]

Curti's publications helped establish intellectual and cultural history as new emphases within the profession. He used the pages of the *Teachers College Record* to promote the application of these subjects to the secondary school curriculum. In one article, he referred to Teachers College as "a pioneer among professional schools of education in trying to acquaint the teacher with the literature of American cultural history."[31] In support of this claim, he cited J. Montgomery Gambrill's 1914 course on social history at Teachers College. Even earlier than this, Charles Beard had offered his own courses at Teachers College utilizing the new approach of interdisciplinary cultural history.

As social reconstructionists, Beard, Counts, Curti, and Dewey advocated the use of history and social science to promote social and educational change. They used *The Social Frontier* to spread their views, hoping to move American culture away from unrestrained individualism and toward the ideal of democratic collectivism. Reforms in education could contribute to this end. In an article entitled "Can Education Share in Social Reconstruction?" published in October 1934, John Dewey wrote: "I do not think . . . that the schools can in any literal sense be the builders of a new social order. But the schools will surely, as a matter of fact and not of ideal, share in the building of the social order of the future."[32] This remark reflects views propounded earlier by George Counts in speeches and publications.[33]

In the late 1930s, the group made plans for an institute of social research at Teachers College that would advance these objectives. The plan was short-circuited when Beard encountered an article in the *New York Times* announcing the intention of the University of Pennsylvania to offer an interdisciplinary program "for students who wish to specialize in the broad field of the development of social and cultural institutions."[34] Because the program sounded too close to their own idea, the group abandoned the project. The Penn program eventually became the first American studies department in the nation.

As program director of the American Historical Association (AHA) convention in 1940, Curti arranged several sessions on "the common man," including full panels on women's, labor, and African American history. Du Bois chaired the session "The Negro in American History" and invited the historian Rayford Logan, of Howard University, to participate. Curti invited Mary Beard to chair the session on women's history. While gratified by the introduction of women's history to the AHA program, she declined the invitation, evidently irked at not being given a role in lining up the other panelists.[35]

Curti became president of the Mississippi Valley Historical Association in 1952 and vice president of the American Studies Association and president of the American Historical Association in 1954. He used his official addresses to these organizations to attack McCarthyism, loyalty oaths, and anti-intellectualism. During the 1950s, he also wrote a high school history textbook with Paul Todd, a revised edition of which is still in print. Like Charles Beard, Curti was "often attacked, especially in the

1950s, for his liberalism, his relativism, and for his defense of unpopular causes."[36]

During Curti's brief tenure at Teachers College, his personal qualities and intellectual stature attracted a wide range of students. Former faculty member Alice Spieseke recalled Curti's pleasure in the contribution to public education made by his teaching at the college. She commented, in particular, on his openness to new ideas:

> He wasn't dogmatic; he wasn't a person who was emphatic in his notions. He was always willing to talk with you about ideas and if you entertained or saw things from a point of view different from his, he would explore it further, never criticize you because you differed from him. Students liked his open-mindedness and that he treated them as equals.[37]

Curti's reputation as a historian sympathetic to the field of black history undoubtedly provided a catalyst for Wright's choice of him as sponsor of her dissertation. During the 1920s and 1930s, many African Americans attended Teachers College with scholarship assistance made available by the Julius Rosenwald Fund and the Rockefeller Foundation. These organizations supported the preparation of scholars and teachers for black schools and colleges throughout the South. In 1938 between two hundred and three hundred African Americans enrolled at Teachers College, constituting almost 10 percent of the student body. These figures represented the college's interest in the "urgent and needy matter of Negro education."[38] Courses and lectures by speakers such as Dr. Mordecai Johnson, the first black president of Howard University, were regularly offered. Seven hundred people came to hear Johnson speak on the topic "The Future Outlook for American Negroes" in 1930. A number of well-known black educators took degrees at Teachers College, including Lucy Diggs Slowe, first dean of women at Howard, and Charles Thompson, dean of the School of Education there. Indeed, Paula Giddings asserts that Howard University "followed the lead of such schools as Columbia University in establishing a Teachers College that offered a more professional, comprehensive, and varied program than the two year normal school,"[39] ties that are more fully documented in Rayford Logan's history of Howard University.[40]

During the summer months, Teachers College offered extension courses in seven states throughout the South and the District of Columbia. Lawrence Cremin indicates that these courses were largely attended by women teachers seeking coursework beyond their normal-school preparation.[41] Over two thousand individuals, only 18 percent of whom had baccalaureate degrees, were registered in extension courses during 1927 and 1928. "At first," Cremin writes, "some felt that the relationship between the two racial groups might be disturbed by a northern university's intrusion into a southern area. But at the close of the year, all those connected with the experiment, instructors, students and local administrators alike, praised the work that had been done."[42]

Under the leadership of Professor Mabel Carney of the Department of Rural Education, a student organization for African Americans was established in 1928.[43] A Midwestern woman, Carney received her education at Teachers College and was appointed to the faculty in 1917. A suffrage supporter, she claimed three lifelong interests: rural education, the welfare of African Americans, and world peace. With support from the Rosenwald Fund, Carney brought James Weldon Johnson, Du Bois, Booker T. Washington, and Mary McLeod Bethune, among others, to participate in a lecture series on "race relations" that regularly drew large crowds.

In her regular report to the president and dean of Teachers College, Carney mentioned professors with a particular interest in "Negro student welfare," including George Counts, Esther Lloyd-Jones, and Sarah Sturtevant. Both Professors Lloyd-Jones and Sturtevant worked closely with Slowe in redefining the role of dean of women from that of matron to expert in the education of women.[44] In 1926 Carney toured Africa, including a trip to Cape Town. Subsequently, she traveled throughout the South, visiting Hampton Institute and Lincoln, Howard, Tuskegee, and Fisk Universities.

Mary Beard and Marion Wright were thus part of an intellectual milieu that included the new social history, social reconstructionism, and the burgeoning social studies movement. Like their male counterparts, they were dedicated to using new forms of knowledge to extend democracy and the benefits of citizenship to women and African Americans. They shared the same progressive faith as the organizational architects of NCSS that social education in the schools could become the conduit for such change. By pressing the boundaries of this movement toward a more complex consideration of gender and race, Beard and Wright provided models for those who would build on their work in subsequent decades.

Mary Ritter Beard (1876–1958)

In the intellectual history of the twentieth century, Mary Ritter Beard's contributions have clearly been overshadowed by those of her husband. Newer considerations of her husband's legacy, however, have made fairer assessments than earlier ones of the depth of their collaboration.[45] In the last twenty years, the women's studies movement has given her ideas a serious reexamination, most recently in a book edited by Nancy Cott that assembles a large number of her letters and, in the introduction, provides a lengthy analysis of her thinking.[46] New editions of a number of Mary Beard's books have also been published. An enigmatic figure in many respects, Mary Beard resists easy labeling, even as feminist. An antiessentialist before the term was invented, she attempted to hold class and gender in balance as she studied the "long history" of women. Because she opposed many prominent women's leaders of the day, was dubious about the merits of the equal rights movement, and wrote history "without portfolio," she became something of a pariah in certain academic circles. Beard remained convinced throughout her life that "sexual equality was a deficient goal for women if it meant measuring up to a male norm."[47] A true radical, she often attacked even those audiences she was invited to address, chiding them for the timidity of their goals and outlooks.

Beard wrote eight books of her own and coauthored seven with her husband. Cott remarks that "like many the accomplished wife of a more famous man, Mary Beard achieved much greater public prominence as her husband's collaborator than she gained on her own as a suffragist, reformer, or author."[48] Upon his death in 1948, "his evaluators read her out of the record, calling *The Rise of American Civilization,* for example, 'his' masterpiece, 'his' greatest work."[49] Her independent publications include *Woman's Work in Municipalities, A Short History of the American Labor Movement, On Understanding Women,* and her magnum opus, *Woman as Force in History.*[50] Beard insisted that the work of citizenship and civilization be redefined to include women's role in sustaining families and communities. Most provocatively, she rejected the feminist claim of women's subordination throughout what she called "long history."

Beard worked for suffrage but opposed Alice Paul's Equal Rights Amendment, a position reflecting her sensitivity to class issues. Along with Florence Kelley and Frances Perkins, whose roots were in the labor movement, Beard believed that "equal treatment of unequals is the greatest inequality."[51] As Beard saw it, such an amendment primarily served privileged women. In her writing, she contrasted the lives of those women who dealt with the "central problems of life" around survival with those of women who wavered "between the will to create" and "the will merely to enjoy."[52] In an essay called "Mothercraft," Beard criticized middle-class women for the "pious precepts" that ignored poor women's "bitter struggle for the barest necessities of life."[53] She cited the "Institutes of Mothercraft" devised by middle-class women for poor women that assumed family dysfunction resulted from maternal failure. Beard rejected both diagnosis and solution, instead arguing for overhaul of a social and economic structure supporting neither mothers nor families.

In this essay and later work, Beard rejected the distinctions other scholars made between "social" and "political" activity, suggesting that "everything that counts is political." In *Women's Work in Municipalities*, she describes the numerous projects undertaken by women's clubs and teachers' associations as political activity. She concludes that narrow definitions of politics had obscured the important contributions women made as citizens.

Charles and Mary Beard relied on creative, popularly oriented approaches to communicating their views. As Nancy Cott comments, "both remained deeply skeptical that conventional establishments of higher learning furthered the goals of democratic progress and social enlightenment."[54] For example, they founded the Workers Education Bureau of America for training in the social sciences as preparation for working-class leadership.[55] This program was affiliated with Brookwood Labor College of Katonah, New York, and resembled the summer school for women in trade unions launched at Bryn Mawr College around the same time.[56] In 1920 Mary Beard wrote *A Short History of the American Labor Movement* as a contribution to the bureau's Workers' Bookshelf series. Throughout her life, Beard produced numerous speeches, radio addresses, and newspaper and magazine articles in an effort to extend the reach of her ideas.

Beard recognized the uneven way that social and political change affected women of different classes and races. During her suffrage days, she was troubled by the manner in which the increasingly conservative mainstream groups excluded African American women for fear of alienating Southern women. Beard's early affiliation with Alice Paul's Congressional Union reflected their shared tutelage under the Pankhursts in England and the more inclusive nature of Paul's group. In the suffrage parade organized by the Congressional Union on the eve of Woodrow Wilson's inauguration, Beard, her husband, and their children joined a group of black marchers in a show of solidarity.[57] In subsequent years, such unity became increasingly rare as the National American Woman Suffrage Association appealed to anti-immigrant and racist sentiment to advance its cause.

Beard wrote a good deal of women's history but found that a key audience for it, the women's colleges, often rejected the conclusions she drew from her research. She rankled at "the false dogma of feminism" that women had never done anything of substance in the world.[58] She faulted the writers of women's studies courses at Douglass and Smith Colleges for suggesting that women have chiefly been victims of history. In the book *On Understanding Women,* she wrote that "in their quest for rights, they have naturally placed emphasis on their wrongs, rather than their achievements and possessions, and have retold history as a story of their long martyrdom."[59] She concluded that these views have contributed "to the tradition that history has been made by men alone, that civilization, at least the evils of it, is the fruit of masculine labors or will, and have demanded that those who have hitherto been nothing should become as near like the males as possible to be something."[60]

Not only did Beard find this conclusion inaccurate, but also she believed it detrimental to women's ability to grasp their future possibilities in society. According to Beard, women's history, correctly done, could create the "female determination of feminine destiny." In a syllabus she prepared for the American Association of University Women (AAUW), Beard suggested that women professors "are sometimes the most hostile to the suggestion" that women's story be added to the curriculum. She asserted that "the 'sexless' education upon which they insist is not, after all, abstract to any great degree. It is basically a sex education—masculine in design and spirit."[61] Her conclusions are echoed by Adrienne Rich in "Toward a Woman-Centered University," published originally as a report of the Carnegie Foundation for the Advancement of Teaching, which invokes Mary Beard at the beginning of the essay.[62]

Beard challenged M. Carey Thomas, president of Bryn Mawr College, for her belief that in shaping women's education, "what was good enough for men was perfect for women."[63] In an address to the AAUW, Beard directly challenged the pursuit of a college education as a means of gaining equality with men. She often stated her fear that establishing women's education on male principles would diminish the force of "enlightened humanism."[64] Each time women demonstrated, for example, that they "could compose just as rigid documents for their doctoral theses as the most sterile man, there was rejoicing by the egalitarians."[65]

An early critical theorist of education, she argued that the so-called democratic education of the day socialized women and girls "to satisfy the political and educational needs of a bourgeois, competitive society."[66] Feminists unthinkingly accepted the rules of the capitalist game, she argued, when they fought for an equal place in an unjust system. Beard became increasingly disillusioned with higher education for women as she came to the conclusion that it inhibited women's interest in social reform by fostering individualism at the expense of commitment to communal life and social change.

A seeming inconsistency in Mary Beard's approach to women's education lies in her refusal to consider a role for vocational education or home economics in the college curriculum. Given her efforts to untangle what she saw as the conflation of the public and private in traditional historiography and her insistence on women's contributions to civilization through their sustenance of families and communities, this opposition needs reconciling. On the one hand, she rejected an education for women based on male values and male standards; on the other, she saw home economics as a form of vocational education that had no place in college and a reversion "from full opportunity for women in public life."[67] Perhaps the best explanation that can be given about this and other contradictions in her work is that while enhancing her freedom to engage new subject matter, her position outside conventional academic life may have cost her the critical scrutiny by colleagues that might have ultimately produced greater consistency in her work.

In *Woman as Force in History*, Beard moved her critique of women's status one step further, calling for a different vision of equality from that of academic feminists. She called female equality not a "woman question" but a "human" one.[68] While championing the view that "women's past history . . . must be regarded as indispensable to the maintenance and promotion of civilization in the present age," she reflected the temper of the post–World War II world, seeing the necessity of utilizing the power of both men and women in the struggle "*against* disruptive forces of barbarism and *for* the realization of the noblest ideals in the heritage of humanity" (emphasis in original).[69] For Beard, the future of civilization itself was at stake. She saw equal opportunity to participate in "the disruptive forces of barbarism" as self-defeating for feminism and for all human beings. True equality, according to Beard, moved womanly values center stage within the culture. Like Peggy McIntosh and Nel Noddings today, she claimed that these values offered the best hope of rescuing Western civilization from its destructive potential.[70]

Mary Beard made a more direct contribution to social education through her coauthorship with Charles Beard of a number of influential textbooks, including *American Citizenship* (1914), *A History of the United States* (1921), *The Rise of American Civilization* (1927), *America in Midpassage* (1939), *The American Spirit* (1942), and *A Basic History of the United States* (1944).[71] Taken as a whole, the Beards' textbooks sought to implement the 1916 NEA report on social studies in the schools. One historian estimated that these books sold over five million copies between 1912 and 1952 and were used in elementary and junior and senior high schools.[72] However, some historians have also taken the position that since they were unable to determine firsthand the nature of the collaboration between the Beards on these books, they have simply chosen to consider them the work of Charles alone.[73] Charles Beard took pains during his lifetime to emphasize the true partnership involved in the production of these books. In fact, he instructed his Macmillan publishers to avoid quoting reviewers who singled him out as the sole author since this was, he asserted repeatedly, false.[74]

In several respects, Mary Beard pushed her husband toward an even broader understanding of social history. In a letter to a friend, she explained that her view of history as the entire story of human life represented a new way of looking at the past for her husband:

> History is in fact the whole story of humankind including literature, philosophy, and biology and everything else. This is the way I see it and having thus seen it, I have in my collaboration with CAB [Charles A. Beard], from its beginning widened politics, war and law and political economy to cover more aspects of human development. CAB has accepted my wide interest and done everything he could to work with me as I have done everything I could to work with him.[75]

A perusal of their textbooks indicates that women's history reaches a level scarcely matched by most current social studies texts. Among the topics discussed are women in colonial times, witchcraft, mothers' pensions, women's clubs, Lowell mills, child labor laws, suffrage, temperance, and tenement house reform. The textbooks treat the following women: Harriet Martineau, Mary Wollstonecraft, Mercy Otis Warren, Abigail Adams, Elizabeth Cady Stanton, Julia Ward Howe, Dorothea Dix, Eliza Pinckney, and Susan B. Anthony, among others. At the end of one chapter of *History of the United States,* students are invited to debate the statement, "Women now have equal opportunities with men."[76]

Beard's last decades were spent in an effort to establish a solid foundation for women's collective memory through establishment of the Women's Center for World Archives. These archives would contain a variety of materials—diaries, household records, shopping lists, correspondence, manuscripts—whatever revealed patterns of women's thoughts, roles, and actions. As part of this project, Beard wished to establish a "true woman's college," a women's research institute, and an academy of women to encourage women to take an interest in their own history. At the same time, she launched several encyclopedia projects, attempting to convince *Britannica* and *Collier's* to augment their treatment of women's history. In the end, her own estrangement from the established institutions of women's education probably best explains her inability to bring these dreams to fruition.

Marion Thompson Wright (1905–1962)

Historians of the traditionally black colleges indicate that male administrators of the early twentieth century typically viewed black coeds as "wild, untamed," and in need of "constant surveillance."[77] As a result, women's activities in such institutions were extremely restricted. Despite, or perhaps because of, the fact that their presence increased during the 1920s to around 20 percent of all graduates of black coeducational institutions,[78] women were often made to feel unwelcome. Relations between women and the administration at Howard University, the preeminent coeducational black institution of higher education, reached a nadir in 1912 when thirty-three female students requested that the president appoint a dean to communicate their needs more effectively to the administration. The request was not granted for a decade, until Lucy Diggs Slowe was appointed in 1922. During the 1920s, the proportion of bachelor of arts degrees awarded to women climbed steeply; by 1930 it had risen to slightly over 50 percent, reflecting black women's response to the articulation of their mission as "racial uplift" through teaching, social work, and voluntarism.[79]

Slowe began her tenure at Howard under the last white president of the school, J. Stanley Durkee. From her earliest days on campus, she criticized the restrictive policies that demeaned women. In 1929, when the first black president, Mordecai Johnson, took over, his generally autocratic approach to administration and his tendency to call all his female professors and administrators "daughter" provoked even greater difficulties.[80] One of the consuming battles of Slowe's life occurred during the years just before her death in the 1930s as she fought Johnson in a public and acrimonious controversy over the role of female students, faculty, and staff on campus.

Slowe charged that black colleges tended to perpetuate a patriarchal outlook with their clear message that black women were expected to serve and not lead. To prove her point, Slowe surveyed forty-four coeducational black colleges and found that women received little in courses, activities, or role models to prepare them for leadership.[81] In 1933, Slowe published an article, "Higher Education of Negro Women," in the *Journal of Negro Education* in which she argued for changes in the treatment of black women by these colleges. Slowe advocated a shift from the old order toward a new approach that would encourage women in "the making and executing of the rules under which they live."[82] In 1936, she invited Mary Beard to Howard to deliver an address on women's history that, she hoped, would "instill confidence in women students."[83]

From the beginning of her tenure, Slowe demanded a role for women on university councils, dormitories for women on campus, and an expanded counseling service for female students. Wright was one of the first female students to spend four years under Slowe's aegis, benefiting directly from Slowe's efforts by gaining a position as a resident adviser in the new female dormitory during her senior year.

Born in 1905 in Newark, New Jersey, Wright graduated at the top of her class, one of only a handful of African Americans at elite Barringer High School. This was a remarkable accomplishment when one considers that Wright dropped out of high school to marry at the age of sixteen and had two children in the subsequent two years before completing her degree. Only because of her mother's pressure and insistence did she return to Barringer; it was also her mother who encouraged her to apply for a scholarship to college. But the offer she received from Howard University placed her in a difficult position.

At that time, Howard's policy prohibited married or divorced women from attending the university. As late as 1913, "Howard's board of directors would vote that any female teacher who 'thereafter married while teaching at the university would be considered as having resigned her position.'"[84] Wright chose to conceal her marriage and children and accept the scholarship. During the 1930s, she divorced and remarried. Even after she returned to Howard as a faculty member in 1940, however, she concealed the existence of her children. She fully understood Baptist minister and Howard University president Mordecai Johnson's views concerning divorce and recognized full well what his judgment would be concerning her earlier deception of the university. She continued to keep her family a secret to most members of the Howard community until her death.

Wright graduated magna cum laude from Howard in 1927 and received a fellowship to study for a master's degree in education. Wright's thesis examined the segregated public school systems of sixteen states. Charles Thompson, dean of the School of Education at Howard, later suggested to Wright that she continue her analysis of school segregation through the study that became her doctoral dissertation at Teachers College.[85]

Wright returned to New Jersey to do a certificate program at the New York School for Social Work, later a part of Columbia University. The curriculum emphasized education and social work in support of the settlement-house movement. Wright used her training as a caseworker for the Newark Department of Welfare and the New Jersey Emergency Relief Administration during the Great Depression in this program and carried these interests into her doctoral work at Teachers College. In 1933 she began a Ph.D. program in history and educational sociology, one of no more than about forty students and very few African Americans matriculating for this degree at Teachers College at the time.[86] During her years at Columbia, she made lifelong friends from among the black intellectuals who studied there, including Walter G. Daniel, later a Howard faculty member as well.

By the late 1930s and early 1940s, Woodson and Wesley's work with the ASNLH had produced noticeable results. Meier and Rudwick report that "there was a quickening of interest in Negro history both among a broader group of black scholars and a small though growing number of whites."[87] Wright's dissertation, *The Education of Negroes in New Jersey*, was an exhaustive and highly original work of scholarship.[88] Wright followed Curti's model in dealing comprehensively with the social, political, and intellectual forces that had shaped black education in the state. Her analysis ranged from the earliest colonial days and Quaker influences to the then current condition of segregated schooling in the southern half of New Jersey. Her work can be characterized as both historical and sociological in its thrust, reflecting not only her theoretical background from her formal education but also the practical experience she had gained as a social worker. She demonstrated the negative and powerful impact racial segregation had on children in the southern counties while extolling the more favorable circumstances of largely integrated education in the northern counties.

Wright documented in great detail the inadequate education for black children that resulted from segregation, including shabby facilities, meager resources, and underpaid teachers. She argued that this inferior education produced numerous deleterious consequences, such as juvenile delinquency. Above all, she made the point that the promises of democracy must be extended to *all* citizens regardless of race. This would be the theme of all her subsequent writing: America must apply its democratic ideals to all its citizens.

Wright clearly owed her greatest intellectual debt to Curti.[89] One of only a handful of scholars nationwide who considered African American history a legitimate dissertation topic at this time, Curti was quoted at some length toward the end of her study:

> Much also depends on the extent to which educators realize that they . . . are deeply influenced by a point of view which they have unconsciously absorbed from their social environment, by a frame of reference which constantly limits their work. Only by recognizing this source of error in their

work, only by analyzing the influences which have determined this frame of reference can they hope to rise above the limitations of their class and personal backgrounds and the more or less obsolete ideas and emotional attitudes related to these. Only by so doing can they become whole-hearted pioneers in the building of a better social order.[90]

This passage from *Social Ideas of American Educators* suggests the importance both Curti and Wright attached to the influence of cultural context in shaping attitudes. In Curti's writing, the potential for using education to change attitudes toward various social groups like women, the working class, and African Americans is stated quite explicitly. Wright's published material over the next two decades repeatedly utilizes similar constructs, carefully and deliberately placing her subject matter in its cultural context. Her writing also exhibits a pronounced moral flavor, yet her condemnation of segregation is tempered by a recognition of the cultural support for racism. She repeatedly appeals to her readers' commitment to democratic values in trying to shift these old and damaging patterns.

Wright was also clearly influenced by Dewey's instrumentalism. In her dissertation, she cites Dewey's *Schools of To-morrow*, written with his daughter, Evelyn, in 1915.[91] This work became the basis for his subsequent treatise, *Democracy and Education*, published in 1916.[92] In the former work, the authors describe a number of experimental schools that were effectively carrying democracy into the new system of mass public education. Among these is a black school in Indianapolis run by William J. Valentine. Valentine later came to New Jersey to head a highly regarded vocational school for African Americans in Bordentown. Wright noted this fact in the bibliography of her dissertation. Dewey characterized the Indianapolis school as a "social settlement" and offered it as a possible model for "solving the race question."[93]

Wright's faith that the democratic process would eventually bring racial equality has been criticized as "naive" by later black historians.[94] However, contemporary historians also recognize the contributions her work made in demonstrating the persistence of a dynamic black culture that had managed to survive the tragedy of slavery and the challenge of Jim Crow. Her "thorough scholarship and faith in the potential of a democratic society . . . exemplified the perspective of those engaged in the finest work being done in Afro-American history at the time," according to one source.[95]

In the 1940s Wright's work "helped spread dissatisfaction" with "the total educational program for Negroes in the state."[96] As a result of her research and the efforts of the NAACP, New Jersey passed a new constitution in 1947, the first in the country to forbid segregation in both the public schools and the state militia. The example of this successful desegregation in New Jersey became a catalyst for the Truman initiative to desegregate the armed forces.[97]

Wright's dissertation brought her to the attention of the national NAACP, which was assembling social science data to prove the widespread and devastating effects of segregation. Wright worked with the team assembled by Dr. Kenneth Clark to gather and interpret materials in support of the NAACP challenge to "separate but equal."[98] Subsequently, Wright used the *Journal of Negro Education* to develop further her own ideas on the effects of segregation. This journal was established by Charles Thompson in 1932 to open the field of policy research to African Americans, who had been "generally ignored by the predominantly white academic journals of their day." Thompson published articles that were "strictly speaking outside the discipline of education and provided an outlet for [Rayford] Logan, [W. E. B.] Du Bois, [Ralph] Bunche, Sterling Brown, and many others."[99]

In New Jersey some African Americans expressed concern over integration because of the success of many black schools in incorporating black history into the curriculum and in hiring African Americans as teachers. In fact, in her article "Mr. Baxter's School," Wright herself had demonstrated the superior education offered by a nineteenth-century black school in Newark.[100] In 1953 she wrote another piece, "Extending Civil Rights in New Jersey," that can be interpreted as an effort to put these concerns to rest. In this case, she provided data indicating that in the six years since passage of the new state constitution, African American teachers had gained an additional 166 teaching positions in New Jersey.[101] She concluded this article with a statement that "New Jersey has blazed trails in the improvement of human relations that merit serious reflection. . . . Let us be vigilant in our efforts to eliminate still further the gaps between democratic ideals and practices."[102] She described the "significant precedent" of the New Jersey Constitution of 1947 in outlawing racial segregation as "an achievement which the NAACP hopes to extend to other states through cases now pending before the United States Supreme Court."[103]

As a faculty member at Howard during the 1940s and 1950s, Wright found herself in illustrious company. In a study that examines the career of Amherst- and Harvard-educated Rayford Logan, Keith Janken comments that "the core of Howard's faculty in the 1930s and 1940s not only was the best of any African-American college, it also rivaled some of the best white universities."[104] This elite group included Alain Locke in philosophy, Ralph Bunche in political science, E. Franklin Frazier in sociology, Sterling

Brown in English, and Charles Wesley and John Hope Franklin in history. Also during this period, Howard's law school trained a cadre of civil rights lawyers who would figure prominently in the legal challenges to segregation in the 1950s.

By comparison with the generation of black historians who came later, Wright's criticism of the white establishment was muted. Her patriotism, optimism about America's future, and faith in the power of education to integrate African Americans into American society sometimes placed her in a paradoxical position. For example, despite being a pacifist, she encouraged black involvement in the armed services during World War II because she found a strong correlation between race and rejection by these groups. She explained this in terms of the inferior education given African Americans, thus suggesting another reason to end school segregation.

During her years at Howard University, Wright served as an assistant editor and regular contributor to the *Journal of Negro Education*.[105] She published a number of articles in the *Journal of Negro History*, winning two awards from this journal, including one for best article in 1943. She worked at the center of highly visible academic efforts to extend the true meaning of democracy to African Americans. Nevertheless, as a woman in this environment, she struggled for recognition, often commenting to friends that her pay and promotions were negatively affected by her gender. During these years, the pressures of this unfair treatment and an estranged relationship with her children produced tremendous psychological difficulties for Wright.

Her writings, speeches, and organizational commitments reflected a measure of agreement with the theme of "racial uplift." Nevertheless, Wright increasingly came to criticize the lack of recognition educated black women received from the community for this work. After Slowe's death, Wright suggested that a full-fledged guidance and counseling program be launched for undergraduates at Howard. Wright became its acting director in 1946, taking on this task along with her responsibilities for coordinating the student teaching program. In 1954 she pursued a postdoctoral program in guidance, counseling, and personnel management at Teachers College, Columbia University, and traveled widely to review such practices at other institutions.[106]

Along with her contributions to journals focused on black experiences in education and history, she published in the *Friends Historical Association Bulletin, School and Society,* and *New Jersey History*.[107] Though not a Quaker herself, she valued their historical contributions to race relations: "By themselves respecting the personalities of the Negroes they attempted to stimulate similar behavior in the members of other groups. By teaching the Negroes to respect themselves they sought to ameliorate the conditions of those who still chafed under the bondsman's yoke."[108]

Wright served as a contributing editor to the *Aframerican Woman's Journal*, the organ of Mary McLeod Bethune's National Council of Negro Women.[109] During the 1950s, like Bethune, she worked in the Women's International League for Peace and Freedom. She also chaired committees for Delta Sigma Theta, her college sorority and an activist black women's organization, on rural education and the expansion of libraries throughout the South. Oral histories done by friends after her death suggest that she saw the position of minorities and women in education in a parallel light. As Walter Daniel put it in a tribute published after her death, "she felt she had to fight the cause for women."[110]

Although she was never a classroom teacher herself, Wright's role as a teacher educator brought many involvements with teachers. She was a member of the NEA and the American Teachers Association (ATA), an organization for black teachers, as well as the Association of Social Science Teachers in Negro Colleges. She promoted African American history through the ATA and the ASNLH. During the 1940s and 1950s, the NEA made an effort at outreach through a joint committee with the ATA to distribute to its members "instructional materials on Negroes." Segregation remained a problem, however, in a number of chapters throughout the country. In 1955, the NEA agreed to work for desegregation as a result of the *Brown* case. However, only in 1966 did the two organizations fully merge.[111]

In 1961 Wright received a grant to sustain her in the writing of a Slowe biography. She submitted a sketch to Radcliffe College for inclusion in *Notable American Women, 1607–1950* but took her own life in October 1962, before this project was completed. Her friends concluded that she had finally succumbed to the depression that had plagued her since her young adult years. As one colleague put it, "There was something in her life she couldn't handle."[112]

John Hope Franklin has called the world of the Negro scholar "indescribably lonely."[113] For Wright, loneliness and depression took their toll in her life.

Conclusion

In conclusion, several points can be made concerning the forms of social education developed by Beard and Wright. Like the founders of the social studies movement, both scholars saw social betterment as the aim of historical and sociological knowledge. Beard's belief that women's history could contribute to a new era for women's citizenship motivated her quest to inaugurate such a field. Similarly, Wright held the conviction that education could contribute to a solution for the complex problem of racism in this society.

The interdisciplinary breadth of Beard's and Wright's approach to knowledge production paralleled that advocated by the new field of social studies, incorporating sociology, economics, vocational guidance, and civics.[114] In their efforts to reconstruct the histories of groups whose records were sparse, scattered, and different from those of more conventional subjects, Beard and Wright stretched historical methodology to include evidence and topics that today figure prominently in many scholars' more interdisciplinary research repertoire. In a similar vein, both women saw the role of educators as multidimensional. Well aware that the demands of educating women and African Americans presented new challenges to schools, Beard and Wright counseled creativity and flexibility in educational means and ends.

Their lives offer examples of the role of the public intellectual, a construction that Thomas Bender used to explain Charles Beard but that applies equally to these two women: "The responsibility of intellect in a democratic society was to enrich politics and culture by proposing in public powerful ideas that invited, even demanded, response."[115] However, as outsiders, they recognized the necessity of being opportunistic in the methods they used to fulfill this function. Beard's recognition of the masculinist quality of virtually all higher education and Wright's acknowledgment of the racist nature of schools mandated new modes of dissemination of their research.

Furthermore, they worked at a time of specialization and professionalization in universities; these trends made popularization of academic research suspect and contributed to their marginalization. It is not surprising, therefore, that their work engendered resistance. Beard provoked resistance from feminists and academics. Wright encountered the sexism of her own institution and the racism of society.

Beard and Wright sought an inclusive understanding of the nature of legitimate knowledge in schools and universities. As empiricists, they could not have failed to notice the limitations of past representations of the world, explaining such deficiencies in terms of the biased norms governing selection of material for curricula. Like academic feminists today, they critiqued the partiality and skewed nature of the "truths" presented by the historical canon. They challenged "the meta-narratives," rejecting the idea "that stories about a single group could be generalized to all humans."[116]

Beard avoided the essentialism of much of women's history by bringing sensitivity to social class from her background in labor history. She steadfastly refused to attach a sense of victimization to women's "long history," as she called it. As feminist theoreticians today attempt to shore up female agency, Beard's ideas have tremendous resonance. Her work invites favorable comparison with that of contemporary feminist scholars like Gerda Lerner and Elizabeth Minnich.[117]

Wright's research stands as a foundation stone for what we today call multicultural education. She struggled with an American exceptionalism "forged around the Black man as an outsider."[118] Her legacy inspired a new generation of black historians, including Spencer Crew, Clement Price, Giles Wright, and others who today hold an annual conference in honor of her memory during Black History Month.

A recently published volume of readings in social studies begins with the assertion that the intellectuals featured in that work "foresaw the need to amend our notions of knowledge, understanding, curriculum, and education to more fully embrace the diversity of this nation." Like that group of scholars, Beard and Wright also recognized that "diversity and mutuality" form "the bedrocks of democratic living."[119] Their models of transformative scholarship suggest the multiple perspectives that have characterized social education from the start.

Writings of Mary Ritter Beard

Mary Ritter Beard, "The Direction of Women's Education," speech given at the Alumnae Luncheon for the Centenary of Mount Holyoke College, 7 May 1937, in *The Centenary of Mount Holyoke College* (South Hadley, Mass., 1937), 44–61.

There is a distinct thing called education—a unit complete in itself. Men created the body, or unit, of knowledge, thought, values and methods called education. It was long in their exclusive guardianship. America pioneered in giving women equal access to this masculine creation and heritage. The great prize has been won at last. Consequently, it is not incumbent upon women to criticize ungratefully this education so lavishly opened to them now; any one who has received it in any institution of learning on the accredited list is fully competent to instruct them; whatever is handed out to them in the guise of education is to be accepted by them as the true substance and sum of education; when they have

*received it they are to regard their minds as trained; and there is nothing more to
be done unless perchance they wish to hand it on to others in the form of adult
education. In short the history of the business is closed like Goethe's book with
seven seals. The victory is good. There is really nothing left but to crown the
heroes and heroines with laurels and sing in unison: "Peace on earth; goodwill to
men.". . .*

*How could any American ever have supposed that any economic, political,
social or intellectual scheme could have rooted itself in any land without the consent and co-operation of women? Throughout the ages of human societies, even
before the founding of colonies in the New World, women had shared in the substance of education devised for and reflecting their class whatever it was. . . .*

*In adopting the illusion that [women] had been nothing with respect to edu-
cation, in cutting loose from their own vast heritage of knowledge, experience,
and thought, in casting off the ennobling memory of themselves, women lost their
bearings as women and therefore as human beings all of whom are either men or
women. Thus when the doors of institutions of formal learning were unlocked for
them, they too lightly accepted as education the body of knowledge and the developing doctrines which the masters of those institutions deemed to be education in
its fullness. . . .*

*In other words, that formal education to which women had access and which
was said to be such a blessing repudiated and condemned every humane tradition of the education which had been woman's heritage from the Enlightenment.
Fortunately, by the time women had been thoroughly imbued with the new
learning, that very learning began to be understood as a hollow mockery of life.
It was so one-sided as to be untrue. It was so unreal as to be false in letter and
in social temper. . . .*

*In this American renaissance and revision, a noted triumvirate of college alum-
nae living in Chicago—Jane Addams, Julia Lathrop, and Florence Kelley—in the
very center of individualistic political economy, history, biology and sociology calling itself science, revived the feminine tradition and accepting the fact that they
were women, though equally educated, offered society and its educational institutions a philosophy and learning less in conformity with the stockyards. . . . This
they did by going outside the academic cloister, by recognizing other life than that
in dormitories, by remaining true to their own experiences and reasoning, by
maintaining close contact with the realities of the common life—in short, by insist-
ing upon that realism which is in fact the essence of the scientific spirit. . . .*

*Before us all indeed is the urgency of an intelligent choice in the direction of
women's education. . . . It is the choice once more between the barracks, the bat-
tlefield, the concentration camp, soldier-breeding and cloistral scholasticism on
the one side; and the home, the arts of peaceful industry, training for life, and the
exchange of cultural values on the other side. . . .*

In the choice which women now make lie the perils of extreme effeminacy no doubt—the preference and quest for ease, comfort and luxury, that is for over-refinement. However, at this hour when the balance is so heavily weighted on the side of militarism and sheer force, the women who know their history and under-stand their role in the processes of a humane civilization can make only one decision. They must cling deliberately and firmly to their principle of history, take their stand for the cause of enlightened humanism, and make their direction of the education of girls serve the ends of that grand cause.

But let there be no misunderstanding of that education. It means no mere instruction in the arts of keeping house, in child psychology, in sex wiles, in mari-tal relations or the technicalities of scholarship and research, however important these may be as subsidiaries. It does mean education based squarely on the feminine principle of history, without surrender to men on the march for the kill, and sensi-tive to the public responsibilities which inexorably flow from that principle. . . .

Woman is *and* makes *history.* Sub specie aeternitatis.

Writings of Marion Thompson Wright

Marion Thompson Wright,"Implications for Education," chap. 15 in *The Education of Negroes in New Jersey,* **Contributions to Education 815 (New York, 1941), 202–11.**

Education for living in a democracy must concern itself, then, with those objectives which will make for integration in community living on the one hand and for individual efficiency on the other. . . . It has been generally conceded that the prime function of the elementary school is that of integration through the development of common habits, ideals, and attitudes. The task of promoting indi-vidual efficiency to the end that each person may be able to make his unique con-tribution to group living is generally deferred to the periods covered by the sec-ondary and higher levels of training. . . .

To propose more democratic policies or practices for the purpose of counteract-ing or superseding less democratic policies or practices is to be forced into a fight against vested interests, social prejudices, customs making for economic and social caste, group exploitation, and various forms of intolerances, many of which have an etiology of long history and considerable strength.

That these defects along with others exist in the social order as it is now consti-tuted cannot be denied. The vital question stands as to what position American educators will take in revising their programs of education. Will they follow the lead of the community in social philosophy and practice or will they themselves set the lead in molding public opinion along the lines of democratic thinking and practice?

As previously indicated, a consideration of the negative and positive components of the subject under study reveals many tendencies, trends, and practices in connection with the education of Negro children in New Jersey. On the negative side, separate schools for colored children in the southern counties have a history of long standing. This investigation has shown that in some instances they evolved during the ante-bellum period of the nineteenth century from the philanthropic motives of groups interested in the welfare of Negroes, bond and free, and continued as a matter of tradition. In other cases separate schools resulted either from the refusal of white citizens to permit their children to attend mixed schools or from the requests of Negroes for separate schools in order to protect their children from humiliation and to provide teaching opportunities for qualified members of their own race. In recent years there has been a tendency for municipalities in northern counties to initiate discriminatory practices against Negroes where the proportion of the Negro population approaches or exceeds ten per cent of the total population. Residential segregation has played an important part in furthering this tendency. . . .

The history of education in New Jersey has also revealed that unequal opportunities have been the usual accompaniment of segregated schools. . . . Recent investigations show that at the present time it is still a matter of inferior facilities, limited opportunities to share in the benefits of the reorganized secondary school, particularly on the junior high school level, instruction in ungraded schools, and fewer openings in the field for teacher training and placement.

On the other hand this historical study has shown several positive components in the educational provisions made for Negro children. Very significant is the fact that New Jersey has never passed a law demanding the separation of the races in the schools, such as exists on the statute books of approximately one-third of the states in the Union, nor has she now a permissive law, as is the case with still other states. . . .

In order to promote these more positive trends toward equal status it will be necessary for the educators of New Jersey to assume the role of leaders rather than that of followers. The situation is weighted in favor of intolerances toward a racial group and makes for deeply seated prejudices against its members. There is lack of respect for the personalities of members of the race and denial of equal opportunities for self development, for community participation, and in many respects there is an exclusion from contacts with or enjoyments of the cultural components of civilization. A strong degree of social inertia must be overcome if these educators are to lead in a program to bring all the school children of New Jersey within the pale of democratic living. Consideration of the means for attaining this goal must take into account the long history and the background factors out of which these social attitudes have evolved, so that instead of deliberately cutting across what happens in many cases to be feelings or emotions with deep-seated roots there will be a re-education of these feelings and emotions along lines that are more constructive and that will make for greater integration on the part of all concerned.

Notes

1. O. L. Davis Jr., ed., *NCSS in Retrospect* (Washington, D.C., 1996); Walter Parker, ed., *Educating the Democratic Mind* (Albany, N.Y., 1996); see also the special issue of *Social Education* (vol. 59, no. 7 [November–December 1995]), "A History of NCSS: Seventy-Five Years of Service," edited by Ben A. Smith and J. Jesse Palmer.

2. Hazel Hertzberg, "History and Progressivism: A Century of Reform Proposals," in *Historical Literacy: The Case for History in American Education*, ed. Paul Gagnon (New York, 1989), 69–99; Murry Nelson, "Emma Willard: Pioneer in Social Studies Education," *Theory and Research in Social Education* 15 (Fall 1987): 245–55; Oliver Keels, "The Collegiate Influence on the Early Social Studies Curriculum: A Reassessment of the Role of Historians," *Theory and Research in Social Education* 8 (Fall 1980): 105–20.

3. See, e.g., Catherine Cornbleth and Dexter Waugh, *The Great Speckled Bird* (New York, 1995).

4. Linda Levstik, "NCSS and the Teaching of History," in *NCSS in Retrospect*, ed. O. L. Davis Jr. (Washington, D.C., 1996), 21–35.

5. Jesus Garcia and Edward Buendia, "NCSS and Ethnic/Cultural Diversity," in *NCSS in Retrospect*, ed. O. L. Davis Jr. (Washington, D.C., 1996), 55–67.

6. For an analysis of the problem of shared authorship and mutual influence between Mary Beard and Charles Beard, see my article "Forceful yet Forgotten: Mary Ritter Beard and the Writing of History," *History Teacher* 31 (November 1997): 9–31.

7. Elaine May, "The Radical Roots of American Studies," *American Quarterly* 48 (June 1996): 179–200.

8. May, "Radical Roots," 180.

9. Dorothy Ross, *The Origins of American Social Science* (Cambridge, Mass., 1991), 162.

10. Hazel Hertzberg, *Social Studies Reform* (Boulder, Colo., 1982), 386.

11. John Dewey, *The School and Society* (Chicago, 1900).

12. Hertzberg, *Social Studies Reform*, 18.

13. Peter Soderbergh, "The Historian and the Schools: Charles A. Beard's Views and Influence on the Teaching of Social Studies in Public Secondary Schools, 1909–1939" (Ph.D. diss., University of Texas at Austin, 1966), 125.

14. Stephen J. Thornton, "NCSS: The Early Years," in *NCSS in Retrospect*, ed. Davis.

15. Michael Whelan, "Albert Bushnell Hart and the Origins of Social Studies Education," *Theory and Research in Social Education* 22 (Fall 1994): 423–40.

16. James Banks, ed., *Multicultural Education: Transformative Knowledge and Action* (New York, 1996); August Meier and Eliot Rudwick, *Black History and the Historical Profession, 1915–1980* (Urbana, Ill., 1986).

17. Benjamin Quarles, *Black Mosaic: Essays in Afro-American History and Historiography* (Amherst, Mass., 1988).

18. Morton White, *Social Thought in America: The Revolt against Formalism* (Boston, 1957).

19. Soderbergh, "The Historian and the Schools," 96.

20. Nancy Cott, ed., *A Woman Making History* (New Haven, Conn., 1991), 15.

21. Mary Beard, *Women's Work in Municipalities* (New York, 1915).

22. Allen Davis, "Memorial to Merle Curti," *American Studies Association Newsletter* 19 (June 1996): 15.

23. Meier and Rudwick, *Black History*, 105.

24. Joan Burstyn, ed., *Past and Promise: Lives of New Jersey Women* (Metuchen, N.J., 1990), 437.

25. Hertzberg, *Social Studies Reform*, 45.

27. Merle Curti, *Growth of American Thought* (New York, 1943).

28. Meier and Rudwick, *Black History*, 105.

29. Merle Curti, *Control of Social Studies Textbooks* (Washington, D.C., 1941).

30. Soderbergh, "The Historian and the Schools"; Andrew Mullen, "Clio's Uncertain Guardians: History Education at Teachers College, Columbia University, 1906–1988" (Ph.D. diss., Teachers College, Columbia University, 1996).

31. Merle Curti, "American Intellectual History in the Secondary Schools," *Teachers College Record* 39 (March 1938): 467–75.

32. John Dewey, "Can Schools Share in Social Reconstruction?" *Social Frontier* 1 (Winter 1934): 11–13.

33. George Counts, *Dare the Schools Build a New Social Order?* (New York, 1932).

34. Lawrence Dennis, *George S. Counts and Charles A. Beard: Collaborators for Change* (Albany, N.Y., 1989).

35. Cott, *A Woman Making History*, 221.

36. Davis, "Memorial to Merle Curti," 15.

37. Alice Spieseke, interview by Hazel Hertzberg, New York, Milbank Memorial Library, Teachers College, Columbia University, 30 December 1978.

38. William Russell, Papers, 1928–1944, New York, Milbank Memorial Library, Teachers College, Columbia University.

39. Paula Giddings, *In Search of Sisterhood* (New York, 1988).

40. Rayford Logan, *Howard University: The First Hundred Years: 1867–1967* (New York, 1969).

41. Lawrence Cremin, *A History of Teachers College* (New York, 1954).

42. Cremin, *History of Teachers College*, 262.

43. Betty Weneck, "The 'Average Teacher' Need Not Apply: Women Educators at Teachers College, 1897–1927" (Ed.D. diss., Teachers College, Columbia University, 1996).

44. Edward T. James, Janet Wilson James, and Paul S. Boyer, *Notable American Women: A Biographical Dictionary* (Cambridge, Mass., 1971).

45. Ellen Nore, *Charles A. Beard: An Intellectual Biography* (Carbondale, Ill., 1983); Peter Novick, *That Noble Dream: The "Objectivity Question" and the American Historical Profession* (New York, 1988).

46. Cott, *A Woman Making History.*

47. Cott, *A Woman Making History*, 2.

48. Cott, *A Woman Making History*, 2.

49. Cott, *A Woman Making History*, 3.

50. Beard, *Women's Work in Municipalities;* Mary Ritter Beard, *A Short History of the American Labor Movement* (New York, 1920); Mary Ritter Beard, *On Understanding Women* (New York, 1931); Mary Ritter Beard, *Woman as Force in History* (New York, 1946).

51. Ann J. Lane, *Mary Ritter Beard: A Sourcebook* (Boston, 1988), 27.

52. Lane, *Mary Ritter Beard*, 152.

53. Mary Ritter Beard, "Mothercraft," *Woman Voter* 1–2, January 1912, 12–13.

54. Cott, *A Woman Making History*, 15.

55. Thomas Bender, *New York Intellect* (Baltimore, Md., 1987), 300.

56. Rita Heller, "The Women of Summer: The Bryn Mawr Summer School for Women Workers, 1921–1938" (Ph.D. diss., Rutgers University, 1986).

57. Barbara Turoff, *Mary Beard as Force in History* (Dayton, Ohio, 1979), 23.

58. Turoff, *Beard as Force in History*, 18.

59. Beard, *On Understanding Women*, 30.

60. Beard, *On Understanding Women*, 30.

61. Lane, *Mary Ritter Beard*, 207.

62. Adrienne Rich, "Toward a Woman-Centered University," in *On Lies, Secrets, and Silences* (New York, 1975), 125–57.

63. Lane, *Mary Ritter Beard*, 156.

64. Beard, *On Understanding Women*.

65. Lane, *Mary Ritter Beard*, 152.

66. Lane, *Mary Ritter Beard*, 158.

67. Cott, *A Woman Making History*, 60.

68. Beard, *Woman as Force in History*, 332.

69. Beard, *Woman as Force in History*, 332.

70. Peggy McIntosh, "Interactive Phases of Curricular Re-vision," Working Paper No. 124, Wellesley College, Wellesley, Mass., 1983. Nel Noddings, *The Challenge to Care in Schools* (New York, 1992).

71. Charles Beard and Mary Beard, *History of the United States* (New York, 1921); Charles Beard and Mary Beard, *The Rise of American Civilization* (New York, 1927); Charles Beard and Mary Beard, *The Making of American Civilization* (New York, 1937); Charles Beard and Mary Beard, *America in Midpassage* (New York, 1939); Charles Beard and Mary Beard, *The American Spirit* (New York, 1942); Charles Beard and Mary Beard, *A Basic History of the United States* (New York, 1944).

72. Charles Ducharme, *Charles A. Beard and the Social Studies: A Book of Readings* (New York, 1969).

73. Cott, *A Woman Making History*, 3.

74. Cott, *A Woman Making History*, 28.

75. Cott, *A Woman Making History*, 245.

76. Beard and Beard, *History of the United States*, 569.

77. Darlene Clark Hine, ed., *Black Women in America* (Brooklyn, N.Y., 1993), 386.

78. Giddings, *In Search of Sisterhood*, 81.

79. Giddings, *In Search of Sisterhood*, 145.

80. Keith Janken, *Rayford W. Logan and the Dilemma of the African American Intellectual* (New York, 1993).

81. Hine, *Black Women in America*, 385.

82. Lucy Diggs Slowe, "Higher Education of Negro Women," *Journal of Negro Education* 2 (August 1933): 352–69.

83. James Anderson, *The Education of Blacks in the South, 1860–1935* (Chapel Hill, N.C., 1988).

84. Giddings, *In Search of Sisterhood*, 43.

85. Meier and Rudwick, *Black History*.

86. Cremin, *History of Teachers College*, 163.

87. Meier and Rudwick, *Black History*, 100.

88. Marion Thompson Wright, *The Education of Negroes in New Jersey* (New York, 1941).

89. Meier and Rudwick, *Black History*, 105.

90. Wright, *Education of Negroes*, 202.

91. John Dewey with Evelyn Dewey, *Schools of To-morrow* (New York, 1915); reprinted in *John Dewey: The Middle Years, 1899–1924*, ed. J. Boydston (Carbondale, Ill., 1979), 207–404.

92. John Dewey, *Democracy and Education* (New York, 1916).

93. John Boydston, ed., *John Dewey: The Middle Years, 1899–1924* (Carbondale, Ill., 1979), 340.

94. Clement Price, unpublished oral history transcript, 9 September 1996, Rutgers University, Newark, N.J.

95. Meier and Rudwick, *Black History*, 105.

96. Marion Thompson Wright, "Extending Civil Rights in New Jersey through the Division against Discrimination," *Journal of Negro History* 30 (January 1953): 91–107.

97. Giles Wright, *Afro-Americans in New Jersey: A Short History* (Trenton, N.J., 1988).

98. Price, oral history.

99. Janken, *Logan and the African-American Intellectual* (Amherst, Mass., 1993), 203.

100. Marion Thompson Wright, "Mr. Baxter's School," *Proceedings of the New Jersey Historical Society* 59 (April 1941): 116–32.

101. Wright, "Extending Civil Rights," 102.

102. Wright, "Extending Civil Rights," 107.

103. Wright, "Extending Civil Rights," 108.

104. Janken, *Logan and the African-American Intellectual*, 203.

105. See, e.g., Marion Thompson Wright,, "Educational Programs for the Improvement of Race Relations: Negro Advancement Organizations," *Journal of Negro Education* 13 (July 1944): 349–60.

106. Walter Daniel, unpublished oral history transcript of interview with James A. Moss, Women's Project of New Jersey Papers, Rutgers University Special Collections, New Brunswick, N.J., 1982.

107. Marion Thompson Wright, "The Quakers as Social Workers among

Negroes in New Jersey from 1763–1804," *Bulletin of Friends Historical Association* 30 (Autumn 1941): 79–87; Marion Thompson Wright, "Have You Met the Social Worker?" *School and Society* 55 (February 1942): 239–41; Wright, "Mr. Baxter's School," 116–32.

108. Wright, "Quakers as Social Workers," 87.

109. Marion Thompson Wright, "The National Council of Negro Women and the Schools," *Aframerican Women's Journal* 2 (Summer 1944): 12–14.

110. Daniel, oral history, 305.

111. Hine, *Black Women in America*, 27.

112. Daniel, oral history.

113. Ducharme, *Beard and Social Studies*.

114. Thornton, "NCSS: The Early Years," 22.

115. Bender, *New York Intellect*. 308.

116. Banks, *Multicultural Education*, 49.

117. Gerda Lerner, *The Creation of Patriarchy* (New York, 1986); Gerda Lerner, *The Creation of Feminist Consciousness* (New York, 1993); Elizabeth Minnich, *Transforming Knowledge* (Philadelphia, 1990).

118. Quarles, *Black Mosaic*, 9.

119. Parker, *Educating the Democratic Mind*, 3.

6

Lucy Sprague Mitchell: Teacher, Geographer, and Teacher Educator

Sherry L. Field

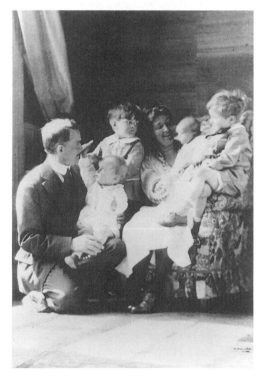

Lucy Sprague Mitchell
Lucy Sprague Mitchell Papers, Rare Book
and Manuscript Library, Columbia University

Lucy Sprague Mitchell was a transcendent educator who envisioned a world in which experiential education was accessible for all young children. Her theories about childhood education richly amplified the body of knowledge about children's social education. As she worked with them, her research led to a greater understanding of children's social worlds through their relationships, language, spatial awareness, and motor activities. An understanding of the relationships of people to the world and to other people were key to a child's education. Mitchell fervently believed that engaging children in geographical and historical explorations was critical to their achievement of relational understanding and general learning. Her viewpoints were widely shared through her writing for children, parents, and educators.

Mitchell's commitment to democratic, inclusive education was the driving force of her adult life. As with her young pupils, she emphasized her own children's development in a child friendly environment and advanced the notion that children were not small adults but people who should be nurtured in every possible way. This included a recognition of children's capacities as active explorers, even researchers and reporters, of their world.

Mitchell also laid the groundwork for the educational institution that would become Bank Street College in New York. Her innovations in teacher education served as a foundation for a movement toward holistic, thorough, field-based experiences. She advocated that teachers of young children use an active curriculum and integrate the social studies in imaginative and meaningful ways. At Bank Street College and through her many public and private school-related workshops, she "taught teachers how to teach by the force of her own example." Indeed, she wanted most to be remembered simply as teacher.[1]

Today, Lucy Sprague Mitchell's child-centered, humanistic philosophies about education are still a basic element of Bank Street College's central mission. But, like that of many of her female peers in social studies education, her legacy has been remembered only dimly, if at all.[2] Perhaps her contributions have been marginalized because she worked outside the mainstream of social studies: she never belonged to the National Council for the Social Studies or the predominant American Historical Association.[3] While she proposed exciting and innovative educational possibilities for children in geography, it was at the time an emerging school subject.[4] Perhaps because, like social studies educators Mary Ritter Beard and Marion Thompson Wright, she had "only indirect ties to the emerging structures within the field," her work was considered less significant than that of those who were working within the field's structure.[5]

Perhaps because she also was an early-childhood educator, the child development theories that hallmarked her work were neither legitimated nor taken seriously by social science educators. Nevertheless, Mitchell's lifework stands as a powerful reminder of some of the earliest thought on social constructivism. She never failed to highlight the critical importance of embracing and enhancing the social world of the child. This chapter, drawn heavily from her autobiography and from her professional writing, recounts a brief history of Mitchell's life, including key events that influenced her contributions to teaching, curriculum development, and teacher education.

Early Influences

Lucy Sprague Mitchell's lifetime (1878–1967) spanned the period from the Victorian era to the space age. Mitchell was born in Chicago, Illinois, the fourth of six children. Her father, Otho Sprague, was a wealthy merchant, and her mother, Lucia, a leader in Chicago's burgeoning social and cultural scene. Lucy was schooled at home with her three younger siblings. Her governess taught reading, mathematics, American and Greek history, drawing, and music. Although she developed a zeal for learning and, at the age of thirteen, decided to "read right around Father's library systematically,"[6] Mitchell remembered life in her Victorian-era home as fairly dark and dismal. She found her father's strict rules oppressive and believed that her father's role in the power structure of the household squelched her mother's creativity and spontaneity. Lucy found, however, that she shared with her father a gift for storytelling. On Sunday evenings, the family would gather in the library for story time, and Otho would entrance his offspring with vivid tales about a family with six children. Together, they were engaged in the magical family's adventures around the world.[7]

Several key events in her early life in Chicago contributed to Mitchell's development as an educator. Often a loner as a child, she explored her neighborhood and city and developed a passion for geography that would continue into her adult life. She watched Chicago's growth from the vantage point of its leaders, a possibility afforded by her family's socioeconomic status.[8] She remembered the panic of 1883 and the depression that followed, the Haymarket riot in May 1886, and the Pullman railroad strike of 1894 as events critical to her personal understanding of the world of business, that of her father and his peers.[9] Throughout her life, Mitchell was burdened by guilt about her wealth. While she was grateful for the educational and career options that her background made available to her, she remained ambivalent about her socioeconomic status.

The cultural growth of Chicago, a source of pride to Otho Sprague and his peers, included the formation of the Chicago Symphony, the founding of the Art Institute of Chicago, and the 1893 World's Fair. Lucy Sprague was fascinated by the majesty of the fair's buildings and by the layout of the grounds. To her, the World's Fair provided an opportunity to systematically explore each building and to have a "great experience in architecture." She also "became an expert Fair guide to [her family's] many guests."[10] Her intellectual independence already established, the fifteen-year-old Mitchell must have found this particular event leading up to the twentieth century a liberating one.

Another lasting influence on Mitchell's life as an educator was her connection to some of the luminaries from social work and the growing field of education. The effect of her acquaintance with Jane Addams, whom she met as a young teenager, was a powerful one. She began regular visits to Hull House and fell "under the spell of Addams . . . who became a symbol of the 'real' world—a world of work, and of people that [Mitchell] longed to reach."[11] No doubt Lucy Sprague was impressed with the scope of Addams's work, which included founding Hull House, supporting women's suffrage, and promoting peace education.[12]

A contrasting professional influence on Lucy's life was her access to the scholars who came to the new University of Chicago. The dinner parties that her father regularly hosted often included members of the university faculty. The reverence Otho Sprague had for scholars was "the kind . . . once accorded the clergy," and he fully supported the new university. Because of this, Lucy Sprague came to know educators well. Alice Freeman Palmer, then dean of women at the new university, lived with the Spragues when she first moved to Chicago. Palmer, who at the age of twenty-seven had been president of Wellesley College, was a strong and enduring role model for young Lucy.[13] After meeting the famous philosopher, Mitchell "read everything that John Dewey wrote" and was profoundly affected by his work the rest of her life.[14] Dewey was a major influence on her eventual choice of a profession.

Lucy Sprague and her family moved to Southern California when she was almost sixteen, in an attempt to help her father convalesce from tuberculosis. She was enrolled in the Marlborough School and ecstatically engaged in the social and educational life of boarding school. It was the first time that Lucy had attended school with other children for an extended period of time. She thrived there and in her senior year received an invitation from Alice Freeman Palmer to enter Radcliffe. Lucy Sprague lived with the Palmers in Cambridge while she was a student at Radcliffe. Her college years were fruitful and meaningful. She graduated with honors from Radcliffe in 1900 and looked eagerly toward her future. To Lucy Sprague, her Radcliffe education allowed her to be free from her family, gain new intellectual interests, and enjoy a newfound self-confidence.[15]

A Working Woman

After graduation from Radcliffe, Lucy Sprague was appointed assistant to Professor George C. Edwards, with the charge to oversee the needs of freshman and sophomore women at the University of California, Berkeley. Student culture at turn-of-the-century Berkeley was male dominated. Prior to her arrival, there were no female faculty.[16] Lucy Sprague found female students to be isolated and ridiculed on campus. Before she was promoted to dean of women in 1906, she tackled the problem of a severe housing shortage for women students, oversaw the establishment of women's social clubs, and advocated self-governance for students. She conducted surveys of women students to determine their academic, social, and housing needs. Her years at Berkeley produced two opposing personal beliefs about her accomplishments there. On the one hand, Lucy Sprague must have felt some professional satisfaction about her administrative accomplishments, for which she was widely recognized by her peers. On the other hand, she wrote: "I wanted to do something more definite, more constructive about the kinds of opportunities the University offered its women students. My early protest against the narrowness of professional training offered had increased rather than decreased. The more I saw of these vigorous western girls, the more preposterous it seemed that they should have no choice except to become teachers—preposterous for them and certainly not desirable for children. For what other professions could the University prepare them? To find an answer to that question became an obsession."[17]

By 1911, Lucy Sprague was determined to find an answer. She took a three-month leave of absence from her administrative and teaching duties and traveled to New York. While there and in her role as dean of women, she hoped to learn about other career opportunities for her university women. She also explored opportunities for her own future and apprenticed with some of the leading women's activists in the city: Lillian Wald, director and founder of the Henry Street Settlement; Florence Kelley, secretary of the Consumers' League; Mary Richmond, who headed the Charity Organization Society of the Russell Sage Foundation;

Pauline Goldmark, research analyst for the Russell Sage Foundation; and Julia Richman, a district superintendent for the New York public schools. From Lillian Wald, she learned about "social, economic, and particularly labor problems in real not theoretical situations." Mitchell described Florence Kelley as a "single-minded human dynamo" who "concentrated on current labor legislation." Mary Richmond's tutelage included investigating cases and writing reports. With Pauline Goldmark, she saw "the passion to gather accurate social facts and interpret them by logical, impersonal reasoning." She wrote that her brief time with Julia Richman "was of tremendous significance. This is the work for me, I thought. Public education is the most constructive attack on social problems, for it deals with children and the future. It requires endless research concerning children and what they need to make them grow wholesomely. It requires experimentation in curriculum for children and in teacher education. It requires an understanding of our culture. It is the synthesis of all my interests, all my hopes for humanity. I returned to Berkeley with a clear focus in my own life."[18]

During her return trip to California, she "wrote like mad," producing a new course proposal and two articles. One of the articles, she noted, was outlined to show the interconnections of psychology, sociology, economics, and anthropology.[19] She believed that an understanding of these interconnections would help students understand human beings and culture in the United States. She was beginning to conceptualize the notion that an interdisciplinary orientation in schools could help children learn about the world and that by actively exploring the world, children could come to understand themselves and each other.

At Berkeley, in addition to engaging in much personal introspection and attempting to determine a realistic place for herself in the field of education, Lucy Sprague was reintroduced to her future husband, Wesley Clair Mitchell, an emerging star in the field of economics. They had met briefly in Chicago when Lucy was eighteen. Lucy did not think of him again until, in an attempt to expand her content knowledge for her own course development, she enrolled in one of the popular economics courses Wesley taught at Berkeley. She was impressed with his teaching style, enthusiasm, and knowledge of economics. Over a period of five years, their relationship solidified, and they were married on 8 May 1912.

The Berkeley years were also ones of personal disjuncture. At times confident of her abilities to bring about social and policy change, especially for her women university students, Lucy Sprague was often equally ill at ease in her role as professor. Recognizing that her career opportunities at this point were guided by men and believing that her appointment resulted in no small measure from her social status, she resisted being what Jane Roland Martin terms "a servant of patriarchal policy."[20] Her letters to Wesley and her memoirs recount her personal struggles and professional dissatisfaction during this time. When she and her new husband moved to New York City in 1913, she resolved to find her niche.

Intellectual Growth and Context

Combining interests in two relatively new fields in education—social reform and the study of education using statistical methods—Mitchell began to learn more about them. She studied research and children's education in practical and theoretical ways. At Teachers College, Columbia University, she attended Edward Thorndike's lectures on educational psychology. Mitchell worked with Dewey, reading his *Democracy and Education* and embracing much of the social philosophy guiding his work. She familiarized herself with the ideas of educators who formed the core of the progressive movement in schools, such as Dewey, Thorndike, and William Kilpatrick. Mitchell learned firsthand of the importance of school setting, curriculum, and teacher training. In her memoirs, she wrote, "[I] began seeking some practical job with children in New York public schools—for public education was then, and has been ever since, the goal of my efforts."[21] By volunteering her services at the Public Education Association, she met Harriet Johnson, then the head of the visiting teachers. In this capacity, Johnson was a liaison between public schools and parents. Mitchell credits her for being a wise mentor and great teacher, for being open minded and experimental, and for being scientific and demanding evidence. Perhaps she admired these qualities in Johnson because she had adopted them in herself. In concert with progressive educators' interest in the psychological testing of children to classify them by mental abilities rather than chronological age, Mitchell volunteered to work with the board of education's Department of Mentally Retarded Children. After consulting with John Dewey, Frederick Ellis, Harriet Johnson, Eleanor Johnson, Elizabeth Farrell, and Lillian Wald, she proposed founding a psychological clinic for testing children at neighborhood schools. The psychological clinic, or survey, received partial funding from the board of education in 1915, and Mitchell served as one of the survey's testers. The psychological clinic would not be Mitchell's lifework, but the knowledge it afforded her about children's capabilities and the learning process would guide her continued work in experimental education.

Partially as an outgrowth of the psychological survey work, in 1916 the Bureau of Educational Experiments (BEE) was formed. This organization was founded to conduct research on children's development and growth in experimental schools and was funded by a generous grant from Lucy Sprague Mitchell's cousin. Organized democratically to be governed by a working council of twelve members and with Mitchell as chair, the BEE determined to "work on a joint study of young children in as free a school setup as we could plan."[22]

Mitchell was introduced by Harriet Johnson to Caroline Pratt at the Play School (which later was named the City and Country School). She was immediately intrigued with the school's approach to teaching children. After observing the first class of four-year-olds, Mitchell found Caroline Pratt's experimental approach to teaching exciting and relevant. She "wanted to be a part of this experiment" and spent the next few years working with Pratt.[23]

The geographical niche that the Mitchells carved out shifted several times in their first few years in New York City. Because of the many projects in which they became involved, they eventually housed themselves, the Bureau of Educational Experiments, and the City and Country School in six houses on West Twelfth and West Thirteenth Streets, where they remained from 1921 to 1938. Lucy Sprague Mitchell became a teacher of young children.

Major Contributions to the Field

In New York City, Mitchell had the financial and social freedom to do the work that she loved. She enjoyed being involved in BEE's many projects and typically met new challenges with zeal. Her role as a teacher, and eventually as a mother, allowed her to become a close observer of children. She noticed that the traditional stories written for children and available to teachers and parents were lacking. Typically full of moral overtones or based upon sagas and epics, the content of storybooks was, Mitchell believed, inappropriate. The language of early storybooks was not inviting to children, and in some cases it even frightened them. Widespread debate over the appropriateness of sharing fairy tales with children began at this time and continues to the present.[24]

Mitchell determined that a better model for children would be stories about their lives and the familiar world around them. Employing familiar topics drawn from children's everyday experiences and using familiar language would honor children's voices. Stories from a child's social world should be considered valued content, Mitchell believed. Such a notion was liberating for children, parents, and teachers. Mitchell was a leader in advocating this radical shift from traditional tales, and the publication of her first book brought her national prominence in children's education.

While working at the Play School, Mitchell clarified her thoughts about the nature and importance to child development of appropriate curricular experiences. She began recording some of the stories that she had found effective for the young children she taught. She also studied the children and their use of language. Mitchell's interest in children's language and their relationships with each other and the world foreshadowed what, some forty years later, was a burgeoning field of study.[25] Mitchell enthusiastically created curriculum materials based upon children's language and experience and became an advocate for their use.

The Here and Now Story Book was published in 1921.[26] The stories it contained, prepared for children aged two to seven, departed vastly from the usual assortment of children's stories that were available at the time. For example, a typical turn-of-the-century storybook written with first- and second-graders in mind contained stories such as "King Alfred and the Cakes," "Julius Caesar," "The Story of Cincinnatus," and "Horatius at the Bridge."[27] The *First Yearbook* of the National Herbart Society (now the National Society for the Study of Education) suggested a social studies curriculum for first- and second-grade children of stories based upon history. Included were stories from the *Iliad,* the *Odyssey,* the *Aeneid,* the *Nibelungenlied,* and the *Arabian Nights,* as well as sagas and stories about King Arthur.[28] Mitchell was appalled by the use for children of stories whose content focused on conquest and violence. She said that her stories were designed to allow children "the opportunity to explore first their own environment and gradually . . . along lines of their own inquiries."[29] She believed that children should hear in their stories about "a world of sounds and smells and tastes and sights and feeling and contacts . . . [and] activities . . . told in motor terms."[30] Additionally, the stories should "raise inquiries" and "open up . . . relationships."[31] In storybooks, and in the larger world, the relationships people had with one another and with the earth were of paramount importance to Mitchell.

Her first book was met with widespread attention and favorable, even glowing, reviews by such educational luminaries as Harold O. Rugg, Elizabeth Jenkins, William Carson Ryan, and Arnold and Beatrice Gesell. For example, the Gesells exulted in their review for the *New York Evening Post Literary Review*: "To blaze a new trail always gives one a sense of adventure. It is refreshing to lay hold of a book which proposes to use a little daring exploration and trial and error in the important field of children's literature. . . . It should give a new impetus to creative work and artistic expression with little children."[32]

To say that *The Here and Now Storybook* was successful is an understatement. Mitchell added a related *Here and Now Primer* in 1924.[33] By the time a second version of stories, *Another Here and Now Storybook,* was published in 1937, the original version of *Here and Now* was in its eighteenth printing.[34] The foreword to *Another Here and Now Storybook* suggests the prior publication's impact. Mitchell wrote that "the children for whom and with whom the first *Here and Now Storybook* was written have come of age" and provided the following vignette: "The proof of the early diet of the *Here and Now Story Book* is now described by a freshman at Stanford University . . . [who said that looking] back as a child . . . 'There is one book lying a little apart from all the rest. It is slightly dirtier than the other[s], rather more ragged. Some of the pages have been scribbled in childish enthusiasm. Its title, still faintly discernible, is *The Here and Now Story Book.* That book is the first one I can remember. I hope it will be the last to be forgotten. . . . I grew up with *The Here and Now Story Book,* and to me, it seemed very real. To me, the stories were all true; they weren't really stories at all, but rather accounts taken from my own life.'"[35]

Mitchell continued to work at the City and Country School until 1929. During this time, the passion inspired by her early explorations in her Chicago neighborhood that began her interest in the study of geography was reignited. She took a leave of absence to work with the American Geographic Society. Mitchell recognized that learning more about urban geography would complement her rationale for teaching urban children about the city, the world they knew best. She spent a year surveying Long Island City. Ever intrepid, she "walked, street by street, across meadows, around the dumping grounds, under the Queensboro Bridge, along the shore of the East River, a box of colored pencils hanging around [her] neck and maps in [her] hands."[36] Her task was to compile detailed information about new buildings, stores, public utilities, public services, and even houses and apartment buildings. She matched population information to the man-made changes her maps recorded and organized it on a series of transparencies. Mitchell's survey related patterns of growth and change and showed how the distribution of people changes in relation to changes in cultural needs. The predictions about the future of the area with which she concluded her report were reanalyzed fifteen years later, and she noted that most had been correct.[37]

As Mitchell's ideas about geography crystallized, she began to conceptualize innovative methods to teach children. In the United States, the nature of geography education was changing during the 1920s and 1930s, just as the larger fields of the social sciences were being reconceptualized as social studies education.[38] Geographic themes were central in several of the books she wrote next for children. In *Horses, Now and Long Ago,* which she described as her own children's favorite, she began with present-day realistic settings then gave a historical overview of horses, an animal with which most children would be familiar.[39] *Manhattan Now and Long Ago* provided a geographic context for learning about the city.[40] *North America: The Land They Live In for the Children Who Live There* divided the continent into regions and related stories of people in the various regions and how the forces of nature influenced their lives.[41] Of these books, *North America* appears to have been the most enduring.[42]

Mitchell's attentions were drawn to a new form of geography. Human geography was a field of study just becoming popular during the Progressive Era. She defined it as "what the earth does to people and what people do to the earth."[43] Mitchell believed that the study of human geography, when complemented by the usual emphasis on the more traditional physical geography, or "earth forces," could provide for children a richer landscape to understand the world. Earth forces, "all things that people found on earth and did not make—climate, soil, land forms, rivers, winds, water, metals, coal, plants, and animals," were important to a child's understanding of geography because they could be experienced directly. Human geography portrayed the Earth–human relationship and provided cultural context. Mitchell encouraged teachers to make geographers instead of teaching geography.[44] Her impassioned geography curriculum work about these topics intensified.

Mitchell's conviction about the importance of geography education in a child's life had two impressive outcomes. First, she invented and began to implement a straightforward system for teaching map skills to children. She was especially interested in children's understanding of the relationships between people and the earth and developed a series of "tool maps" on which children could work out basic geography relationships. To help children recognize complex Earth-human relationships, individual maps were to be "intellectually superimposed" after their introduction. The first tool maps were handmade, large graphic relief maps painted in oils on oilcloth. Unlike elevation maps with unrealistic colorations, these maps resembled real life. Later, twenty transparent maps were created for use over a base map in a variety of combinations and for multiple purposes. Mitchell hoped that these would be widely available to teachers.

Problem solving was a desired outcome of children's direct experience with maps. Mitchell described one group of nine-year-olds who solved complex problems the pioneers faced during westward expansion, using methods not dissimilar from those used today. She presented the children with a scenario of settlers traveling by covered wagon, starting at Independence, Missouri. The pupils were to find the best route to Oregon or California. On Mitchell's huge oilcloth graphic relief map, the children began their research and reported their conclusions. Delving into source materials—other source maps, pictures, accounts of pioneers, and stories—the children discovered the topography, flora, and fauna of the United States. Using watercolors so that their pictures could be washed off and the maps used again, the children painted their symbols all over the map and eventually found an appropriate route. Their map represented earth forces of topography, climate, vegetation, and wild animals, as well as people who had to decide how to reckon with the earth forces.[45] This example demonstrated preferred methods for engaging children in problem solving by integrating geography, history, science, drama, and art.

Young Geographers: How They Explore the World and How They Map the World, which Mitchell described modestly as a "small book for teachers," was published in 1934.[46] It stands as a seminal work in children's geography education. Written for teachers, *Young Geographers* provided an explanation of how children explore the world, a chart and expanded description of the stages of development of children's geographic thinking from infancy to twelve years of age, and a procedure for mapmaking with children. Teachers were advised to use various types of maps, and illustrations accompanied salient points. The final segment of the book contained fifteen pages of photographs of children at work on their maps, a variety of classroom and outdoor settings. and final products. For example, several Little Red Schoolhouse children are pictured in their large, open classroom in which a spacious corner of the room is covered with various stages of block building to demonstrate their organization of people, boats, and automobiles. The caption reads: "Six year olds playing river and city work activities after trips to the Manhattan water-front. The floor scheme is a spontaneous crude map with rough orientation. It is a 'tool map' used for play."[47] Children at the Spring Hill School in Litchfield, Connecticut, are pictured outdoors creating a huge outline of the United States. The photograph is captioned: "Outdoor map of the United States (60' x 80') with 5 foot high Rockies made by Ten-Year-Olds. An electrified train later crossed the continent. Natural resources such as iron, copper, coal and oil were buried in the correct locations. The map was used as a tool map for both play and information."[48]

Mitchell sought to further geographic inquiry in a new way that would increase its prominence in the curriculum. She felt that by combining the geography and history curriculum for older children, it could become as challenging and exciting as the "Here and Now" curriculum suggested for younger children. The nature of relationships would continue to figure strongly in a geography- and history-based curriculum. She wondered: "Could not the human geography approach be made—the study of ways of living that people developed be related to the lands they used? But how could the far away and long ago be made as 'alive' to children as the here and now?"[49] She "worked out . . . the kind of maps that should be used, the kind of stories that must be found or written, the kind of source material that must be gathered."[50]

Mitchell left her work at the City and Country School and began an association with the Little Red Schoolhouse, an experimental school in Greenwich Village. Here she was able to try out many of her instructional ideas. She started by teaching kindergarten children. She had thirty-nine students in her first class. Extensive records were kept about "what the group as a whole and what each child did in block-building, drawing, painting, and carpentry; verbatim notes of group discussions; accounts of trips with preparatory and follow up activities and discussions; spontaneous conversations and stories; diary accounts of dramatic play and map-making."[51]

One approach paramount to Mitchell's teaching was to provide for children direct experiences. She noted that typically the school curriculum was based on the idea that children learned conceptual information by hearing or reading, through words that often were unrelated to children's experiences. When her kindergarten students misnamed a tulip when she brought into class a rose or daisy, she took the children to a nearby flower market. Once there, she discovered that the children named indiscriminately the flowers that they encountered. Mitchell noted that the children were being trained to use word symbols without having the concrete experiences to internalize the symbols.[52] Furthering children's experiences in their neighborhoods was a key step toward direct discovery. By enlarging the walls of the schoolhouse to include the community, children's capacity for language and discovery surged.

Little Red Schoolhouse children took many field trips in their neighborhood and in the larger world. Once back in the classroom, the children would construct the environments they had just learned about. Their construction materials were blocks, boxes, modeling clay, and other objects in the school. Early on, a field trip to the Gansvoort Farmers' Market was enriched for the children when they had the opportunity to talk to a farmer, who carefully explained the process of planting, growing, and gathering his crop of turnips and told the children about the route he took to the market. The children were given several turnips, which were the object of discussion back in the schoolroom. When asked where the farmer got his turnips, one child confidently replied, "From the A&P!"[53] This response helped clarify the need for direct experience. Mitchell observed that these children had learned about the farmer but not the farm. When the children's play with toy horses indicated that they did not know what a horse eats, a visit to a nearby livery stable was scheduled. During the trip, children saw horses sleeping, eating, and working, and they got to take a short ride on a horse. The visit was followed by a whole group classroom discussion that led to the children's construction of the livery-stable site. They added the horses' environment, stables, stalls, water troughs, wagons, and appropriate food for the animals to their neighborhood schema of block-building.[54]

Comparing rural and urban life seemed to be a natural part of the environmental studies Mitchell favored. It remains today as a basic element of the elementary social studies curriculum.[55] The city children who attended Little Red Schoolhouse had difficulty thinking and learning about life in the country unless they had direct experience with it. Another innovative aspect of their schoolwork grew out of this realization. It was decided that young children would spend the month of June at an empty settlement camp and learn about life in the country. The first trip included kindergartners and first graders; the school's director, Elisabeth Irwin; two of the students' mothers; fellow teacher Rhoda Harris; and Mitchell. While this first June country stay was not without its problems, such as children's anxiety at having left their mothers and fear of the outdoors, it was also full of rich experiences. The children visited a farm, ate outdoors, and experienced a real country environment, complete with trees and ponds. The country visit became a routine part of the school curriculum. Mitchell recalled her experiences at the Little Red Schoolhouse as profitable ones, during which she was "earnestly trying to understand children and to work out a curriculum that fitted them."[56]

Later, Mitchell wrote a book devoted to the exploration of communities and their inhabitants. On the basis of her numerous experiences and what she had learned about taking field trips with children, Mitchell published *The People of the U.S.A.: Their Place in the School Curriculum.*[57] The book was also an outlet for Mitchell to advance her ideas about intercultural education, and extensive resource lists for teachers' use were provided. Included were suggestions for urban, rural, and suburban field trips for children, as well as teachers' notes about helpful resources. Mitchell called the second half of the book "Knowing People through

Cultural Differences and Ties" and provided general information about cultural groups; arts, music, and dance; and regions. Mitchell believed that for the child, "the more he knows [about people and places] through personal contact, the better for his social growth."[58] Although it was published after the United States entered World War II, the volume supported learning about people who had emigrated from all over the world. For example, fifteen references were suggested about German immigrants or stories related to Germany, and ten titles were given for Italy. As World War II progressed, elementary social studies in the United States adjusted to include more of an emphasis on geography, civics, and economics. Discussions of teaching children to be tolerant and to move toward peaceful overtures were commonplace in educational materials and policy directives during this period.[59]

Mitchell progressively turned her attention from teaching children to teaching teachers. She compared the pioneering status of the field of teacher education in the 1930s to the infancy of the child-development field when she began her career in education in 1916.[60] Bank Street evolved from the early work of the Bureau of Educational Experiments. Initially, in 1930 it was a cooperative school for experimental teachers. The BEE library seemed to be a popular meeting place for experimental-school teachers, or, as Mitchell called them, "eager pioneers," who sought a synthesis of, and understanding about, implications for the latest early-childhood research. A physical move from the BEE's location at Twelfth and Thirteenth Streets to 69 Bank Street symbolized for Mitchell and her colleagues the beginning of a new era of research, in which they could test their findings as well as gather data. That work was to be with teachers who were as interested in the burgeoning field of child development as were the researchers. An innovative training process was necessary during which teachers could engage in various child-centered experiences.

In spite of the financial hardships suffered nationally during the Great Depression, Bank Street College grew in size and stature, combining the work of the BEE, the Cooperative School for Student Teachers, and the research staff. Located at the site of a Fleischman's yeast factory, the four-story building was renovated to include a nursery school and playground on the upper floors and a school for older children and offices for the research staff on the lower floors. The renovated building retained much of its original character and many of its unique architectural features. For example, Mitchell described the structure's four stories and huge basement as having columns similar to those at the Egyptian temple at Karnak.[65]

Teacher education was an emerging field, and Bank Street moved to the forefront with its progressive programs. Plans were made for its pre-service teacher-education students to have experiences in one or more of eight cooperative schools: in Manhattan, Brooklyn, Staten Island, Old Greenwich, Litchfield, Connecticut, Flourtown, Pennsylvania, and Morristown, New Jersey. The schools were varied in population, location (urban, rural, suburban), teaching styles, and types of programs. Most unusual was the mission of Bank Street to immerse preservice teachers in the task of learning as children would. The goals of the school were to "help students develop a scientific attitude towards their work and toward life. To us this means an attitude of eager, alert observations; a constant questioning of the old procedure in light of new observations; a use of the world as well as of books as source material; an experimental open-mindedness; and an effort to keep as reliable records as the situation permits in order to base the future upon actual knowledge of the experience of the past."[62] That students were to develop the attitude of "artist" and to embrace a sense of joy and relish toward life and work was another overarching goal at Bank Street.

The curriculum was active and exciting for Bank Street students, just as it was to be for children. Lucy believed that experimental education of adults included many of the same elements necessary for the education of children. Having large blocks of time to work and study together cooperatively was a predominant feature of the Bank Street program. For example, students were placed in schools Monday through Thursday morning; from Thursday afternoon through Saturday, they did intensive coursework on campus. During the on-campus, weekend work, students were offered firsthand experiences in Bank Street studio and laboratory settings and through fieldwork. Students' coursework was specifically designed to be supplemented by observation and real-life experiences. Additionally, students were to "wake up atrophied senses" and to enjoy new experiences in teaching practice. They did this by using forms of painting, modeling, music, language, and dance to enrich a child-centered curriculum of reading, writing, arithmetic, carpentry, and mapmaking.

Bank Street students were also to give back to the community. One morning a week for one semester, students were required to volunteer for social organizations. While volunteerism swelled in classrooms across the country during World War II, Bank Street's requirement for social activism predates by sixty years the current interest in service learning in grades K–16.[63] Lucy taught language development and environment courses at Bank Street. And she led her Bank Street students on extended field trips, just as she had done with her younger students. They visited labor unions, political rallies, tenements, subsidized housing, detention centers, and courts. Mitchell and her students took longer "field trips" to more distant sites every spring. Some destinations included coal-mining towns, steel mills, and the Tennessee Valley Authority. Students learned about each area "from its geological beginnings to its contemporary socio-economic structure."[64]

Just as Mitchell had devoted attention to writing curriculum materials and books for children, she engaged in writing for teachers. With fellow Bank Street staff members, she published *Know Your Children in School*, which included classroom vignettes organized by grade level from kindergarten through sixth grade. Taken from the records of the Bank Street Workshops, the stories were written to show the "typical needs of children . . . and how a school may be a place for children to grow in."[65] As Bank Street matured, a much needed connection to the community of inservice teachers was made. Workshops for inservice education were first offered in 1943, initially to help teachers implement a new curriculum adopted by the New York City Board of Education. Teachers met after school at Bank Street to discuss issues and solve problems. By 1946, evening courses were added to Bank Street's offerings for inservice teachers, and they attracted some five hundred students each semester. The master of science degree was added to Bank Street's School for Teachers degree options in 1950, necessitating a name change to Bank Street College of Education.[66]

Mitchell's role in the operation of Bank Street, while still substantial, decreased during the 1940s and 1950s to include only the Division of Studies and Publications and the Writers' Laboratory. By 1948, Mitchell no longer taught classes or workshops. She chaired the Working Council until 1950 and served as acting president from 1953 to 1956. President John Niemeyer always called Mitchell Bank Street's "first president."[67] She continued her service as a trustee at Bank Street until her death in 1967.

A Life to Remember

Lucy Sprague Mitchell's legacy is that of an egalitarian educator whose ideas about social education for children and teachers have well withstood the passage of time.[68] The following glimpses into schools reflect Mitchell's pedagogy. Their settings could be classrooms of the 1920s or of the 1990s. Children in preschools and primary schools listen to stories whose authors were influenced by Mitchell's theories about the use of active language. They retell stories to a classmate or to their teacher. Other students are asked to solve a problem. They may be given the task of constructing a model of the community one hundred years ago. Younger children build models of their classroom, school, or neighborhood, after a visit to the community. Their tools likely are blocks and other manipulatives. Older children learn about maps in a developmentally appropriate and sequential fashion. They all learn in various ways about the *here* and *now,* as well as the *there* and *then.* Several generations of children have been the beneficiaries of experiential learning practices such as those advocated by Mitchell.

Sustained advocacy for radical departure from the traditional methods of teaching the social studies was another of Mitchell's passionate contributions. She believed that children should not only hear and read about the social studies but also must live them. They were, simply, to become geographers and historians through problem solving, mapmaking, field trips, and working with one another.

Innumerable parents and teachers were directly or indirectly guided by Mitchell's humanistic approach to education, her storybooks for children, her instructional texts for adults, and her other professional writing.[69] Her work at Bank Street remains perhaps her strongest legacy, and it is there that her presence abounds. Mitchell should be respectfully remembered not only as teacher but also as woman, wife, mother, and colleague. The following words were written about the aims for Bank Street students, but they could just as easily describe Lucy Sprague Mitchell's impressive and rewarding life, during which she was able to "feel in herself, her work, her play, her social relations, her whole life, a response to her total environment . . . the habits, culture, and institutions of her time."[70]

Writings of Lucy Sprague Mitchell

Lucy Sprague Mitchell, *The Here and Now Storybook* (New York, 1921), 4–8.

In looking for content for these stories I followed the general lines of the school for which they were written. The school gives the children the opportunity to explore first their own environment and gradually widens this environment for them along lines of their own inquiries. Consequently I did not seek for material outside the ordinary surroundings of the children. On the contrary, I assumed that in stories as in other educational procedure, the place to begin is the point at which the child has arrived,—to begin and lead out from. With small children this point is still within the "here" and the "now," and so stories must begin with the familiar and the immediate. But also stories must lead children out from the familiar and immediate, for that is the method both of education and of art. Here and now stories mean to me stories which include the children's first-hand experiences as a starting point, not stories which are literally limited to these experiences. Therefore to get my basis for the stories I went to the environment in which a child of each age naturally finds himself and there I watched him. I tried to see what in his home, in his school, in the streets, he seized upon and how he made this his own. I tried to determine what were the relationships he used to order his experiences.

Lucy Sprague Mitchell, *Young Geographers: How They Explore the World and How They Map the World* **(New York, 1934), 12–15.**

To base a curriculum for small children upon a study of their environment seems at first glance preposterous. For modern children are born into an appallingly complicated world. . . .

[One] question is, are the teachers among those who live in a world the functioning of which they do not understand? If so, children will have as little chance to explore their surroundings, as little chance to pursue a laboratory method in their classroom as in their homes.

And it must be said that many schools have, even yet, failed to modify their classroom procedures since the days when children's homes brought them into intimate casual relations, often work relations, with the production of clothes and food and when transportation was readily understood through animals. . . . [Students] pass on to subjects labeled "history" and "geography" with little or no help in understanding the lives of the people around them or the way their practical needs are met. Not often do they develop the habits of first-hand observation and experimentation and the attendant "relationship thinking"—an expression we use as a short cut to the cumbersome statement that all thinking is seeing relations. . . .

In a like manner, . . . the subject matter of geography will be developed logically irrespective of the locality or information a child may gather from the kind of community he lives in. Many geographies for children still assume that the whole should be presented before the part. So they begin with the earth as a sphere, divided by longitudes and latitudes, zones and hemispheres. Communities assessed in terms of their world importance rather than of their familiarity, will be placed upon this globe, the direction and length of rivers, the height of mountains, the boundaries of nations—all these locational geographic facts appear successively in a geography curriculum arranged according to the logic of the content. Geography has fared even less well than history: the "here" has been even more slighted than the "now."

Lucy Sprague Mitchell and Johanna Boetz, *The People of the U.S.A.:*
Their Place in the School Curriculum **(New York, 1942), 5–6.**

America, perhaps more than any other country, is composed of groups with
differing backgrounds: social, economic, religious, regional, national, racial. . . .
How can schools help children really to know "the other fellow"?

Children begin with a narrow group experience. . . . [T]hey may still remain
within the narrow boundary of social or economic or racial group. Their lives will
not necessarily bring them into close contact with members of different work
groups, different regional, national or racial groups. They may know about them
but yet not know them.

Perhaps the greatest challenge to democratic education is to find a way to
know people so that, in a measure, we take them on as a part of us and our group.
Here, as always, we must look for those direct experiences which create a thought-
provoking and feeling situation different from that created by reports of the expe-
riences of others. Nor does social osmosis between differing social, economic,
national and racial groups necessarily take place by mere physical proximity.
Even if children pass members of other groups in the street or even if they sit
beside them in school, they may not see them from the inside; they may not under-
stand their ways and interests, they may not widen their own group to include
them. They may still only know about them and not know them.

Children may become old without ever growing beyond the group they were
born into or by chance have become identified with through a later work group.
Often this means that they carry through life a body of prejudices. For the reverse
and ugly side of group loyalty often means a prejudice against, or at any rate a
limited understanding of, those not included in one's own group. . . . Democrat-
ic education means a widening of the group one is interested in or whose inter-
ests one can understand both logically and emotionally. Ideally one's group
should grow to include all people, no matter what their nationality, race or eco-
nomic or social status.

Notes

1. Mary Phelps and Margaret Wise Brown, "Lucy Sprague Mitchell," *Horn*
Book Magazine 13, no. 3 (May–June 1937): 159–63.

2. See, e.g., Nel Noddings, "Social Studies and Feminism," *Theory and*
Research in Social Education 20, no. 33 (Summer 1992): 230–41; Margaret Smith
Crocco, "Mary Ritter Beard and Marion Thompson Wright: Shaping Inclusive
Social Education," *Theory and Research in Social Education* 25, no. 1 (Winter 1997):
6–33; O. L. Davis Jr., ed., *NCSS in Retrospect* (Washington, D.C., 1996).

3. Mitchell belonged to the Society of Women Geographers. After the 1938

International Geographic Association Meeting in Amsterdam, she traveled with seventeen other members to Asia. (Lucy Sprague Mitchell, *Two Lives: The Story of Wesley Clair Mitchell and Myself* [New York, 1953], 487).

4. Salvatore J. Natoli, "The Evolving Nature of Geography," in *Social Studies and Social Sciences: A Fifty-Year Perspective,* Bulletin No. 78, edited by Stanley P. Wronski and Donald H. Bragaw (Washington, D.C., 1986), 28–42.

5. Crocco, "Beard and Wright," 10.

6. Lucy Sprague Mitchell, *Two Lives,* 58.

7. Joyce Antler, *Lucy Sprague Mitchell: The Making of a Modern Woman* (New Haven, Conn., 1987), 11.

8. See, e.g., Bessie Louise Pierce, *A History of Chicago* (Chicago, 1957); David F. Burgh, *Chicago's White City of 1893* (Lexington, Ky., 1976).

9. Mitchell, *Two Lives,* 62–64.

10. Mitchell, *Two Lives,* 71.

11. Mitchell, *Two Lives,* 60.

12. Aline M. Stomfay-Stitz, *Peace Education in America, 1828–1990* (Metuchen, N.J., 1993), 59.

13. Palmer resigned her presidential position after marrying George Palmer, a Harvard professor. She chose to work on a consulting basis thereafter. Her role as dean of women at the University of Chicago required her to be in residence only twelve weeks a year.

14. Mitchell, *Two Lives,* 74.

15. Antler, *Lucy Sprague Mitchell,* 54.

16. Antler, *Lucy Sprague Mitchell,* 108.

17. Mitchell, *Two Lives,* 207.

18. Mitchell, *Two Lives,* 150.

19. Mitchell, *Two Lives,* 210.

20. Jane Roland Martin, "Excluding Women from the Educational Realm," *Harvard Educational Review* 52, no. 2 (1982): 133–48.

21. Mitchell, *Two Lives,* 250.

22. Mitchell, *Two Lives,* 273.

23. Mitchell, *Two Lives,* 151.

24. Bernice Cullinan, Lee Galda, and Bee Cullinan, *Literature and the Child,* 3d ed. (Fort Worth, Texas, 1994), 158–99.

25. Shirley Brice Heath, *Ways with Words: Language, Life, and Work in Communities and in Classrooms* (Cambridge, England, 1983); Judith Wells Lindfors, *Children's Language and Learning,* 2d ed. (Englewood Cliffs, N.J., 1987).

26. Lucy Sprague Mitchell, *The Here and Now Storybook* (New York, 1921).

27. James Baldwin, *Fifty Famous Stories Retold* (New York, 1896).

28. National Herbart Society, *First Yearbook* (Chicago, 1902).

29. Mitchell, *Here and Now Storybook,* 4.

30. Mitchell, *Here and Now Storybook,* 6.

31. Mitchell, *Here and Now Storybook,* 28–29.

32. Arnold Gesell and Beatrice Gesell, review of *The Here and Now Storybook,* by Lucy Sprague Mitchell, *New York Evening Post Literary Review,* 7 November 1921.

33. Lucy Sprague Mitchell, *Here and Now Primer: Home from the Country* (New York, 1924).

34. Lucy Sprague Mitchell, *Another Here and Now Storybook* (New York, 1937).

35. Mitchell, *Another Here and Now Storybook*, xxiv.

36. Mitchell, *Two Lives*, 423.

37. Mitchell, *Two Lives*, 424.

38. Natoli, "Evolving Nature of Geography"; Barbara J. Winston, "Teaching and Learning in Geography," in *Social Studies and Social Sciences*, ed. Wronski and Bragaw, 43–58. Hazel Hertzberg, *Social Studies Reform, 1880–1980* (Boulder, Colo., 1986); David W. Saxe, *Social Studies: The Early Years* (Albany, N.Y., 1991); Murry Nelson, "The Early Years: 1921–1937," *Social Education* 59, no. 7 (November–December 1995): 399–408.

39. Lucy Sprague Mitchell, *Horses, Now and Long Ago* (New York, 1926).

40. Lucy Sprague Mitchell and Clara Lambert, *Manhattan Now and Long Ago* (New York, 1926).

41. Lucy Sprague Mitchell, *North America: The Land They Live In for the Children Who Live There* (New York, 1931). Mitchell, *Two Lives*, 430.

42. E.g., it was the only one of Mitchell's books listed as a resource for teachers in Ruth Tooze and Beatrice Perham Krone, *Literature and Music as Resources for Social Studies* (Englewood Cliffs, N.J., 1955).

43. Mitchell, *Two Lives*, 424.

44. Lucy Sprague Mitchell, "Making Young Geographers Instead of Teaching Geography," *Progressive Education* 5 (July–September 1928): 217–23.

45. Mitchell, *Two Lives*, 426–27.

46. Lucy Sprague Mitchell, *Young Geographers: How They Explore the World and How They Map the World* (New York, 1934).

47. Mitchell, *Young Geographers*, 89.

48. Mitchell, *Young Geographers*, 96.

49. Mitchell, *Two Lives*, 408.

50. Mitchell, *Two Lives*, 410.

51. Mitchell, *Two Lives*, 416.

52. Mitchell, *Two Lives*, 416.

53. Mitchell, *Two Lives*, 418.

54. Mitchell, *Two Lives*, 418.

55. Salvatore J. Natoli, ed., *Strengthening Geography in the Social Studies*, Bulletin No. 81 (Washington, D.C., 1988).

56. Mitchell, *Two Lives*, 422.

57. Lucy Sprague Mitchell and Johanna Boetz, *The People of the U.S.A.: Their Place in the School Curriculum* (New York, 1942).

58. Mitchell and Boetz, *People of the U.S.A.*, 9.

59. Sherry L. Field, "Scrap Drives, Stamp Sales, and School Spirit: Examples of Elementary Social Studies during World War II," *Theory and Research in Social Education* 23, no. 1 (Winter 1994): 441–60.

60. Mitchell, *Two Lives*, 469.

61. Mitchell, *Two Lives*, 468.

62. Mitchell, *Two Lives*, 470.

63. Sherry L. Field, "Roosevelt's World War II Army of Community Service Workers: Children and Their Teachers," *Social Education* 60, no. 5 (October 1996): 280–83; Rahima C. Wade and David W. Saxe, "Community Service–Learning in the Social Studies: Historical Roots, Empirical Evidence, Critical Issues," *Theory and Research in Social Education* 24, no. 4 (Fall 1996): 331–59; A. S. Waterman, ed., *Service-Learning: Applications from the Research* (Mahwah, N.J., 1997); N. A. Glasgow, *Taking the Classroom into the Community: A Guidebook* (Thousand Oaks, Calif., 1996).

64. Antler, *Lucy Sprague Mitchell*, 318.

65. Lucy Sprague Mitchell et al., *Know Your Children in School* (New York, 1954), 15–16.

66. Mitchell, *Two Lives*, 473.

67. Antler, *Lucy Sprague Mitchell*, 343.

68. E.g., her theories about children's sensory experiences and learning and acquisition of map and thinking skills are cited frequently in Carol Seefeldt, *Social Studies for the Preschool–Primary Child*, 3d ed. (Columbus, Ohio, 1989). Seefeldt's is one of the only textbooks written specifically about young children's social education.

69. Lucy Sprague Mitchell authored or coauthored six books for adults, twenty-three books for children, and twenty-eight journal articles or book chapters.

70. Lucy Sprague Mitchell, "A Cooperative School for Student Teachers," *Progressive Education* 8, no. 3 (March 1931): 251–55.

7

Bessie Louise Pierce
and Her Contributions to the Social Studies

Murry R. Nelson

Bessie Louise Pierce
Courtesy of the Department of Special Collections,
University of Chicago Library

In 1925 Bessie Louise Pierce was elected vice president of the newly formed (in 1921) National Council for the Social Studies (NCSS), and the next year she was elected president of that group. This was by no means a given, since no accepted line of succession from vice president to president of the organization existed until 1930. At her election as president, Bessie Pierce was forty-four years old and an associate professor of history at the University of Iowa. How she came to be such a prominent figure in social studies, yet without being viewed as a significant figure in the field, and where her career moved after her election and service to NCSS is the focus of this chapter.

Early Years

Bessie Pierce was born in Caro, Michigan, on 20 April 1888 but was raised in Waverly, Iowa, where her family moved shortly after her birth and where her father owned and operated a dry-goods business. She attended high school in Waverly and then enrolled at the University of Iowa, where she received a degree in history in 1910. For the next six years Pierce taught in high schools in Sanborn, Iowa, and in the larger town of Mason City. During these years she almost certainly raised questions to herself regarding the best ways to teach students history as well as the best ways to train teachers to teach history better. In 1916 she was offered the position of instructor in history and head of the social studies department at the laboratory school of the University of Iowa. The lab school there was based on John Dewey's lab school at the University of Chicago and was one of the best in the country at that time, with faculty actively engaged in research and writing as well as teaching. Clearly, the intellectual atmosphere was to Pierce's liking; she was inspired to begin summer course work at the University of Chicago that led to her master's degree in history in 1918.

Professional Beginnings

At about this time Pierce joined the American Historical Association (AHA) and became actively interested in the discussions about the teaching of history in schools. She also became acquainted with Professor Arthur M. Schlesinger of Ohio State University and his work in the AHA. In the fall of 1918 Schlesinger accepted a position as professor of history at the University of Iowa, and Pierce enrolled in a Ph.D. program in history with Schlesinger as her adviser. She also remained an active teacher in the lab school until the 1920–21 academic year, when she became an instructor of history in the Department of History at Iowa. Her decision to return to Iowa's lab school in 1918 was not made without second thoughts. That fall she had been offered a position to begin 1 January 1919 at the University of Kansas lab school as supervisor of the history and science group, though her official rank would be assistant professor in what today would be called a tenure line. Pierce was nominated for the position by Rolla Tryon, whom she had had as a professor at the University of Chicago.[1]

First Professional Writings

After returning to Iowa, Pierce began writing and publishing her research and comments on the nature of history teaching in schools. Already known by some leaders in the field through her association with the University of Chicago and her work at the lab school in Iowa, Pierce expanded her reputation through her publication in the *Historical Outlook*, the most well known journal in the area of history teaching. In March 1919 she published "An Experiment in Individual Instruction in History," most likely the research conducted for her master's degree. Taking as her point of departure the work published in 1916 by another professor at Iowa, E. E. Lewis, who observed and recorded the rate of questioning by history teachers, Pierce designed a plan for allowing students to work with a teacher individually and then set about training another student in what we might recognize as the Lancasterian method. This method, first devised at the turn of the eighteenth century, involved a "master" who would ground in knowledge a number of older and brighter students, each of whom would then seek to teach the material to a small group of subordinates.[2] In Pierce's study, one group of students used this method. Her other group of students had group recitations and questions with the teacher. Pierce concluded that students seemed to do slightly better with the method involving the master and tutors, but those who used the individual method all gave it a solid endorsement except for one girl. Pierce then attempted some correlational analysis that, by today's standards, seems crude in both its methods and its pupil classification. Nevertheless, Pierce asserted the great utility of individual instruction to a teacher who wishes to see children succeed "commensurate with their ability."[3]

The next year Pierce published, again in the *Historical Outlook*, "The Socialized Recitation." This article addressed the question-and-answer sequence in a history classroom and offered an alternative to the "old method" in which there was "a tendency toward pupil-passivity." Pierce felt that, in contrast to this superficial study of history, "the socialized recitation" also allowed for the development of positive attitudes toward the subject studied and broadened the student's ability to express his or her opinion, even critically but always "in the spirit of good-will." Being "socialized" in Pierce's view meant that students would develop the social attributes necessary for being effective members of a community.

Pierce noted that some teachers try to imbue such feelings by having a student lead the class, but she questioned whether the students are really "socialized" through this method and asked what the role of the teacher ought to be under those circumstances. In the socialized method, students are "taken into the confidence of the teacher, and the scheme is explained carefully and thoroughly, [and] the average high school class will co-operate irrespective of the length of time in which they have been taught by other methods." Pierce provided two stenographic reports of work in the same school. Though the method seems a bit simplistic in its training and rapid success, Pierce made cogent arguments and clearly affected many readers of the journal. She also revealed herself as an early qualitative researcher.[4]

Early Involvement with the NCSS

By 1921 Pierce had shifted to her role as instructor in the University of Iowa's Department of History, but her focus and interests remained similar. When the National Council for the Social Studies was formed in 1921, she was an early member and by 1922 had become a member of the NCSS Executive Committee, composed of the four officers of NCSS and three other members. The first NCSS vice president was Rolla Tryon, Pierce's former professor at Chicago. Tryon was a professor of the teaching of history and had recently published a teaching-methods book on history and social sciences for elementary and secondary schools. He later authored one of the volumes (*The Social Sciences as School Subjects*) of the massive AHA study on the social studies in the schools. NCSS had also established an advisory board with members from other history and social science organizations that had been a part of the Joint Commission on the Presentation of Social Studies in the Schools along with NCSS.[5] The commission later became part of the executive council governing body of NCSS. One of the two AHA representatives to this joint commission was Arthur Schlesinger, Pierce's mentor at the University of Iowa. (The other member was Henry Johnson, of Teachers College, Columbia University.) So Pierce was "connected" when she joined NCSS, yet she never felt totally a part of it and became inactive in the organization shortly after serving as president.

In November 1921 Pierce published another piece in the *Historical Outlook*, "A Survey of Methods Courses in History."[6] This was the result of a survey she had conducted of twenty-six institutions training teachers in the teaching of history. Through this survey Pierce found out, and shared with the professional community, the qualifications of the teachers of such courses, the length and demands of instruction, the number of students trained, and the content of the courses. Among other recommendations, her conclusions called for more than a one-semester course in methods related to teaching history for those preparing to enter that field.

Early Involvement with the AHA

Shortly after the publication of that article, Pierce attended the annual meeting of the AHA held in St. Louis in December 1921. If the information in the annual reports of the AHA is correct, this was the first AHA meeting she attended. At this meeting Pierce was a discussant for two papers given under the general title "Conference upon Desirable Adjustments between History and the Other Social Studies in Elementary and Secondary Schools." Her responses were later published in the *Historical Outlook*.[7] One of the two presenters was Rolla Tryon, and that may have been one reason that Pierce was commenting. In her remarks, Pierce made a point that speaks to the fears and hopes of those of us in the field today. She noted that to most people more social studies or other social sciences means less history. She commented that historians "naturally object to giving time to other social sciences which we have felt justly is ours." Different arrangements had been tried to mollify all parties concerned but to no avail. "The ideal arrangement, of course, would make it possible for the social studies to be presented by people so well trained in all of the subjects that there would be constant correlation."

Pierce's attendance at the AHA meeting and her presentation were highly unusual; she was one of the few women members of the AHA and one of only 58 women (of more than 350 people) who are listed as attending that meeting and one of only 4 women who appeared on the program. Despite her successes as a scholar, Pierce was always acutely aware that, because she was a woman, people held low expectations of her ability. She was clearly a highly motivated and capable scholar, but she recognized early on that this would not be sufficient to convince skeptics of her abilities and commitment to the field. After attending the AHA meetings in 1921, Pierce became a regular attendee for most of the following years. In 1922 she was cited as a member who greatly assisted the Joint Commission on the Presentation of History in the Schools, and at the December 1923 AHA meetings held in Columbus, Ohio, Pierce made a presentation entitled "The Attack upon History Textbooks" at a "History in the Schools" session. The title and topic were provocative enough that at least two popular media outlets, the *New York Evening Post* and the *New Republic,* requested advance copies in order to print excerpts to coincide with the meeting.[8]

In 1925 she was named a member of the AHA's Program Committee for the 1926 and 1927 meetings. This coincided with her assumption of the office of vice president of NCSS, which was probably a factor in her being named to the committee, though that alone would not have been a sufficient reason to do so.

It was at about this time that Pierce turned away from NCSS interest and focused much more on her involvement with the AHA. There does not seem to be any one reason for this change of interest. It may have been that she felt she had done as much as she could within NCSS. It might also have been that she felt herself more concerned with history and concomitant issues that she felt were most appropriately addressed within the AHA forum.

It is interesting to note that Pierce was not asked to serve on the Committee on History and Other Social Sciences in the Schools, later renamed the Commission on Social Studies in the Schools, which created and shepherded the massive seventeen-volume study on aspects of this topic. In studying the AHA documents it is clear that the chair of that committee for many years, A. C. Krey, was essentially given carte blanche in naming the committee. Krey's views were quite strong in many areas. A medieval historian, he had considerably less respect for people interested in history teaching in the schools who did not have a degree in history.[9] But Pierce did have a degree in history, taken under Arthur Schlesinger, and her research and publication in the area certainly warranted strong consideration for a position on the committee. Nevertheless she was never appointed to it, although she did author, in 1933, a volume for the commission study and engaged in a great deal of written communication with many of her fellow authors, particularly Charles Beard and Charles Merriam, in this massive study, "Investigation of Social Studies in the Schools." In a note to Jesse Newlon, who was apparently acting as a kind of bursar for the commission, Pierce displayed the honest and self-effacing qualities that are evident in her correspondence:

> As you know, I was compensated for two months of work on the document which I felt was as generous as need be although, of course, I put much more than two months of work upon it. However, if you feel that your Committee would care to pay for the typing service which will be necessary in the revision which Professor Hayes thought should be made I should be very grateful. Whatever amount up to $25.00 you would feel right would be very satisfactory and very helpful. However, do not feel obligated to do this for I am glad to take care of the matter if it seems wiser to do so.[10]

Besides the national publications noted earlier, Pierce authored a number of papers for the *University of Iowa Extension Bulletin*, particularly for a College of Education series that began in 1924. These articles included "Aids for History Teachers," "The Correlation of History and Geography," "The High School Library," and "Textbooks in United States History," as well as a longer volume, *Social Studies for the Junior High School*. In 1923 Pierce completed her doctoral dissertation at the University of Iowa under Schlesinger and was promoted to assistant professor in the history department.

Pierce maintained cordial relations with her peers in the AHA but never became overly friendly. She was always frank and critical, but proper, in her interactions with her colleagues, particularly her male colleagues. She was less wary with women colleagues and, her correspondence indicates, often insightful in recognizing the way women were perceived by male peers.

In a letter to Pierce in 1943, Jeannette Nichols, president of the Middle States Council for the Social Studies, who possessed a Ph.D. degree but was known most often as the wife of Roy Nichols, a professor of history at Swarthmore, offered belated congratulations for Pierce's promotion to the rank of full professor in the University of Chicago's history department, which she joined in 1929. Nichols indicated that the promotion was overdue and clearly intimated that Pierce's status as a woman had impeded her rightful progress:

> I want you to accept my congratulations for that [promotion], because there really are very few women who have won the rank in our No. 1 institutions. The fact that they did not grant it as soon as they should of (sic), does not alter the more important fact that your achievements were such that they won the promotion.[11]

In her reply Pierce thanked Nichols and expressed her relief at the promotion, since there had been a great deal of anxiety on the part of associate professors since university president Robert Maynard Hutchins had decided to change many of their appointments to term and not permanent appointments. Pierce noted, "I do not think that many in the upper ranks worried unduly but it does give a sense of security, especially in these days of insecurity and when one is a 'mere woman.'"[12]

In a 1944 letter to Nellie Neilson, Pierce expressed her great pride in Neilson's selection as the first woman president of the AHA and in Neilson's typifying "the best in the profession, both personally and academically."[13] Neilson, in a reply to Pierce, noted that her own heart attack and passing out during the middle of an address concerned her because she hated to "set that sort of record for a woman as president."[14] Neilson went on to note that she had had a bad heart for a long time but tried not to let it stop her.

Lengthier Research Studies: Policy and Ideology and the Notions of Citizenship

In 1926 (the same year that Pierce was promoted to associate professor of history at Iowa), Knopf published a revision of her dissertation on the manipulation of school curricula, *Public Opinion and the Teaching of History*. This work constituted a new, hybrid direction for Pierce and her research. Whereas previously she had concentrated on the methodology of secondary teaching, her work now reflected a growing concern with the relationship between educational policy and national ideology. This would remain important to her and her writing for the rest of her professional career.

Pierce's dissertation work involved compiling information from numerous political and community service organizations and seeking their input, as well as research on how public opinion affected the teaching of history in the United States from the early 1800s until the present date. One-third of the book focuses on statutory regulations in the teaching of history, with a last chapter dealing only with disloyalty charges against teachers since 1917. These largely related to teachers who supported peace initiatives or were pacifists but were often labeled traitors for not being openly supportive of America's war efforts. The best known of these were teachers in New York City tried under the Lusk Laws. These laws mandated loyalty oaths and gave the Commissioner of Education of New York the sole right to refuse to issue such a certification of loyalty to any teacher. Most certificates were denied because of perceived "pro-

Germanism," but some were denied for Communist Party membership, both of which were viewed as seditious or treasonous under the addition to the law made in 1917.[15]

Pierce was particularly interested in seeing how teachers and districts were altering or had altered their teaching as a result of "patriotic" concerns. Regarding the "German cause" in World War I, Pierce quoted observations about this subject, such as those of Charles and Mary Beard in their *History of the United States*, then attempted to find more details by contacting organizations in order to validate the claims made by the Beards and other historians.

The second part of *Public Opinion and the Teaching of History* in the United States, "The Activities of Propagandist Agencies," has two lengthy chapters, one on attempts to control textbooks and the other on the attacks on history textbooks since 1917. The appendices include the infamous "Lusk Laws of New York regarding Instruction in Patriotism and Citizenship, the Flag, Textbooks and Qualifications for Teachers," as well as similar laws or mandates in California, Boston, New York City, and Wisconsin. Her work revealed how difficult it was to teach without indoctrinating and the cost of resisting such inculcation of students. One is struck by how far academic freedom has advanced but also how far it still has to go. Taking Pierce's work together with Howard Beale's two books on censorship and academic freedom written in the 1930s as part of the AHA Commission on the Social Studies, one can capture a broad perspective on this issue from the late nineteenth century through the first third of the twentieth century.

Pierce made great efforts in *Public Opinion and the Teaching of History* "to narrate without partiality or prejudice the facts relating to the subject under discussion."[16] In a letter to Pierce, Merle Curti wrote, "I envy your objectivity. I am afraid I could never have so skillfully let the material speak for itself."[17] Pierce had been concerned with the ideas of citizenship and the responsibilities of citizenship since she had been a high school teacher. Her dissertation work moved her into an area of neutrality as she described the goals and intentions of organizations that espoused citizenship education. It is this neutrality that is frustrating to scholars trying to get her views on the duties of the citizen and the notion of citizenship education. Besides being vehemently against censorship of any type, Pierce seemingly failed to distinguish between the messages of the KKK, the Boy Scouts, and the American Legion, for example. This failure to make a distinction is related to Pierce's belief that given the opportunity to examine all of these organizations and others, students will have the tools from their training in school to determine the organizations and ideas that will further democracy and the human condition. Telling students what to do would have been antithetical to her ideas of informed choice. In 1929 she wrote, "The teacher of history and the other social studies is thus confronted by a myriad of forces endeavoring to draw him hither and thither. Independence from such forces comes only through wide and accurate information and by the integrity of purpose to teach the truth."[18]

In spite of Pierce's efforts at neutrality in her examinations of textbooks, at least two of her own views of the good citizen come through. First, in *Civic Attitudes in American School Textbooks*, she finds repugnant the loyalty laws that cause precensorship of textbooks. She echoes the protest of the American Historical Association in that regard and finds most apt the *New York Times*'s declaration that as a result of the censorship, "it was inconceivable that any honest man would wish to write textbooks in history for children under such statutory principles."[19] Second, in that same book she notes the less flattering way texts address the citizens and governments of other nations. The fact that she found this disturbing reflects larger views of global citizenship.

Pierce's earlier writings and practices were often more revealing. In an article published in 1920 she revealed a practice that she followed in her high school history teaching and also provided insight into her beliefs about the responsibilities and practices of good citizens. Pierce first quoted favorably from Alexander Inglis's discussion in *Principles of Secondary Education* of the social and civic value of history. Inglis saw factual teaching and modern application as two facets of history teaching and of useful civic values. Much more important, he noted and Pierce agreed, were the "real *attitudes* developed through the study of the subject" (emphasis in original).[20] Pierce devised her "socialized recitation" to develop these real attitudes or indirect values. The structure of the socialized recitation seems to be a possible blueprint for Pierce's views of citizenship in the larger societal context:

> In the first place, each pupil should be made to feel his responsibility for the conduct of the class during the whole recitation hour. Here is found the development of the community instinct as distinguished from an individualistic attitude. The pupil should feel himself an integral part of the group, should feel that it is his duty as well as his privilege to contribute to the fullest of his capacity, and to use his influence to lead others to do likewise. He should be trained to assume the part of critic, but only in the spirit of good-will. In the second place, there should be a development of self-expression and of individuality through the necessity of active participation

for each person. Third, the work should be so organized in the lesson assignment that the time lost in questioning in the ordinary recitation can be spent in class discussion. In the fourth place, the work should be so assigned that there will not be a departure from the work in hand.[21]

In 1927, in a volume edited by Milo Hillegas called *The Classroom Teacher,* Pierce presented notions consistent with these ideas that offer teachers direction in leading students to informed decisions as citizens. She stated that "The teacher of civics should not confine herself to one book in the presentation of her subject. Supplementary reading wisely selected is a most valuable aid in the teaching of civics."[22]

In addition Pierce advocated that the civics classroom should be a laboratory in which "suitable tools for work such as bulletin boards, wall maps and charts, as well as books and visual aids" are provided. "Upon the bulletin board should be clipped materials appropriate for fostering the day's work. These might include newspaper articles, "copies of city ordinances, statutes, and other official papers and pictures from magazines and the Rotogravure section of the Sunday papers."[23] In addition extracurricular activities "should provide opportunities for developing leaders, for solving problems of social interest, and for motivating the work of the classroom."[24]

Pierce's dissertation and subsequent book helped establish her reputation concerning the external forces that bear on history teaching and curriculum. At the same time, Pierce continued to write about the teaching of history in school. In 1925 she wrote an article for the *Historical Outlook* entitled "The Social Studies in the Eighth Grade."[25] This article was a mixture of survey information, review and listing of resources for teaching social studies, and commentary. In the survey Pierce provided extensive descriptions of social studies in three sites around the nation. The resources included textbooks for eighth-grade use, visual aids, and course requirements in states with mandates for eighth-grade social studies or history. Pierce included a section authored by her sister, Anne, on using music in American history classes.

In late 1924 or early 1925 Pierce was appointed chair of the NCSS Committee on Standards of Teaching. In 1925 the committee presented its report to the whole council. In secretary Edgar Dawson's report of 1925 on this subject, he noted that of the ten points made in the committee's platform, the last was the most interesting, that is, "the teaching load for social studies in the high school should never exceed four periods a day."[26]

The University of Chicago and Later AHA Activity

In 1929 Pierce accepted the offer of the Local Research Committee to come
to the University of Chicago as an associate professor of history and head
of the History of Chicago Project, which was to integrate economic, political, and sociological studies and uncover new areas for research. Pierce's
mentor, Arthur Schlesinger, had left Iowa for Harvard the year before,
and Pierce saw this project as something that she could work on for many
years. Pierce recast the project into an extensive history of the city in four
volumes covering the period from 1673 to 1915.[27] Ultimately the Chicago
history project lasted more than forty years, and the last volume remained
unfinished at Pierce's death.

After beginning the Chicago project, Pierce still maintained an active
interest and involvement with other social studies and school history
notions. In 1930 she authored *Civic Attitudes in American School Textbooks*,
an examination of attitudes contained in texts not only from history but
also from civics, economics, sociology, political problems, geography, foreign languages, music, and basal readers.[28] In addition she read sixty-
three courses of study published by state departments of public instruction and city school systems. Her findings were again limited to
describing, not assessing. She found that all of these sources expressed
civic attitudes, though none of the attitudes seemed particularly surprising. She commented neither on whether it was appropriate for these
resources to be doctrinaire nor whether she agreed with any of the attitudes that the works sought to inculcate.

In 1926 the AHA's Committee on History and Other Social Sciences in
the Schools, later renamed Commission on the Social Studies, conceived
of a massive project, "Investigation of the Social Studies in the Schools,"
that extended for more than seven years. Led by A. C. Krey, the chairman
of the commission and director of the investigation, and George Counts
as research director, this commission of the AHA published seventeen
volumes. Pierce wrote volume 3, *Citizens' Organizations and the Civic
Training of Youth*.[29] Consistent with Pierce's approach, this was a relatively "neutral" study in which Pierce presented information on more than
two hundred organizations. Most of this was simply transmission and
compilation of data generated by the organizations themselves via survey questionnaires, the most popular means of gathering social science
data at that time. Pierce had used a similar technique in her dissertation;
to avoid duplication to any great extent, she omitted or passed over
briefly those groups treated in her earlier study. She noted that "the purpose of the study is purely objective and no attempt has been made to

assess the value or the effectiveness of the programs."[30]

This volume consisted of eight parts. Part 1 examined educational and civic policies of patriotic organizations such as the U.S. Flag Association, the American Citizenship Foundation, the Daughters of the American Revolution, the American Legion, and the Veterans of Foreign Wars. Part 2 was devoted to the educational and civic policies of military groups like the Navy League, the Reserve Officers Training Corps, and Citizens Military Training Camps. Pierce had a very hard time separating the goals of these groups from those in the first part of the study. Finally, the third part discussed the programs of peace organizations like the National Council for the Prevention of War and the American School Citizenship League, which sprang from the National Peace Congress in 1908.[31] Part 4 focused on fraternal groups such as the Freemasons but also included in this genre the Ku Klux Klan. Pierce traces the KKK's nativist beginnings and presents most of its beliefs and policies through its own publications. She is nonjudgmental in detailing their accusations against Jews, Roman Catholics, Bolsheviks, and immigrants. Not one word in this chapter mentions African Americans in any way. The actions of the Klan would seem to have warranted a harsher appraisal, but Pierce is consistent in not evaluating any of the groups in her study nor endorsing or disavowing any of their actions.

Part 5 examined religious and racial groups. It is here that Pierce mentions that the National Association for the Advancement of Colored People opposed the Klan. This section included groups like the Ancient Order of Hibernians in America, the Order of Scottish Clans, and the Federation of Polish Hebrews. Part 6 addressed youth movements, including the Girl Scouts and Boy Scouts, the Junior Red Cross, the YMCA and YWCA, the Young People's Socialist League, and organizations devoted to character education. Part 7 was devoted to business and labor groups, and part 8 examined groups on both sides of the issue of Prohibition.

Overall, Pierce's aim in the book was to lay out the policies and goals of all groups discussed. In reading this book, one is struck by Pierce's ability to remain nonjudgmental, particularly regarding reckless or radical groups. Clearly, she perceived this stance as necessary in allowing readers themselves to assess specific groups. History at this time was wrestling with the goal of becoming more scientific, a social science rather than one of the humanities, where more latitude for interpretation and judgment existed. Pierce may have felt constrained because of this ethos, especially in light of her gender. Pierce felt the pressure of the need to be taken seriously as a historian. She was consistently very careful in her work not to be controversial since this might call into question her credentials (and those of other women).

This approach to publication was in sharp contrast to Pierce's dealings with students and professional peers. In these, she was deliberate, critical, and brutally honest. In a 1930 letter to a former student at the University of Iowa who had delayed the beginning of a Ph.D. program and now sought Pierce's guidance in doing his work at Chicago where she had just begun, Pierce noted that "unless you are fully desirous of going forward with the doctorate at this time, it would seem to me that it would be well for you to do something else."[32] In a 1945 letter to Allan Nevins, Pierce discussed the circumstances of her relationship with a former graduate assistant:

> You will perhaps be interested to know that Mr. Destler was one of my first assistants on the History of Chicago, and although he was an able young man, his contributions to the project were such that I found it best not to ask him to remain after that year, even if he had wanted to. Like many young people, he may be searching for the unusual.[33]

Sometimes, Pierce deprecated her own contributions to projects by referring to her comments as not very useful, or words to that effect. Over the years of communicating with Conyers Read, the executive secretary of the AHA, he always wrote to her with the familiar address, "Bessie." Nevertheless, Pierce continued to address him deferentially as "Mr. Read," as she did with almost all males. Even she and her old adviser, Arthur Schlesinger, exchanged letters as "Mr. Schlesinger" and "Miss Pierce" as late as 1939, after they had known each other for nearly twenty years. Admittedly, it was a more formal time, yet Pierce did write to almost all the women that she knew using their first names. Such male-female relationships must have been difficult, since any uninvited informality on the part of the woman might have been interpreted as being too forward. Thus, it was not until Read insisted that she call him "Conyers" or that he call her "Miss" or "Dr. Pierce" that she finally agreed to a new arrangement.

In many exchanges with Read, Pierce displayed a critical and thorough command of issues and offered candid and straightforward assessments. She was insightful in her comments about people and positions for AHA leadership, often balancing abilities against timing. In a lengthy letter she weighed Schlesinger's feeling that "new blood" should be brought into some committees against the need for both continuity and Schlesinger's breadth of vision.[34] Clearly, Pierce understood what was at stake in a variety of situations and on numerous issues, yet her candor seems to have been governed by a sense of appropriateness about expressing those views that depended heavily on matters of deference and context.

Pierce's involvement with the AHA in the 1930s and 1940s was considerable. In 1939 she was appointed a member of the AHA's Committee on Appointments, which meant that she had a hand in all of the committee compositions of the organization and as a member of its executive committee.[35] For the decade of the 1930s, Pierce was the only female on the AHA Executive Committee. That committee appointed the executive board of *Social Education*, the journal of NCSS; the executive committee of that executive board; and *Social Education*'s advisory board, among whom were some of the most prominent educators in social studies and history at the time. These included Charles Beard of Columbia University; Erling Hunt and Merle Curti, both of Teachers College, Columbia University; Edgar Wesley of the University of Minnesota; Howard Wilson and Arthur Schlesinger, both of Harvard University; James Michener of Colorado State College of Education; Ernest Horn of the University of Iowa; Daniel Knowlton of New York University; and I. James Quillen of Stanford University.[36]

As the 1940s progressed, the board of *Social Education* came under the exclusive control of NCSS, as the AHA's involvement waned. By 1940 the ratio of appointments was nine by NCSS and three by the AHA.[37] Certainly Bessie Pierce's close contacts in both organizations made her input about these appointments vital, although officially the managing editor of NCSS made the formal recommendations for these posts.[38] It is clear that Pierce dedicated a lot of time and thought to her assignment on the executive committee, as she often offered her views in writing regarding potential appointments and her suggestions occasionally resulted in altered assignments being made. In a letter about the continued appointment of Arthur Schlesinger to the Social Science Research Council (SSRC), she suggested to Read that Schlesinger's presence on the SSRC would be essential to the field of history and the AHA. The appointment was subsequently continued.[39] In addition to her work on the executive committee, Pierce was also a member of two special committees charged with recommending wartime policy on education to the federal government.[40]

Final Projects

During the 1930s and 1940s Pierce devoted a great deal of time and effort to writing high school and college textbooks in history, none of which was ever published. One source explains these later developments in Pierce's career in this fashion:

After a manuscript on martial music written with her sister failed to interest publishers, she collaborated with David Behan on a twentieth-century American history text and with Gene Lavengood on a general history of the United States. For more than fifteen years, these projects distracted her from teaching and supervision of the History of Chicago Project without producing the additional income she had hoped they would provide.[41]

Pierce's proposed project with her sister Anne stemmed from both personal interest and family loyalty. Anne taught music education at the University of Iowa. She asked Bessie to prepare a brief discussion about the background of American patriotic songs for Anne's students. The sisters then used the manuscript with pupils at the University of Iowa lab schools, where it was well received. The two sisters then tried to find a publisher to make the material available to schools throughout the country. Most of this work was done in the late 1930s and early 1940s. In 1949 Pierce was still seeking a publisher; at that time, she acknowledged that the material was no longer up-to-date and additional material would be needed. As she noted in a letter at that time, "Perhaps the subject matter is inopportune, but when the manuscript was prepared we were in the midst of war."[42]

In 1953 she retired from the University of Chicago, and in 1972 she moved back to Iowa City in order to spend as much time as possible with her sister. Pierce never married, though she reflected on her status with at least a bit of humor. In the letter mentioned earlier in which she discussed with Conyers Read their modes of address, she commented, "Parenthetically, don't 'Dr.' or 'Miss' me. The former I abhor and the second I can't help."[43]

Bessie Pierce died in 1974 after many years away from active involvement with social studies education. Nevertheless she was a pioneer in the field and remains a woman worthy of respect not only for all that she did but also for the exigencies that she faced in a male-dominated field.

Writings of Bessie Louise Pierce

Bessie Louise Pierce, "The Socialized Recitation," *Historical Outlook* 9, no. 5 (May 1920): 189–90.

What, then, should be the qualities of the socialized work which will distinguish it from the usual "pounding-in-of-information" plan? In the first place, each pupil should be made to feel his responsibility for the conduct of the class during the whole recitation hour. Here is found the development of the community instinct as distinguished from an individualistic attitude. The pupil should feel himself an integral part of the group, should feel that it is his duty as well as privilege to contribute to the fullest of his capacity, and to use his influence to lead others to do likewise. He should be trained to assume the part of critic, but only in the spirit of good-will. In the second place there should be a development of self-expression and of individuality through the necessity of active participation for each person. Third, the work should be so organized in the lesson assignment that the time lost in questioning in the ordinary recitation can be spent in class discussion. In the fourth place, the work should be so assigned that there will not be a departure from the work in hand.

Bessie Louise Pierce, "The Social Studies in the Eighth Grade," *Historical Outlook* **16, no. 7 (November 1925): 315–17.**

The "socialized" recitation in a variety of forms has appeared, considered by its advocates as best adapted to develop initiative, self-reliance and a social attitude in the pupil. The teacher has been told that persistently excessive teacher-participation in the classroom is an evidence of poor instruction. As a result, many teachers have so completely subordinated themselves that a near anarchism has ensued, undermining the values possible in the new type of work. . . .

Much has been written about the need and value of standardized tests, but as yet little has been accomplished. The future, moreover, does not hold out many promises until a greater uniformity in programs and in subject-matter can be brought about.

Bessie Louise Pierce, *Public Opinion and the Teaching of History in the United States* **(New York, 1926).**

History for the sake of propaganda is not a unique possession of any one country. It has been employed in the name of "patriotism" by many nations. Livy extolled Rome, Green exalted England, Bancroft eulogized the exploits of the founders of America, and Treitschke and Nietzsche pictured the glories of an imperialist regime in Germany. As a result, there has developed an overwhelming pride in national and racial attributes and achievements. From such a source has sprung much of the hereditary enmity between France and Germany. Indeed, it has been said that an analogous situation exists in the United States. . . .

Propagandist history, however, is not merely an instrument of the ultra-nationalist. By the pacifist it may be employed to depict with a vivid gruesomeness the horrors of war; by it the militarist may demonstrate the advantages of prepared-ness; the racially conscious may narrate, in their history, achievements of their heroes to the exclusion or derogation of those of other groups; the religious enthu-siasts may commend the contributions of their sect to the neglect of others; and economic and social organizations may seek to serve their particular purposes. Demands for revised history textbooks, such as emanated during the World War, to teach the point of view of then current, are but a recent instance of a practice as old as the teaching of history.

Bessie Louise Pierce, "Propaganda in Teaching Social Studies," *Histor-ical Outlook* **20, no. 8 (December 1929): 387–89.**

The word "propaganda" as commonly used today does not mean disinterested information. Indeed it connotes an ulterior purpose, which may be good or bad. When it concerns itself with education and the schools, it may become especially vicious, because it generally develops a regimentation of thinking away from which education is supposed to lead. . . .

But partisan history in America has not been demanded solely on the basis of sectional controversies. Racial, religious and patriotic groups have also asserted their individual claims and endeavored to make Clio a special pleader. . . .

But the story is not yet told, for direction of teaching is not confined solely to the field of history. Included in an ever-widening circle are the subjects of civics and economics, the former a special concern of organizations promoting instruc-tion in "American institutions and ideals."

The teacher of history and the other social studies is thus confronted by a myr-iad of forces endeavoring to draw him hither and thither. Independence from such forces only comes through wide and accurate information and by integrity of pur-pose to teach the truth.

Notes

1. Letter from H. Nutt to B. Pierce, 23 October 1918, Pierce Papers, University of Chicago.

2. A. Meyer, *An Educational History of the Western World* (New York, 1972).

3. B. Pierce, "An Experiment in Individual Instruction in History," *Historical Outlook* 10, no. 2 (February 1919): 86–87.

4. B. Pierce, "The Socialized Recitation," *Historical Outlook* 9, no. 5 (May 1920): 189–93.

5. M. Nelson, "The Early Years, 1921–1937," *Social Education* 59, no. 7 (Novem-ber–December 1995): 400.

6. B. Pierce, "A Survey of Methods Courses in History," *Historical Outlook* 8, no. 9 (December 1921): 315–18.

7. B. Pierce, "Discussion of the Papers," *Historical Outlook* 12, no. 9 (December 1921): 86–87.

8. Letter from C. Puckette to B. Pierce, 11 December 1923; and telegram from (n.i.) Knipfing to B. Pierce, 31 December 1923, Pierce Papers, University of Chicago.

9. E. Wesley, interview by author, 23 May 1974, Stanford, Calif.

10. Letter from B. Pierce to J. Newlon, 13 January 1931, Pierce Papers, University of Chicago.

11. Letter from Mrs. R. Nichols to B. Pierce, 9 October 1943, Pierce Papers, University of Chicago.

12. Letter from B. Pierce to Mrs. R. Nichols, 12 October 1943, Pierce Papers, University of Chicago.

13. Letter from B. Pierce to N. Neilson, 4 January 1944.

14. Letter from N. Neilson to B. Pierce, 7 February 1944, Pierce Papers, University of Chicago.

15. B. Pierce, *Public Opinion and the Teaching of History in the United States* (New York, 1926).

16. Pierce, *Public Opinion*, viii.

17. Letter from M. Curti to B. Pierce, 12 June 1933, Pierce Papers, University of Chicago.

18. B. Pierce, "Propaganda in the Teaching of Social Studies," *Historical Outlook* 20, no. 8 (July 1929): 387–89.

19. *New York Times*, 19 April 1923, as quoted in B. Pierce, *Civic Attitudes in American School Textbooks* (Chicago 1930), 234.

20. Alexander Inglis, *Principles of Secondary Education* (Riverside, N.Y., 1918), 547, cited in B. Pierce, "Socialized Recitation."

21. Pierce, "Socialized Recitation," 189.

22. B. Pierce with H. C. Hill, "Civics," in *The Classroom Teacher*, ed. Milo E. Hillegas (Chicago, 1927), 24.

23. Pierce, "Civics," 30.

24. Pierce, "Civics," 80.

25. B. Pierce, "The Social Studies in the Eighth Grade," *Historical Outlook* 16, no. 7 (November 1925): 315–17.

26. E. Dawson, "Report of the NCSS Secretary," *Historical Outlook* 16, no. 8 (December 1925): 395–401.

27. J. Meyer, "Guide to the Bessie Louise Pierce Papers," 1981, Joseph Regenstein Library, University of Chicago.

28. Pierce, *Civic Attitudes in Textbooks*.

29. B. Pierce, *Citizens' Organizations and the Civic Training of Youth* (New York, 1933).

30. Pierce, *Citizens' Organizations and Civic Training*, ix.

31. The driving force of this group was Fanny Fern Andrews. Her work with the American School Citizenship League and with educating for peace is examined thoroughly in a recent dissertation by Julie Weber, "Fanny Fern Andrews and

the Development of the American School Peace League" (Ph.D. diss., Pennsylvania State University, 1997).

32. Letter from B. Pierce to D. Nelson, 1 April 1930, Pierce Papers, University of Chicago.

33. Letter from B. Pierce to A. Nevins, 4 December 1945, Pierce Papers, University of Chicago.

34. Letter from B. Pierce to C. Read, 20 November 1939, Pierce Papers, University of Chicago.

35. Letter from D. Perkins to B. Pierce, 9 January 1939, Pierce Papers, University of Chicago.

36. Minutes of the meeting of the Executive Committee of the AHA, 5 November 1939, Pierce Papers, University of Chicago.

37. Minutes of the meeting of the Executive Committee of the AHA, 5 November 1939.

38. Letter from B. Pierce to C. Read, 27 November 1939, Pierce Papers, University of Chicago.

39. Pierce to Read, 27 November 1939.

40. Meyer, "Guide to Pierce Papers," 4.

41. Meyer, "Guide to Pierce Papers," 4.

42. Letter from B. Pierce to Mrs. E. Newsome, 27 May 1949, Pierce Papers, University of Chicago.

43. Pierce to Read, 27 November 1939.

8

Rachel Davis DuBois:
Intercultural Education Pioneer

O. L. Davis Jr.

Rachel Davis DuBois
Courtesy of Carol Davis

G entlemen, I will not resign."

Rachel Davis DuBois's response was definite. She was a social studies teacher at Woodbury (New Jersey) High School, and members of the board of education had requested that she tender her resignation. They acknowledged her teaching abilities, but they were responding to pressure from the local American Legion post. According to the Legionnaires, her positions on peace and racial equality were inconsistent with the sentiments of the citizens of Woodbury. The year was 1926.

DuBois was not just another teacher at the high school. The central issue was not her teaching; the flash point was the school's recent assembly programs. DuBois coordinated those programs, and that year they focused attention on the development of "sympathetic" attitudes toward other nations and races. The February schedule featured contributions of blacks to American life. For the first of that month's assemblies, Dr. William Pickens, DuBois's friend and the field secretary of the National Association for the Advancement of Colored People (NAACP), addressed the high school's students. Tensions in the community rose. Just days before members of the board visited DuBois, the board officially canceled the second assembly program of the month that had been planned by some of the small number of black students in the high school. DuBois could only despair at the board's decision. To resign her position as a teacher of civics and history, however, would be to teach her students the wrong lesson about the nation and its constitution. Subsequently, she wrote an open letter to the board and demanded a public hearing that would deal with her beliefs, especially those about her loyalty to the United States. The hearing was never held; the board reappointed her for the next year. Moreover, DuBois and her Woodbury students resumed their series of assembly programs, among the first of her self-styled "intercultural education" activities.

For Rachel Davis DuBois, this deeply unpleasant experience was but another obstacle in her life. She had confronted others and would deal with still more. Without realizing that she had launched the intercultural education movement, she undertook small, doable steps within the realities of the times; she would take the movement much further. For her, its goals were decidedly simple but never simplistic: she sought to facilitate the building of community, understanding of neighbors, and improved relations between people. Her conception of means continued to be practical.[1]

Scenes from a Committed Life

Little in Rachel Davis DuBois's early life might have predicted her involvement in intercultural education. But that she would be deeply committed to peace was a given. Born 25 January 1892, she was the second of six children in her southern New Jersey Quaker family. Generations of her Davis family had farmed the same property for nearly two centuries. As a child, Rachel became good friends with black workers in her home and on the farm. The established institutional segregation of the region and the times, however, divided her and her white neighbors from blacks when they attended school. Even so, her routine involvement in Quaker religious practices and thought provided the seeds for her expanding sense of commitment to social justice. In the life of Quaker meetings, particularly, she embraced the understanding of "God in every man." This idea grew into a steady companion throughout her life.[2]

Young Rachel Davis attended the small rural common school near her farm home. She completed her unremarkable secondary education at Pilesgrove High School, only recently converted from a fee-paying academy. She enjoyed dramatic activities, but few of the courses attracted her attention, although she ranked fourth in her class of thirteen when she graduated in 1909. That she developed an interest in attending college was an anomaly within her circle of friends. Simply, graduates of her high school did not attend college. From a seamstress aunt, she heard of Mount Holyoke College and applied for admission, but it rejected her because her high school was unaccredited. She remained at home for the next year and gained admission to Bucknell University in Leesburg, Pennsylvania. The rural Quaker girl from southern New Jersey felt distinctly out of place throughout her Bucknell years. Majoring in natural science, she became involved in various public speaking and dramatic activities. Still, she never felt accepted socially. She graduated in June 1914 and, unable to pursue a career in science because of her gender, turned to teaching as her only reasonable prospect for a job. Rejected by the school of her first choice, she accepted her first full-time post at Glassboro (New Jersey) High School to teach algebra, biology, and American history.

In particular, because of her lack of preparation, she feared her assignment in history. Too, her students disliked the idea of retracing the history that they had studied in previous courses. She sought some means of survival for both her students and herself. She intuitively seized upon dramatization of historical situations as a possibility, a decision that yielded both heightened interest and mutual satisfaction. She also learned that she enjoyed teaching history and social studies.

Rachel Davis married Nathan Steward DuBois on 19 June 1915. He had courted her by correspondence while she attended college, but she routinely rejected his proposals of marriage until she held her teaching position. They agreed that, if they did not have children, she would continue her career. Furthermore, and unusual for the times, they developed what they considered to be a 50-50 marriage.

Continuing to teach in Glassboro, she began to examine the depth of her Quaker commitment to pacifism. She could not avoid the times in which she lived. The United States slowly drifted into preparation for its entrance into the Great War then consuming the European powers. When war did come to the nation, DuBois decided that she must act firmly on her beliefs. She did not have to wait long to be tested.

In 1917, Glassboro school officials directed teachers to sell war savings stamps to their students. DuBois decided that she could not follow this mandate and told her superintendent of her decision. He responded, "Well, we don't have to yell it from the housetops, do we?" Other American teachers were not as fortunate as she; many were dismissed from their teaching positions because of their refusal to engage in such activities or to sign loyalty oaths. Not only did the superintendent permit DuBois to continue to teach, but also he had such confidence in her that he appointed her acting principal of Glassboro High School when he departed for military service.

Just two years after the end of the world war, she faced a major turning point in her life. It followed her attendance at the First International Conference of Friends in London in August 1920. The assembled Quakers testified and listened to reports about conditions of society and peace in the postwar world. To DuBois, much of the commentary was grim, and it profoundly shocked her. She sat quietly as she listened to riveting accounts of continuing Allied blockades of food and coal from Germany, of the conditions in India under British imperial rule, and of the paternalism shown black South Africans by whites. She felt especially empty when she heard vivid descriptions of the often callous and brutal treatment of black Americans by white Americans. These reports of reality, especially those from her own country, shattered DuBois's theoretical illusions. Within the life of the conference and its aftermath, she developed an emboldened commitment to Quaker ideals. Its expression was her mutual pledge with other young Quakers, "Let us build the world as it ought to be in the midst of things as they are."

DuBois confessed to herself that she did not know enough about the social problems in her own country. Until she knew more about these conditions, she believed that she could not teach history and social studies effectively. Thus, when she returned from her European trip, she resigned her position at Glassboro High School and began to work as a volunteer for several organizations concerned about American social problems. In 1921 she made a fact-finding trip to the South. She visited schools for blacks. She met George Washington Carver. She attended meetings of farmers. As she prepared her report, she read a recent article by W. E. B. Du Bois. She recognized that in her recent experiences she had discovered the direction of her life's work: the betterment of race relations. Subsequently, she joined the NAACP and, throughout the rest of her life, she was an activist in its causes.[3]

For DuBois, her decision was practical not simply theoretical. She set out to learn more about blacks in American life. She read, and she sought black friends. She established a committee whose purpose was to abolish prejudice against blacks. She worked to enroll blacks in de facto segregated Friends schools. Her work took her away from the familiar region of Philadelphia and southern New Jersey to other parts of the nation. Pacifism was a way of life to DuBois, but race relations remained at the center of her being.

In 1922 she journeyed to Europe a second time to attend an international conference of women. This meeting had been called by the Women's International League for Peace and Freedom to raise nations' consciousness about the inequities of the Treaty of Versailles. On the voyage to Europe, Jane Addams, the conference chair, invited DuBois to study the treaty with her and others in preparation for the sessions. When DuBois returned to the United States, she wrote an eight-session discussion guide, *War and Its Consequences,* for use in American high schools and colleges. She also joined an automobile caravan to witness for pacifism on its tour through New York, New Jersey, and Pennsylvania. By the summer of 1924, she was ready to return to teaching. She became a social studies teacher at Woodbury High School.

Finding her civics textbook inadequate, DuBois replaced it with *Americanizing Our Foreign-Born,* one of Harold Rugg's new social studies pamphlets. Her concern about the school's weekly assembly program, however, quickly became prominent. Asked by her superintendent to coordinate the programs, she readily agreed with only one proviso, that she could do what she wanted to do. She began to plan programs that would highlight America's cultural diversity as well as educate students about minority groups. Fortuitously, during the following summer, she attended the NAACP annual meeting, met W. E. B. Du Bois and

Langston Hughes, and, on the West Coast, investigated the effects on Asian-American communities of the recently passed Exclusion Act. Back at Woodbury in the fall of 1925, she convened a committee of teachers to work with her on the year's series of assembly programs.

DuBois suggested that two programs on the same general topic be planned for each month. The first of these programs would offer speakers, artists, or musicians of a particular culture; for the second program, an ethnically mixed group of students would enact aspects of the featured culture. After each assembly program, teachers would follow up with discussions and presentations of additional information. This program format became known as the Woodbury Plan and constituted DuBois's first deliberate educational activity in what soon became known as intercultural education. Except for the board's dramatic cancellation of the February program on black American culture and DuBois's refusal to resign, the basic pattern of the assembly programs continued for that semester and for the next several years. In the third year of the program, she compared attitudes of Woodbury seniors to those of seniors at a nearby school and found that Woodbury students were more tolerant than their counterparts on international and interracial topics.

By the end of the decade, DuBois realized that she again needed to know more. She wanted to continue to build her ideas about intercultural education. Thus, she resigned her Woodbury position and enrolled for graduate study at Teachers College, Columbia University. DuBois was not content simply to pursue a graduate degree. She worked intimately with groups of schools to alter students' international and intercultural attitudes. She worked with teachers and administrators to organize assembly programs and guided teachers' planning for follow-up activities. Long aware of the biases and distortions in textbooks, she researched and wrote supplementary materials for use in established courses. In 1934, DuBois organized what later became the Service Bureau for Intercultural Education, the most prominent vehicle of her work in intercultural education. Her efforts during this period raised the national profile of intercultural education both as ideal and as practice. Nevertheless, several administrative and financial tensions, clearly fed by gender discrimination, prompted DuBois to resign from the bureau in 1941. That same year, after more than a decade of living separately, she and her husband divorced.

The forced departure from her organization and the dissolution of her marriage could have broken weaker individuals. Clearly, DuBois became dispirited. However, she redirected her energies. For DuBois, multicultural education was a committed way of living, not simply activities undertaken at school.

Intercultural Education in Schools:
Practices and Programs

DuBois, largely unprepared academically to teach history and social studies, became a social educator out of opportunity and personal conviction. Through her teaching and civic actions, particularly in race relations, she came to believe that conventional school programs would not advance students' understandings, attitudes, and actions to help create a more just American society. On the other hand, her teaching experience at Woodbury High School convinced her that changed school practices could influence students in positive directions. She left Woodbury never again to teach regularly in the schools, but not because she had failed. Rather, on the basis of her success, she wished to influence additional teachers in many more schools to develop instructional practices that fostered intercultural education. For the decade of the 1930s, living in New York City, she worked tirelessly toward her objective. She not only pursued graduate studies but also crafted practical programs in a number of schools and built an organization that attracted national attention to its focus on intercultural education. This work, DuBois's most impressive contribution to social education, nevertheless remains obscured.[4]

Never constrained by an elegant theory, DuBois simply did what she understood could be done. She essentially followed the Quaker precept "to build the world as it ought to be in the midst of the things as they are." Also, she worked so that she fostered civic and international peace. Her actions consequently drew especially sharp criticism even from like-minded educators who desired programs set within more comprehensive theory as well as from those who claimed that her programs were inadequate because of their limited scope. DuBois's intercultural education stressed cultural uniqueness—differences—in society and among minority and immigrant groups. It avoided the blandness of an emphasis on cultural similarities. It acknowledged the risks attendant on attention to exception at a moment in history when commonality and order were prized. Her actions were practical.

Not unlike many beginning graduate students fresh from classroom teaching, DuBois took her ideas about multicultural assembly programs with her to her program at Teachers College, Columbia University. Assembly programs at the time were common features of American schools' weekly schedules, but most suffered from mind-numbing superficiality and a lack of focus. DuBois sought to replace this void with serious-purposed programs that highlighted minority and immigrant groups.

Consequently, during her first years of graduate study, she worked with teachers and administrators in schools in the Philadelphia, Washington, D.C., and New York City areas as they developed freshened and focused assembly programs according to DuBois's Woodbury Plan. Throughout this period, she routinely administered attitude inventories to students in the participating schools. Research legitimation of the programs was a necessary prelude to expansion of her ideas in schools across the nation.

DuBois recognized that intercultural assembly programs, no matter how dramatic and interesting, were insufficient. Indeed, her plan included follow-up discussions and presentations by teachers as a part of their regular courses. Her development with colleagues of specially prepared pamphlets and bibliographies about different cultural groups added greatly to the value of her programs. To be sure, these materials were consistent with her overriding aim to spotlight ethnic differences as specific contributions to an American society that continued to develop. In these curriculum materials, she presented what some have called a "sanitized ethnicity." Titles included "German Contributions to Physics," "Jewish Orchestra Conductors in American Life," "Italian Immigration: A Brief Survey of the Italians in Colonial America, and Since," "The Negro Contribution to Folk Music in America," and "Japanese Flower Arrangement." None of the curriculum materials focused on aspects of life that seriously divided Americans. Nevertheless, these pamphlets likely were the first materials deliberately fashioned for use in ethnic studies programs in American schools.

In 1934 DuBois took a major step to further popularize her intercultural education activities. She organized the Service Bureau for Intercultural Education with financial support of the American Jewish Committee. For the first time, DuBois opened an office for her operations. The very name of the new group symbolized its role. It existed to be a "service" to teachers rather than to advocate particular means of intercultural education. Thus, it served both as a clearinghouse for information and as an agency that produced special curriculum materials. With federal government depression-era assistance during its first year, DuBois's bureau employed a staff of twelve to conduct research into various ethnic histories and contributions. This team produced seventy-four pieces of curriculum materials.[5]

By the beginning of the 1934–35 school year, the Service Bureau had organized a special intercultural education project that involved fifteen schools in the New York metropolitan area. The project followed the general procedures, including the Woodbury Plan, that DuBois had elaborated during the previous several years. In this project, DuBois expanded her research attention to the impact of the programs on minority students. Of special interest in this project was the participation of New York City's Benjamin Franklin High School, an East Harlem school with large enrollments of second-generation Italian and Puerto Rican students. Leonard Covello, its principal, led the school's involvement with the project, and afterwards he and a number of Benjamin Franklin teachers continued their association with Service Bureau programs. Significantly, and perhaps extravagantly, the project staff attributed increased academic motivation and improved discipline in the participating schools to the continuing effects of the program. DuBois's focus on separate cultures rather than a generalized social harmony apparently was successful, but it was to attract challenges within a few short years.[6]

As the comprehensive demonstration and evaluation project wound down, DuBois found that the Service Bureau's financial support had disappeared. She recognized that one way for her operations to survive was to affiliate with a larger and more solvent organization. On the advice of members of the Service Bureau's board, she supported an invitation from the Progressive Education Association (PEA) to absorb the bureau into its structure as its Commission on Intercultural Education. This new relationship appeared to be a satisfactory fit for both groups. As matters turned out, the relationship was tortured from the outset and doomed to failure. DuBois, however, managed to maintain her programs.[7]

The PEA failed to interest financial supporters in the work of its new commission. Some prominent PEA leaders, in addition, criticized DuBois's work as conceptually and programmatically inadequate, a foreshadowing of judgments later made by Hilda Taba and others. Still other PEA officials suggested that DuBois was a poor manager of resources. In 1938, only two years into the relationship, the PEA board dismissed DuBois from her position and marginalized the work of the commission.

DuBois rebounded from these setbacks with her usual enthusiasm. Soon, she and her reconstituted Service Bureau were involved in a high-visibility, federally sponsored national radio project, appropriately entitled *Americans All—Immigrants All*. The program staff hired DuBois to conduct research for the twenty-six-program series and to supervise follow-up activities of the 1938–39 broadcasts. Significantly, the American Jewish Committee funded some of her activities through a grant to the Service Bureau. Nonetheless, DuBois again found herself in the center of controversy as a result of the mixed and inconsistent purposes of the project. DuBois, true to her principles, effectively urged creation of programs that highlighted distinctive minority and national groups. Critics, especially attuned to the escalating international tensions of the late 1930s, noted that her "separate approach" tended "to glorify" ethnicity and to subvert the clear and present need for national unity. The series, when broadcast, attracted far less dissent than critics anticipated; indeed, it enjoyed popular success. It also received a number of awards for broadcast excellence. The Service Bureau, as a series cosponsor, received an avalanche of requests from schools across the nation for its curriculum materials and for its advice about establishing local projects in intercultural education.[8]

Then at the peak of their work and recognition, DuBois and the Service Bureau were ill prepared for the next series of jolts. Within two years, DuBois would be forced to resign and the bureau would change both its focus and its aim.[9]

At the heart of the controversy lay two continuing public problems: financial support and perceptions that DuBois no longer could exercise capable leadership of the bureau's operations. Both reasons appear slightly disingenuous in retrospect. Certainly, DuBois failed to garner financial support; some colleagues attributed some of this disappointment to the fact that she was a woman. She was prickly and contentious, certainly strong-willed, on occasion, but the Service Bureau was her organization, or so she thought. She had founded the bureau and nurtured its work under severe constraints. Nevertheless, even the men whom she recruited to the bureau's board apparently found her to be "difficult." In several ways, her gender appeared to a board majority to be at the root of her leadership problems. Conceptually, however, the dispute fundamentally centered on the bureau's focus.

Subsequently, the bureau's board appointed a man, Stewart Cole, to direct the organization. Cole and board members, almost all of them men, questioned the pluralist position of DuBois and the bureau. They immediately began to shift the bureau's emphasis toward respect for a national culture with limits to expression of cultural differences. This action represented dimensions of the continuing dispute about pluralism in American life that has erupted throughout the twentieth century.

The move to oust DuBois from the Service Bureau gained momentum. The final straw was an evaluation of the bureau's work by an independent panel. The panel praised the bureau for its pioneering work but identified a number of concerns, all related to DuBois and her initiatives. Most important, it dissented from her fundamental assumptions about the relationship of the bureau's special school programs to students' attitudes and prejudices. Simply, as the nation edged ever closer to war, the evaluation committee emphasized that Americans should work for unity in defense of democracy and that cultural differences that contributed to possible disunity should be avoided. In May 1941 the end arrived. The bureau's board asked DuBois to resign. Unlike the situation fifteen years earlier when she refused to resign her teaching position, DuBois silently left the bureau. Subsequently, the bureau enjoyed several years of vigorous activity, but it followed a different path from the one that DuBois had blazed.

DuBois, however, transformed defeat into new opportunities. She was 50 years old and out of a job. Within a year, she completed her long-delayed doctoral dissertation at New York University and formed a new organization, the Workshop for Cultural Democracy, as a means to further her interests. She and associates continued to work in schools, but they mainly used her new Group Conversation Method to expand their attention to the relations of adults with one another. DuBois, having offered the first university course in intercultural education at Boston University in 1933, continued to teach part-time at universities. Over the next half-century, she continued to labor for civil rights and social justice. She received the dubious honor of a summons to appear before Joseph McCarthy's Senate investigative committee as well as the special affirmation of honorary doctorates from two universities. She died at age 101 in Woodstown, New Jersey, on 30 March 1993.[10]

For DuBois and Intercultural Education, A Legacy Reclaimed

Following her forced departure from the Service Bureau, Rachel Davis DuBois largely disappeared from the American educational landscape. She continued to work in schools for several years, but her prominence in education quickly receded.

Several factors help explain this phenomenon. Intercultural education, to be sure, lost credibility during World War II, and even the restructured Service Bureau came to stress democratic human relations and intergroup education rather than intercultural education. Certainly, differences between DuBois's vision of intercultural education and the newer slogans of human relations and intergroup education remain unclear. A reasonable distinction, however, insists that her intercultural and antiracist programs (e.g., assemblies, pageants) were never simply for display. She intended them to be preludes to person-to-person interactions and conversations to build community.[11]

DuBois also no longer wrote for educational publications, and her name was lost from reviews and bibliographies. In addition, because the field of education remains notoriously ahistorical, most newcomers to educational practice and scholarship have not become aware of her and her work. Moreover, DuBois and intercultural education, although prominent for a time, were marginal to the field's institutional structures. For example, DuBois never became involved in mainstream professional education associations; she was an "outsider" in both educational practice and research. Intercultural education, as well, had no convenient home within the curriculum; as a citizenship initiative, it sought to influence students throughout the curriculum. It "belonged" neither to a single school subject or administrative function nor to any group of subjects or functions. Simply, it was an external advocacy that was not claimed even by the social studies.

Stark evidence of DuBois's abrupt loss of prominence and influence is easy to assemble. For example, two major books and a review of research published within a few years of her resignation from the bureau illuminate the extent of educators' inattention to, and devaluation of, her work.

In the 1945 volume *Democratic Human Relations: The Sixteenth Yearbook of the National Council for the Social Studies*, DuBois received scant reference. William Van Til, then a writer on the staff of her former Bureau of Intercultural Education, and Hilda Taba coedited this volume. In particular, Taba dismissed efforts like those undertaken by DuBois, but without specifically mentioning her, and characterized them as minor attention to "pageants and festivals." However, Wilbur Murra's chapter, "Materials and Sources," listed a number of curriculum materials issued by the Service Bureau under DuBois's leadership. He also judged that *Americans All: Studies in Intercultural Education*, published in 1942 and including attention to DuBois-led projects, was one of two books that "outrank all others in importance, inclusiveness, and usefulness for teachers."[12]

DuBois's contributions also are virtually absent from William Heard Kilpatrick's and William Van Til's 1947 edited volume, *Intercultural Attitudes in the Making*. That Kilpatrick dismissed her work might have been expected because, six years earlier, he chaired the Service Bureau's board when its members decided to dismiss DuBois. Another obvious example of the disregard of her work is noted in Lloyd A. Cook's 1947 review of research on intergroup education. In that review, DuBois and her work went unmentioned.[13]

DuBois's reputation continues to languish in obscurity even as the contemporary multicultural education and ethnic studies movements have gained strength. Some current scholars, to be sure, likely know of her through caricatures of her work by Taba and others. On that basis, they reasonably may regard her work as emblematic of their derision of "foods and festivals," a superficial and unworthy approach to multicultural education. However, her work—even her advocacy of, and reports about, neighborhood and home festivals—was robust and stimulated deepened interactions and conversations between people from different ethnic and social groups. Its significance increases when understood within the context of the interwar period of American life. Regrettably, however, she and the corpus of her prolific work stand largely unrecognized as a precursor to the multiculturalism of the present day.[14]

DuBois, for all her alleged faults, was never one-dimensional or simplistic. She clearly merits recognition as a pioneering social educator who merged her deep religious commitment to social justice with her concern for improved school programs about minority and immigrant groups. She sought to build an America as it ought to be within the milieu of her times. A good portion of her success lay in her practical attempts to do all that she could do.

Writings of Rachel Davis DuBois

Rachel Davis DuBois, "Exploring Sympathetic Attitudes toward Peoples," *Journal of Educational Sociology* 9 (March 1936): 391–94.

Much, we decided, as a result of past experiences in the schools, can be done in an incidental way in the classroom toward enriching the day-by-day classwork, and also by a well-planned use of assembly, homeroom periods, and extracurricular activities. Since by sympathetic attitudes is meant not pity, not toleration, but thinking, feeling, acting together, we made use of the following three approaches in the organization of our activities. . . .

The Intellectual Approach: Though these three approaches overlap somewhat, it was found that the classroom affords the best opportunity for the intellectual approach. Facts omitted in ordinary textbooks and reading materials about various groups were woven into the regular work. . . .

The Emotional Approach: We made effective use of the assembly for the emotional approach. As Murphy reminds us in his Education for World-mindedness, *"since feelings are the springs of conduct" and "any education which neglects them is limited in its effectiveness,"[5] we see the importance of the kind of experiences that a colorful and dramatic performance can give to the students. We found that when a young Japanese woman demonstrates the beautiful Japanese flower arrangement, or an outstanding Negro author reads selections from the*

Negro poets, the students have a reaction that they cannot gain by mere reading or by other more or less purely intellectual experiences. . . .

The Situational Approach: By the situational approach we provided situations in which the students might meet members of the various culture groups and thus have an opportunity to put into practice their new attitudes. . . .

Since we believe that the school cannot solve this problem alone, but only as it works in unity with the community, we multiplied these intimate face-to-face contacts by inviting community leaders to the school functions.

---

5.   Albert J. Murphy, Education for World–mindedness *(New York, 1931), 307.*

Rachel Davis DuBois, "Can We Help to Create a Cultural Renaissance?" *English Journal* 27 (November 1938): 735–36.

A cultural renaissance depends on a lively spirit of creativity in the arts. Real art grows out of experience. The art of a nation then should spring from the experience of all the elements which make up that nation. Our lack of creativity today is caused by our long denial of the experiences of large numbers of individuals who are a part of us. Our social worlds continue to frown upon people for being what they are or for expressing what they feel. . . . But for every Jim Tully, James Weldon Johnson, and Louis Adamic, there are millions of first- and second-generation individuals who, because of the denial of their heritage, are so ashamed of their backgrounds that they become parts of a dull mass of uncreative citizens.

This condition exists everywhere in America. Indeed, the normal community in the United States is made up of people with many different cultural experiences. . . . Yet, although the individuals that make up our cities and counties rub elbows on the streets, their most meaningful experiences go on behind closed doors.

Although there can be no one key to these doors, no one answer to such a complex social problem—that of so synthesizing our cultural elements in a dynamic and creative way that a renaissance will emerge—yet the first step which must be taken if we are to translate these meaningful cultural experiences into art is to develop some pride in being what we are. For it is in our cultural backgrounds that our emotional roots are fastened. . . .

It should not be assumed, however, that no sharing takes place unless we consciously do so. In fact, some sharing goes on in a dynamic society even against our wills. The participation of the Negro in American life is an interesting example.

Rachel Davis DuBois and Emma Schweppe, eds., *The Germans in American Life* (New York, 1936), 2–3.

Changes come slowly. We bring into each new day our former selves. Differences in culture persist. For young people differences that set them apart from the dominant group mean strains and open rebellion against the forces making for a continuance of the old culture. For the mature these differences add to and intensify social and economic handicaps. For the dominant group they mean the establishment of attitudes of superiority. These attitudes of superiority widen the differences felt by all.

The "melting pot" theory has utterly failed to build adequately for all peoples concerned. . . .

Giving all they have to give and receiving equally and so maintaining the strength of each heritage brought to the shores of America, means a respect for personality, a respect for differences in culture.

Notes

1. Rachel Davis DuBois, *All This and Something More: Pioneering in Intercultural Education* (Bryn Mawr, Pa., 1984), 54–59.

2. Information about this and subsequent scenes portrayed in this section were drawn from DuBois's autobiography, *All This and Something More*. See esp. chaps. 1–5. See also Nicholas V. Montalto, *A History of the Intercultural Education Movement, 1924–1941* (New York, 1982), 77–148.

3. W. E. B. Du Bois, "The Dilemma of the Negro," *American Mercury*, October 1924, 179–84.

4. The general overview of DuBois's concentrated work in intercultural education, especially her development of the Service Bureau for Intercultural Education, was drawn from her autobiography, *All This and Something More*, 62–98; and Montalto, *Intercultural Education Movement*, 109–23.

5. See also Rachel Davis DuBois, "Can We Help to Create an American Renaissance?" *English Journal* 27 (November 1938): 733–40.

6. See also Rachel Davis DuBois, "Developing Sympathetic Attitudes toward Peoples," *Journal of Educational Sociology* 9 (March 1936): 387–96; Rachel Davis DuBois, "Intercultural Education at Benjamin Franklin High School," *High Points* 19 (December 1937): 23–29. See also Leonard Covello, *The Heart Is the Teacher* (New York, 1958), 190–92.

7. Montalto, *Intercultural Education Movement*, 124–48. See also Rachel Davis DuBois, *Adventures in Intercultural Education: A Manual for Secondary School Teachers* (New York, 1938); Rachel Davis DuBois and Emma Schweppe, eds., *The Jews in American Life* (New York, 1935); and Rachel Davis DuBois and Emma Schweppe, eds., *The Germans in American Life* (New York, 1936).

8. Montalto, *Intercultural Education Movement*, 149–70.

9. Montalto, *Intercultural Education Movement*, 218–67.

10. Rachel Davis DuBois, *Get Together, Americans* (New York, 1943); Rachel Davis DuBois, *Neighbors in Action: A Manual for Local Leaders in Intergroup Relations* (New York, 1950). For an elaboration of the Group Conversation Method, see Rachel Davis DuBois and Mew-Soong Li, *Reducing Social Tension and Conflict* (New York, 1971). Andy Wallace, "Obituaries: Rachel D. DuBois, 101; Champion of Dialogue across Racial Barriers," *Philadelphia Inquirer,* 5 April 1993; Bruce Lambert, "Rachel D. DuBois 101, Educator Who Promoted Value of Diversity," *New York Times,* 2 April 1993, LB7.

11. DuBois's goals are remarkably consistent with those of the English-Scottish philosopher John Macmurray, also marginalized in this same period. See recent reprints of his *Freedom in the Modern World* (London, 1932; reprint, Atlantic Highlands, N.J., 1992) and *Persons in Relations* (London, 1961; reprint Atlantic Highlands, N.J., 1991).

12. Hilda Taba and William Van Til, eds., *Democratic Human Relations: Promising Practices in Intergroup and Intercultural Education in the Social Studies: Sixteenth Yearbook of the National Council for the Social Studies* (Washington, D.C., 1945). See esp. chap. 2 by Hilda Taba, "Curriculum Problems," 21–62; and chap. 10 by Wilbur Murra, "Materials and Sources," 280–336. C. O. Arndt et al., *Americans All: Studies in Intercultural Education: Fourteenth Yearbook of the Department of Supervisors and Directors of Instruction* (Washington, D.C., 1942).

13. William Heard Kilpatrick and William Van Til, eds., *Intercultural Attitudes in the Making: Ninth Yearbook of the John Dewey Society* (New York, 1947); Lloyd A. Cook, "Intergroup Education," *Review of Educational Research* 17 (October 1947): 266–78.

14. James A. Banks, *Teaching Strategies for Ethnic Studies*, 5th ed. (Boston, 1975); Marilynne Boyle-Baise, "Bleeding Boundaries or Uncertain Center? A Historical Exploration of Multicultural Education," *Journal of Curriculum and Supervision* 14 (Spring 1999): 191–215; Michael R. Olneck, "The Recurring Dream: Symbolism and Ideology in Intercultural and Multicultural Education," *American Journal of Education* 99 (February 1990): 147–74.

9

Composing Her Life:
Hilda Taba and Social Studies History

Jane Bernard-Powers

Hilda Taba
Courtesy of Mary Durkin

"We have to furnish children with an opportunity to cultivate their
ways of democratic living together."

—Hilda Taba, *Dynamics of Education*

Hilda Taba was a major contributor to curriculum theory and practice in
the twentieth century who profoundly influenced social studies curriculum and instruction. Her career stretched across four decades of the twentieth century (1932–1967), and her writings, relationships, and ambitions
were patterned by the social and political dynamics of the times. These
included shifting international boundaries, armed conflicts, racial and
ethnic tensions, and prejudice. Seemingly boundless intellectual energy
and curiosity galvanized Taba to bore into the psychological, social, and
structural elements that constitute learning for individual students,
groups, and teachers. She was passionate about the potential of curriculum to affect students, teachers, and ultimately society. She was capable of
conceptualizing and articulating the complexity of teaching and learning
about social education and social science issues in classrooms. Moreover,
she was courageous enough to put her theories to the extended test of
practice.

Most important, she believed in democracy and the potential of individuals to think for themselves and make reasoned decisions. As an ado-
lescent when Estonia fought Russia for political independence
(1918–1920), she knew firsthand what political repression meant.[1]

Taba occupies a unique position in this biographical compendium
because her formative years were spent in another country. She came to
the United States and to social education with an appreciation for democracy, using the lens of an outsider who knew about life without freedom
of expression and ideas. Because she had not come to the United States
along with family, nor did she join family here, her identity as a social
educator was not sustained and shaped by family and community roots
in the United States, as was the case with some other women considered
in this volume. Unfettered by the need to defend her own community
identity, she had a broad notion of international civic culture and a critical eye for ethnocentrism, stereotyping, and prejudice.

Taba was also a mainstream educator. Her writing and work was with
and about teachers and curriculum. While her Estonian background put
her on the margins in one sense, she found herself at the center of social
education in another sense. Her doctoral work was done at Teachers College with progressive educators such as John Dewey, Henry Bode Boyd,
and George Counts, all of whom were attempting, to one degree or another, to influence the social order through the progressive education move-

ment.[2] She worked on two very significant national curriculum projects: the "Eight-Year Study" (1933–ca. 1940) and the Project in Intergroup Education in Cooperating Schools (1944–1950).[3] She held a position as director of the Curriculum Laboratory at the University of Chicago (ca. 1940–1944) in what has been called the "golden age" of that university— so designated because of pioneering work taking place there in sociology and human relations, among other fields. She returned to the University of Chicago with her intergroup project in 1948. In the later years of her career, she took a position at San Francisco State College (1951) and directed a sixteen-year-long major curriculum project and collaboration with a school district. This project produced a textbook series and resulted in one of the most important research projects in the field to date.[4]

Despite being "an internationally-recognized authority in the field of human relations and curriculum development," Taba is only minimally acknowledged in either curriculum histories or social studies curriculum history.[5] For example, when Herbert Kliebard, in *The Struggle for the American Curriculum, 1893–1958,* cites individuals influential in curriculum development he focuses on Ralph Tyler.[6] Likewise, *The American Curriculum: A Documentary History* does not reference Taba.[7] Two recent works on social studies historiography by Saxe and Lybarger fail to acknowledge Taba's work. Lybarger's chapter on the historiography of social studies in the *Handbook of Research on Social Studies Teaching and Learning* and Saxe's historical review published in *Review of Educational Research* overlook Taba's contributions, as does the 1980 special issue of *Theory and Research in Social Education* on the history of social studies.[8] Taba sits alongside the other scholars profiled in *"Bending the Future to Their Will"* because the bulk of her writing and curriculum work was concerned fundamentally with citizenship education. She spent two decades following her graduation from Teachers College, Columbia University, working on the questions and complexities of democratic living in relation to school curriculum.

Because Taba's work was complex and many distinct aspects exist within her intellectual portfolio, this chapter will focus primarily on her work and writing in progressive education and human relations education (1924–1950). Using interviews with people who knew her and her writings, I will address the broad questions: Who was Hilda Taba? What were her educational interests and work? What is the relationship between her ideas as represented in her writing and feminist perspectives of citizenship education suggested in the introduction to this volume? The broad question underlying this chapter concerns the significance of her work to the domain of civic education.

Biographical Foundations

Taba was born in a small village in southeastern Estonia on 7 December 1902 to a schoolmaster and his wife. Her identity as a schoolmaster's daughter was probably central to her work and writing in civic education.

Estonia is a former Soviet Socialist Republic bounded on the north by the Gulf of Finland, on the south by Latvia, and on the west by the Baltic Sea. Denmark, Sweden, Poland, and Russia number among the countries that laid claim to Estonia for over two centuries. Russia was a tenacious and invasive force in Estonian history, and the repressive aspects of occupation were familiar to Estonians, especially in the nineteenth and twentieth centuries. For at least two centuries, Estonians fought and lobbied for basic rights: first the right to own land and then, in the nineteenth century, the right to education.[9]

According to historian Evald Uustalu, schools were established in the mid-nineteenth century and played an important role in Estonian modern history. Ninety-five percent literacy was achieved by 1870, and the schools were a major factor in an Estonian "national awakening" and desire for self-determination.[10] Moreover, teachers served as the intelligentsia and political leadership of Estonia in the late nineteenth century. It is highly likely that Taba absorbed some very important lessons about democracy and education from her father and the company he kept. Her parents and grandparents knew how fragile democratic institutions and rights were.

This fragility in Estonia was a pivotal influence in Hilda Taba's life and career. Taba's identity as an Estonian, with all of its political and social complexity that evolved over her lifetime, and her identity as a newcomer to the United States who was undoubtedly subjected to the prejudices that accompanied speakers of "foreign languages," influenced her work and professional choices. She was passionate and articulate about the aims and means of teaching children for democratic living.

Taba's mother was instrumental in her educational background in a very specific sense. She supported her daughter's education in the Kanepi parish school where Mr. Taba worked and then at the Voru's Girls' Grammar School.[11] When Hilda decided not to pursue a normal-school education but instead chose to go to Tartu University, her mother supported that decision as well. Taba's father had identified her brother as the first child allowed to attend university, in accordance with family and patriarchal custom. Hilda's mother, uncharacteristically defying family conventions and her husband's wishes, insisted that Hilda also attend college; the family had to sacrifice for Hilda's education. Hilda's godmother helped to pay for her undergraduate education and subsequent schooling as well.[12]

This story in Taba's life is clearly gendered, yet Taba was not a feminist in the conscious way that many of her contemporaries were in the Western world. In the first two decades of the twentieth century, many women in England and the United States lobbied for women's suffrage, access to education, higher wages, and economic protections for women. In Estonia, the Constitution of 1920, organized after the war of liberation from Russia, granted women the right to vote and ensured women's freedom to organize and pursue professional goals.[13] Yet very little evidence of feminist consciousness exists in Taba's writing throughout her career. She apparently did not conceive of education as a potential source of social change for women generally.

Nonetheless, Taba was aware of gender discrimination and identified it as a problem when it came up in her intercultural education work. She noted this in her book on school culture when she pointed out the problems associated with selecting jobs as "boys' jobs" or "girls' jobs" in schools.[14] Moreover, Taba had firsthand experience with gender discrimination. When she finished her doctoral work at Columbia University in the early 1930s, she applied for a job at Tartu University in Estonia. Despite her impressive credentials from Teachers College, the hiring committee turned her down. "Male candidates were more preferred than female candidates at this time," according to Edgar Krull, a Taba scholar from Tartu University.[15] She was bitter about this fact—and talked about her disappointment with colleagues on more than one occasion.[16]

Throughout her life, ambition and intellectual strength drove Taba to challenge herself. When she finished her undergraduate education at Tartu University in the department of philosophy, she seized the opportunity to travel to the United States and continue her studies. At the age of twenty-four she was presented with "the opportunity" to do postgraduate work in the United States with the support of a grant from the Rockefeller Foundation. She came to Bryn Mawr College in 1926 with travel money gathered from "the sale of cattle on the family's farm, a government grant and loan, along with funds from her Godmother."[17]

This journey across continents seems remarkable to me. Elise Boulding, writing in the *Underside of History*, observes, however, that the world looked very promising to women beginning their careers in 1920s. These women were "world shapers" in a way that women born after 1940 cannot easily imagine.[18] It is also evident that Taba had both courage and imagination to travel by herself to a country where she was not fluent in the language and where she knew she would have to support herself. She was a remarkable young woman who distinguished herself through life choices that were by no means gender typical.

Progressive Education and Taba

Taba's intellectual engagement with progressive education began before she came to the United States. Her affinity with this movement grew out of her own experiences with fragile democratic processes in Estonia and the spread of John Dewey's ideas to her country. In the window of opportunity between World War I and World War II, following a war of liberation, Estonia experienced a renaissance of ideas. Theater developed, book publishing increased substantially, and Tartu University reorganized and thrived.[19] Dewey's notions of democracy and education circulated throughout the School of Philosophy at Tartu University at the time that Taba was doing her undergraduate studies.

The Department of Education at Tartu was headed by a progressive educator named Professor Pold, who included Dewey in course readings on modern curriculum and educational sciences.[20] Pold introduced a curriculum that offered comparative perspectives on education. His students were encouraged to critique and analyze original works of "world-renowned educators," and Dewey was included in the group. Taba was thus being educated in a period of great intellectual and political change. She was introduced to ideas about the connections between democracy, civic identity, and social education that paralleled those being discussed in graduate schools in the United States.

Given the absence of personal papers, little is known about Taba's voyage from Estonia and adjustment to life in the United States. What is known is that while she was working toward her master's degree during the academic year 1926–27, she continued to pursue her interest in progressive education and curriculum reform. She read works by Boyd Bode, the progressive educator, and visited the Dalton School in Massachusetts, an institution that individualized instruction by issuing monthly cards to students that identified instructional assignments.[21]

Some of the basic directions of her future work were developed during this period. Thus, it is in one sense not surprising that she chose to pursue doctoral work at Columbia, a place where curriculum change and democratic education were being discussed with notable passion by the faculty. On the other hand, it is amazing that a comparatively recent immigrant to the United States who spoke English as a second language would end up in one of the cradles of progressive education thought.

Taba began her doctoral work at Columbia in 1927. It was an intellectually exciting time to be there, and she had the opportunity to work with two of the most influential progressive educators of the period, John Dewey and William Kilpatrick. In an intellectually charged atmosphere,

Taba developed her ideas about democracy, curriculum reform, progressive education, and human development.

When Taba began her work at Columbia, the Progressive Education Association (PEA) was eight years old and growing. John Dewey was on the eve of his presidency. Patricia Graham's history of progressive education outlines the evolution of the movement and the PEA, noting that the individuals who were drawn under the umbrella of progressive educational reform differed in their visions and goals. Postwar progressive education was dominated by education professionals who worked in large teacher-preparation institutions such as Teachers College, Columbia University, and who focused on teaching and learning in conjunction with the emergent fields of psychology and social science.[22] William Kilpatrick, George Counts, Boyd Bode, and John Dewey were the faculty members who were most influential in Taba's education; they all are acknowledged in her dissertation.

These prominent progressive educators were among the leaders of discussions carried on over several years about the essence of progressive education. While the movement began as a reaction to traditional education and schooling that focused on discipline in the classroom, recitation, and memorization of subject matter content, it grew into a critique of schooling in relation to democratic society. The significance of child-centered education in relation to the movement as a whole, and the relationship of schools to democratic ends and means, evolved into competing themes in the PEA agendas during the 1930s.[23]

Taba was involved in these discussions. In 1932, she articulated her response to mentors' and colleagues' views in her dissertation entitled "The Dynamics of Education: A Methodology of Progressive Educational Thought."[24] This work provides the evidence for Dewey's alleged observation that Taba was possibly the brightest student he had ever had. The book sets out the fundamental premises and roots for much of her subsequent work.

Taba's European education is evident in her dissertation: she drew on highly diverse and sophisticated bodies of work. For example, in making her initial arguments about the essential nature and processes of education, she drew from physics and philosophy. Learning and the study of learning, she argued, should not rely on conceptions from traditional science that are dependent on the observation, prediction, and measurement of static phenomena; they should reflect instead contemporary physics' acceptance of the dynamic nature of the universe. Hence "becoming, meaning cumulative, qualitative change, is one of the most fundamental aspects of organic phenomena," she argued.[25] "Reality is not to be found in isolated existences but in dynamic forms and process" that are organically interrelated and interdependent.[26] This notion of the dynamic nature of reality was the basis for her theories about curriculum and learning.

Like her mentor, Dewey, Taba put experience and education in a partnership. She elaborated in her dissertation on the importance of experiences, noting that the relationship of educational experiences is ontological. By this she means that an education "rich in media and materials" will yield an experience that will stimulate more aims and experiences.[27] Taba thus characterized experiential learning as "constructive"—foreshadowing constructivist educational ideas of the 1980s and 1990s.[28] Furthermore, she argued in the chapter on the aims of education that learning is relational, "with the individual at one end of the relation and the objective values of the environment—physical, cultural, social, all subject matter of learning and experience—at the other end." Learning is what happens between these two and comes out of these two.

Democracy, a centerpiece of progressive education writing and thinking, was also central to Taba's work. Reflecting her own past and Dewey's influence, she wrote, "We have to furnish children with an opportunity to cultivate their ways of democratic living together."[29] She proposed that teachers help children evolve their own ways of living together democratically. The critical phrase in this regard was, for Taba, "their own ways." She addresses education in Soviet Russia in this context, noting that Russian education was very successful in teaching children and adults about the ultimate aims while denying them the "participation in the construction" of such aims.

While a number of other important themes emerged in the dissertation that Taba pursued throughout her career, three stand out. First, she emphasized the importance of effective evaluation while severely criticizing reliance on objective testing.[30] She also addressed the limitations of teaching facts without providing students with powerful generalizations or concepts to orient them to these facts. And finally, she considered the relationship between subjective experience and objective experience in the construction of reality and meaning.[31]

Taba's legacy at Teachers College was substantial. The book based on her dissertation and introduced by Kilpatrick was received with "high praise," according to the editor of *Progressive Education*. What seems most evident about Taba's experience at Columbia is that the faculty recognized her impressive abilities and encouraged her academic pursuits. Judging from her work, she was not intimidated by ideas or by people, and she was confident enough of herself to articulate her criticism of progressive education. Her article "Progressive Education—What Now?"

published in *Progressive Education* in 1934 was a call to action for progressive educators who had become mired in slogans and incomplete ideas and projects. She did not shrink from offering serious criticism and taking a stand. Patricia Graham cites this piece as one of the "most coherent" articles on this subject.[32]

It is also significant that in this article Taba called for a total reorganization and development of curriculum in social sciences in light of its promise "to become the major center of educative experiences for adolescents."[33] Taba clearly had a vision of where social studies curriculum should be going, She provided the theoretical grounding in psychological concepts and experiential education that would become the hallmarks of social education in the 1960s.

Progressive Education's Eight-Year Study

The next phase of Taba's career involved school- and project-level curriculum development and evaluation. It seems remarkable that Taba was not recruited by the University of Chicago, Columbia, or another major university. I can only speculate about whether her gender became an issue, even though it did not seem to affect her work as a student at Teachers College.

Following her unsuccessful effort to gain a job at Tartu University, Taba returned to the United States and took a job in 1933 at the Dalton School in New York, a school with a progressive outlook that became part of the PEA's landmark Eight-Year Study. This study, also called the "Commission on the Relation of School and College" or the "Thirty-Schools Project," examined progressive schools' curriculum and students. It was a substantial research project designed to evaluate how students from progressive schools fared in college.[34]

Ralph Tyler from the University of Chicago was hired to conduct the evaluations for the Eight-Year Study; in that context he met Taba at the Dalton School. Like many others before him, he was very much impressed with her knowledge. Tyler asked her to join him on the evaluation team at Ohio State University as a consultant concerning evaluation of social studies teachers. This was the first step for Taba in a productive professional and personal relationship that would last for decades and result in substantial collaboration.

At Ohio State, Taba focused on "social sensitivity" in the curriculum of the thirty schools involved in the study. This was referred to as a general concern of the project and reflected the goals of progressive education in general: preparing students for effective democratic participation. It was also a good fit with Taba's general interests indicated in her dissertation and her writing about progressive education. She was very much interested in meaningful civic education curriculum and in the needs of adolescents. As she wrote in her 1934 article in *Progressive Education,* curriculum with stated objectives like "living together cooperatively" that did not become meaningful and could not be measured undermined progressive education.[35] The evaluation project provided Taba with an opportunity to test her ability to participate in the development of a curriculum and evaluation project that was "socially oriented [and] integrated" and sprang from student interests.[36] Social sensitivity is and was complex and difficult to define and measure. Not surprisingly, Taba was disinclined to develop a paper-and-pencil test as the exclusive measure of social sensitivity. Thus, she identified behaviors and attitudes that she characterized as dispositions that seemed to represent social sensitivity—cautioning that they were not to become icons. For example, Taba identified "the disposition to look under the surface of social phenomena and to discover the underlying conflicts and problems in social life contributing to a particular phenomenon."[37] She then developed multiple means of assessment, including observation of group activities, informal conversations, anecdotal records, reading records, and book reviews. This entire project was written up and became part of the literature on the Eight-Year Study.

Taba's participation in the Eight-Year Study was important in her career for a least three main reasons. First, her passionate interest in curriculum was developed in this project, along with her impressive ability to tackle complex and sensitive topics related to civic education. Second, she was able to consider the relationship between curriculum and evaluation. As Ralph Tyler acknowledged, Taba well understood the relationship between curriculum and evaluation and was willing to provide "helpful and promising means by which the various evidence may be interrelated and significant interpretations made."[38] Finally, Taba found in Tyler a colleague who was interested in, and appreciative of, her sophisticated perspectives on curriculum. It was in the context of their work together in Ohio that Taba and Tyler developed the framework that became known widely as the "Tyler Rationale."

Taba discussed her role in this development in the preface to her book *Curriculum Development: Theory and Practice.* She wrote that after a "rather confusing meeting on curriculum planning in the 1930's," she and Tyler "began to elaborate a scheme for a sequence of questions to be asked and an order of steps to be taken in planning curriculum." She applied these steps to her work in the Eight-Year Study and, in her words, "continued testing and refining the scheme and building a theoretical rationale for it."[39] The fact that she was not given credit publicly by Tyler for her substantial role in the Tyler Rationale was most likely the basis for Mark Isham's observation in his article on Taba that she was not aggressive in seeking personal credit for her ideas and thus some of her major work was credited to other people.[40]

In 1938 when the evaluation staff moved from Ohio State to the University of Chicago, Taba went along and became director of the Curriculum Laboratory and a member of the faculty, a position she held until she assumed her position with the Intergroup Education Project in 1944.

Intergroup Education

Intergroup education, also known as intercultural education, developed in the 1920s coincident with an upsurge in Ku Klux Klan activities and anti-Catholic and anti-Jewish sentiment in the Midwest and the eastern United States. Rachel Davis DuBois is credited with spearheading the movement and marshaling leadership and support from a phalanx of organizations that grew up in the 1920s and early 1930s.[41] These included the National Conference of Christian and Jews (NCCJ), the American Council on Education, the Julius Rosenwald Fund, and the American Council on Race Relations.[42] The movement, made up of a loosely affiliated group of organizations, emerged in a period of renewed racism to improve intergroup relations and "to maintain national unity as the country struggled through a major Depression and another world war."[43]

Intergroup education started out as education for the public in general and within a decade had turned to public education and schools. The PEA established a Commission on Intercultural Education, which existed from 1937 to 1942. Subsequently the commission developed into a national project that attracted a number of progressive educators, including Kilpatrick, Harold O. Rugg, and Counts, who saw intergroup education as a potential means to realize democracy through the schools.[44]

Interest and activity in intercultural education escalated in the 1940s. It is evident from the promotional newsletter *Intercultural Education News* that the leaders of the movement were very much concerned about race relations, national unity, and the image of the United States. The newsletter banner in 1944 read "Understanding, Cooperation and National Unity Among the Cultural Groups in America."[45] The reality was that democracy looked a little fragile in this mid–World War II period. Demonstrations in Detroit in 1943, Japanese internment camps, anti-

German and anti-Italian sentiment, a growing realization of the Holo-
caust and anti-Semitic passions, and the spread of "enemy propaganda
which make capital of our race discrimination" reminded Americans of
this fragility.[46] Reports of actions taken against Jews in Germany were
disturbing to many in the United States. Anti-Jewish sentiment in communities in the United States was even more disturbing. Thus, the grand
educational projects that foreshadowed today's multicultural education
were developed and disseminated through the newsletter and other
media.

Intercultural Education News provides an informative history of the
breadth of intergroup activities that were in place before Taba joined the
staff of the Intergroup Education Project. There were articles about workshops, consultancies, school materials, and general resources being
offered by the Bureau of Intercultural Education along with pieces by
social scientists and educators such as John Dewey, Gordon Allport, Kurt
Lewin, Allison Davis, Robert Havighurst, and William Kilpatrick.[47] The
scholarship of social scientists such as Allport, whose work on prejudice
was highly influential, was sought to inform the work in public schools.
Kilpatrick, Taba's thesis adviser, was chairman of the Service Bureau for
Intercultural Education, with which Rachel Davis DuBois was involved,
and was influential in recruiting the articles and support of these social
scientists.

The period of greatest expansion in intercultural education was the
mid-1940s (1944–1948), when the NCCJ funded and launched the Intergroup Education in Cooperating Schools Project. Taba directed,
researched, and wrote about this project with her colleagues. Herbert Sea-
mans, the staff executive for NCCJ's educational programs, and Howard
Wilson, social studies specialist from the Harvard Graduate School of
Education and editor of the Harvard Educational Review, had originally
conceived of the project. Wilson went to Taba to ask her to direct the pilot
project, Intergroup Education in Cooperating Schools (1945–1948), which
eventually developed into the Center for Intergroup Education at the University of Chicago (1948–1951).[48]

Taba was an excellent choice for the job. Intergroup education was a
logical extension of her thesis work, her book The Dynamics of Education,
her tenure with the Eight-Year Study, and her associations with progressive educators. Democratic education, or civic education, was at the heart
of the project and central to the thrust of her work as it was evolving. Her
strong feelings are evident in her statement that "the United States had
been one of the few countries with freedom to experiment in human relations. There could be . . . no glib excuses for the glaring inequalities to be

found in civil rights, nor for the discrimination practiced in education, employment, and civic participation."[49]

Taba headed up a summer workshop at Harvard University in the summer of 1944 that resulted in an article published in the *Harvard Educational Review* on workshops and intercultural education. She edited, along with William Van Til, publications director for the Bureau of Intercultural Education, *Democratic Human Relations: Sixteenth Yearbook of the National Council for the Social Studies.*[50]

These efforts brought Taba greater exposure as she took the reins of her new school-based project with the same intense, focused energy that she had brought to the Eight-Year Study. As was true of her writing about progressive education, she approached the work critically. She believed that intercultural education efforts had been too loosely organized and based on "ill conceived" methods. In the introduction to her book *Intergroup Education in Public Schools,* she characterized the early work as "running to a fire without knowing whether they had water or gasoline in the hose."[51] She chastised educators for preaching "about the evils of prejudice" when there was little evidence that such preaching changed students' attitudes. Piecemeal programs without coherent foundations and techniques, and verbal exhortation in lieu of indirect and subtle techniques were the heart of the problem of intergroup education curricula, according to Taba's analysis.

Typically, Taba assumed a great deal of responsibility in attempting to create an ideal curriculum project that delivered on what it set out to do. The scope of the project was daunting. Eighteen school districts, located in communities throughout the United States, were selected on the basis of ethnic, racial, and socioeconomic diversity. School district commitment, teacher interest, and the identification of potential leadership roles for school districts were the qualities that Taba and her staff identified as critical for the success of the project.[52]

Taba brought together a staff of educators with diverse backgrounds—teachers and social scientists—to develop methods for creating locally directed and created projects. The five principles established by Taba and the staff reflect the complexity of her theoretical understanding and her fundamental belief that schools could play a pivotal role in educating future citizens only when the process is done comprehensively and with integrity. Taba's five cardinal principles about intergroup education were:

1. Effective programs needed to be comprehensive: they could not be founded on a single approach nor focused in a single area of school activity.

2. A method of program planning was needed that assured a balanced and organic growth toward the four main objectives by coordinating the unique contributions of each subject area or activity to each objective.

3. Programs had to be developed in which basic concepts were taught cumulatively through all levels, with an appropriate differentiation in content and in context.

4. School programs needed to provide for growth in four distinct areas—ideas and concepts, sensitivities, thinking, and skills—simultaneously in a balanced fashion and in a dynamic interaction.

5. The schools needed to work in coordination with other agencies in the neighborhood and in the larger community.[53]

The intergroup education staff consisted of eight people who went out to eighteen sites, or seventy-two schools and community groups, over a period of two years. The eight people would enter the field for approximately six weeks at a time to work with the projects and then come back together for a week to share results and successes.[54] In keeping with Taba's belief that locally determined, comprehensive programs were the only way to work, they tackled an incredible variety of classroom, school, and community projects.

Of necessity, the staff worked closely and collaboratively, and the week they had together was very important to them all. According to Elizabeth Brady, one of the eight staff people, the week of intense interchange with Taba sitting in the circle was intellectually stimulating and very gratifying. Brady described Taba as a first-rate professional who had a first-rate mind, both qualities evident in their reflective and generative work together.[55] Taba's leadership gifts included a mature ability to collaborate and to foster collaborations. Her staff members were given a great deal of responsibility, and they apparently thrived, given the eight publications and many articles generated from the findings of the project.

Relationships were a central aspect of Taba's working style; that was true for both the staff working in concert with each other and the staff working in relationship with people at the sites. Given the potentially sensitive nature of beliefs and attitudes about ethnic groups, social class, and race, the staff spent two to three days getting to know the people at the site before beginning to talk about potential projects. Staff were expected to maintain a heightened sensitivity to interpersonal issues, and many examples described in *Intergroup Education in Public Schools* reflect this orientation.

Drawing on her dissertation and Eight-Year Study work, Taba continued to assert that curriculum was a far more complex endeavor than had been realized or articulated before and that intergroup relations had to be approached with a sophisticated understanding of how attitudes were formed and sustained and how learning and relearning of these attitudes took place. She was particularly sensitive to the inadequacy of teaching about cultural attitudes, norms, and practices that left out the sensitivities and general background of the students and their families. Curriculum had to be organic. She wrote in *Dynamics of Education:* "The Curriculum cannot be regarded as a dead and summative body of all the materials, experiences and activities contained in the educational process. It is a living whole, comprised of experience actually going on in school. As such it is what it becomes in practice."[56]

The curriculum methods and materials used by staff were progressive and innovative in the context of the mid-1940s. They included, for example, role playing about social values and sociodrama adapted to the needs of students. Taba utilized her own staff to provide training in role-play techniques and would also look for local people with such skills. Fanny Shaftel, professor emerita from Stanford University, who coauthored *Role Playing the Problem Story,* was hired by Taba and her staff to train teachers in role playing for social value identification and processing.[57]

Curriculum processes also included one of the cornerstones of current multicultural instruction: literature and discussion groups. As Taba characterized the process, one of the challenges to maintenance of core democratic values was ethnocentrism. Therefore, one of the goals of intercultural education was "to expand people's capacity for understanding across barriers" and bridging "cultural and psychological distances."[58] "Reading ladders" were compilations of books and readings used by schools to this end that were viewed as especially successful. The processes of group discussions were developed for teachers and students, as were conflict resolution processes.[59]

Taba was prescient in her perspectives on the content of intergroup curriculum. She argued that any a priori determination of issues or teaching generic ideas about stereotyping was not effective. In a sense she was making an argument that is very close to the contemporary notion of context in educational research. Rather than assume that intergroup education should focus on national concerns such as "Negro-white relations, conflicts among religious groups, or prejudice against ethnic groups," she chose to define difference locally and contextually.

She wrote:

[F]or example, ingroups and out-groups form in schools on such bases as ownership or non ownership of cashmere sweaters, ability to afford coke sessions in the drugstore or inability to afford them, taking a college-preparatory program or general curriculum, the lowest or highest grade in school, and the social clique. While the problems of race were uppermost in some, problems of newcomers or religious differences were more important in others. The matter is further complicated by the fact that these several dimensions tend to cross, reinforce, and confuse each other. Economic differences, for example, affect almost any other dimension of group differences.[60]

She encouraged teachers to examine critically their fields of concentration in order to identify the dominant needs of a subject area. For example, she posited that teachers of American history needed to help students develop a realistic concept of the United States as a multicultural society. She critically noted that students in the United States tend to learn "a good deal about the traditions of New England, about the values of Nordic white men, and about the Protestant religious ideals." Courses of study needed to reflect accurately the values and aspirations of other American cultural groups, and this effort needed to go far beyond special units that celebrated the "contributions" of different racial and ethnic groups.[61]

She understood the notion of ecology in reference to schools and communities. The efforts of the intergroup education staff focused on issues such as segregation in community swimming pools; misconceptions of student behavior and diverse family values; and relationships between families and ethnic groups in a community. One particularly important example from the project involved a school staff's identification of a significant problem in their school: tardiness. Teachers assumed that Mexican American students who were late were not interested in school. The teachers were asked to research the reasons for tardiness and, according to the published account, discovered one young boy whose job involved picking up coal from coal trains in the railroad yard before school. If the trains were late, so was the boy. In another case the family did not own a clock and no one was home when the boy had to leave for school. With the collection of data—action research on a school problem—the staff changed the focus of their interests to the general conditions under which children lived and then extended that to "whether or not the curriculum and, indeed, the whole school program was out of step with the cultural learnings and needs of the Mexican-American children."[62]

Hilda Taba and her intergroup education staff developed a sophisticated and comprehensive view of the complexity of multicultural curriculum and multicultured relations in schooling and community. It rivals work done in the 1990s. Issues of gender and salience; the problems experienced by newcomers, as she called them; economic instability; housing patterns; community relations; fear; and the relationship of school issues to community issues were all tackled by Taba and her staff, working in concert with site faculty. Community relations projects and boards, integrated services, conflict resolution skills being taught to community people and school people were all part of the intergroup education projects.

The project and the work are distinctive in the history of social studies education and social justice projects. In addition to her remarkable ability to link theory with practice, to think conceptually and systemically as she did with intergroup education, and to organize and implement an authentic curriculum change program, Taba was a significant contributor to civic education.

Taba projected into her work in citizenship education—what she called learning for democracy—a profound sense of ethics. Taba was consistent in her compassion and caring for the young people, teachers, and families in the communities where she worked. For example, she cared about the Spanish-speaking families who were distanced from the American mainstream culture by issues of class, status, and language. She recognized the importance of building bridges to families who were discouraged from participating in their schools. She argued that it was the responsibility of the school to provide meaningful curriculum in the classrooms, on the playgrounds, in the school organizations, and everywhere that involved children and parents. Meaningful curriculum was for Taba an ethical issue; it was untenable that schools and teachers would talk about social justice and undermine it by neglect or purposeful contrary action.

Her work in curriculum calls up the 1970s feminist slogan that the personal is political. While Taba was not a feminist in the sense that she did not identify in that way her connections to women and/or her beliefs about women as a group, there are connections in her work to feminism. To generate theory and to speak about it was for Taba only half the work. She generated the theory and then went out into the sites where women and children gathered in schools and community organizations to test out the theory that ultimately was to improve the quality of life for all. Notions of democratic understanding had to emerge from the experiences of the people. Teaching from political abstractions could not be effective unless the abstractions were generated from, and connected to, the real-life experiences of people, especially children.

In a fundamental way, Taba was distinguished from her male mentors at Teachers College and connected to women who were part of the progressive education movement because she "talked the talk" of education for democracy and then went out to "walk the walk." She went out into schools and communities, working directly with people, touching lives and creating new expectations of schooling and curricula.[63]

Writings of Hilda Taba

Hilda Taba, "Curriculum Problems," chap. 2 in *Democratic Human Relations: Promising Practices in Intergroup and Intercultural Education in the Social Studies: Sixteenth Yearbook of the National Council for the Social Studies,* ed. Hilda Taba and William Van Til (Washington, D.C., 1945), 60–62.

No matter what the specific curriculum pattern, certain characteristics stand out as desirable in programs of intergroup education.

1. A curricular pattern should allow for continuity and consistency in content, in interpretation, and in kinds of growth fostered. Concepts such as the dignity of human beings irrespective of race, creed, or national origin cannot be developed in a short period, nor by incidental emphases in different subjects, nor through differing and even inconsistent treatment on different grade levels. Understanding of the roots and consequences of prejudice cannot be compressed into one period of time, no matter how concentrated the study. A slow and gradual exploration of its manifestations in a variety of contexts is needed before concentrated attention to it can be effective. One can dramatize the problem of anti-Semitism in an assembly program, but comprehending its causes and consequences requires a more prolonged experience, through all grade levels.

The need for continuity and consistency stands out still more sharply when programs are viewed from the angle of expected changes in students. Changing attitudes on supposed racial inferiority of Negroes takes much information, experience, and reflection, for such attitudes stubbornly resist change. Prejudice and biased forms of thinking cannot be successfully modified by a casual and brief analysis of them. These are matters to be learned by repetitive experiences and practice over a long period of time, with leisure to absorb ideas and insights, to reflect upon them, and to gather them into new orientation. All of this points toward the wisdom of planning whatever is done in social studies over the whole span of education, instead of concentrated doses in isolated spots. Each unit and each learning activity should take its proper place in a cumulative sequence.

2. It is highly important that curriculum planning in social studies be done with an eye on what goes on in the rest of the school. For one thing, intercultural education involves more than can be accomplished in social studies alone, no matter how broadly conceived. It is therefore wise to draw on experiences in other fields and in other activities in school for additional knowledge, insights, and appreciation. For example, literature can provide an avenue for understanding the variety of human values, problems, and actions that supplement the concepts of cultural diversity developed only in part through social studies. For a humanized understanding of intergroup relations the kinds of insights that come from reading Black Boy or Grapes of Wrath, and Patterns of Negro Segregation or Factories in the Field must come together. Activities that develop students' ability to identify themselves with other people, such as dramatics and assembly programs, drive home emotionally and forcefully the points made in the social studies classroom. Facts learned about anti-Semitism could find application in planning the student council or organizing a party. Principles learned about fair play should become part of the students' behavior toward other students in the classroom, in the hall, on the athletic field. Concepts of economic status and its implications in acceptance and rejection in personal social relationships should find an expression in a keener appraisal of personal relations at school dances and in school clubs. A survey in the community made under the supervision of a sociology teacher could lead to a constructive action no matter how small, involving perhaps other teachers or groupings than the particular class.

It is evident that throughout the school emotional, intellectual, and practical experiences should not be separated from each other. These experiences must not be permitted to foster conflicting ideas or mutually inconsistent attitudes through curricular departmentalization. To achieve unity, it seems necessary to coordinate the program in social studies with the overall program in the school. The best work is done if teachers in all subject fields in the school do cooperative planning and use cooperatively the experiences of students. Schools have recognized this problem of over-all planning.

Some have issued statements of philosophy. Many school systems are surveying their current practices and appraising them as to scope, consistency, overlapping, and omissions. Committees are at work to map out as comprehensive and consistent approaches as possible throughout all subject areas as well as the over-all school program. Such cooperative undertakings undoubtedly will eventuate in a more workable curriculum in each field. These cooperative efforts also hold the promise of integrating the programs in these schools.

Notes

1. Toivo U. Raun, *Estonia and the Estonians* (Stanford, Calif., 1987), 107–11.
2. For a complete account of the history of the Progressive Education Associ-

ation, see Patricia Graham, *Progressive Education: From Arcady to Academe* (New York, 1967).

3. Graham, *Progressive Education*, 133–35; see also Wilford Aiken, "The Story of the Eight Year Study," in *The American Curriculum: A Documentary History*, ed. George Willis et al. (Westport, Conn., 1993), 285–93.

4. Walter C. Parker, "Achieving Thinking and Decision-Making Objectives in Social Studies," in *Handbook of Research on Social Studies Teaching and Learning*, ed. James Shaver (New York, 1991), 349–50.

5. "In Memoriam." News release, San Francisco State College, 1967.

6. Herbert Kliebard, *The Struggle for the American Curriculum, 1893–1958* (New York, 1987), 210–11.

7. George Willis et al., eds., *The American Curriculum: A Documentary History* (Westport, Conn., 1993), 285–93.

8. Michael Bruce Lybarger, "The Historiography of Social Studies: Retrospect, Circumspect, and Prospect," in *Handbook*, ed. Shaver, 3–15; David Warren Saxe, "Framing a Theory for Social Studies Foundations," *Review of Educational Research* 62, no. 3 (1992): 259–71; Paul Robinson, "The History of Social Studies," *Theory and Research in Social Education* 8, no. 3 (Fall 1980). Mark Isham's article "Hilda Taba, 1904–1967" (*Journal of Thought* 17, no. 3 [1982]: 108–25) is an exception to this generality. O. L. Davis was the general guest editor for that issue of the journal. Taba is also included in *Notable American Women*; see Natalie Naylor, "Taba, Hilda," in *Notable American Women: The Modern Period*, ed. Barbara Sicherman and Carol Green (Cambridge, Mass., 1980), 670–72.

9. Evald Uudstalu, "History," in *Aspects of Estonian Culture*, ed. Evald Uudstalu (London, 1961), 42–43.

10. Uudstalu, "History," 43–44.

11. Edgar Krull and Arvo Marits, "Hilda Taba and Estonian Educational Science" in *Jubilee Conference, Hilda Taba–90, Invited Addresses and Reports* (Tartu, Estonia, 1992), 52. Hereafter cited as *Jubilee Conference*.

12. Mary Durkin, interview by author, tape recording, San Francisco, July 1998. Durkin was a colleague from Contra Costa (Calif.) County schools who collaborated with Hilda Taba in the Taba Project.

13. Raun, *Estonia and the Estonians*, 133.

14. Hilda Taba, *School Culture* (New York, 1955), 76.

15. Krull and Marits, "Taba and Educational Science," 52.

16. Durkin, interview.

17. Krull and Marits, "Taba and Educational Science," 53.

18. Elise Boulding, *The Underside of History: A View of Women through Time* (Boulder, Colo., 1976), 755.

19. Raun, *Estonia and the Estonians*, 133.

20. Krull and Marits, "Taba and Educational Science," 52.

21. Kliebard, *American Curriculum*, 210, 211; Isham, "Hilda Taba," 109.

22. Graham, *Progressive Education*, 12, 12, 61.

23. Graham, *Progressive Education*, 67. See also the publication *Progressive Education*, vols. 7–17.

24. Taba, *Dynamics of Education*.

25. Taba, *Dynamics of Education*, 18.

26. Taba, *Dynamics of Education*, 20.

27. Taba, *Dynamics of Education*.

28. For a discussion of constructivist curriculum, see Jon Snyder, Frances Bolin, and Karen Zumwalt, "Curriculum Implementation," in *Handbook of Research on Curriculum*, ed. Philip Jackson (New York, 1992), 414–15.

29. Taba, *Dynamics of Education*, 215.

30. Taba, *Dynamics of Education*, 177.

31. Taba, *Dynamics of Education*, 41–50.

32. Hilda Taba, "Progressive Education—What Now?" *Progressive Education* 11 (March 1934): 162–67; Graham, *Progressive Education*, 77. See also Aiken, " Eight Year Study," passim.

33. Taba, "Progressive Education—What Now?" 167.

34. Graham, *Progressive Education*, 133–35. See also Aiken, "Eight Year Study," passim.

35. Taba, "Progressive Education—What Now?" 164.

36. Taba, "Progressive Education—What Now?" 168.

37. Hilda Taba, "Social Sensitivity," in *Evaluation in the Eight Year Study*, Bulletin No. 6, Progressive Education Association (Columbus, Ohio, 1936), 5.

38. Ralph Tyler, preface to *Evaluation in the Eight Year Study*, Bulletin No. 6, Progressive Education Association (Columbus, Ohio, 1936).

39. Hilda Taba, *Curriculum Development: Theory and Practice* (Burlingame, Calif. 1962), vi; for the four questions and comments, see also Elizabeth Brady, "Intergroup Education in Public Schools, 1945–51," in *Jubilee Conference*, 20.

40. Isham, "Hilda Taba," 108.

41. Maxine Sellers, "Historical Perspectives on Multicultural Education: What Kind? By Whom? For Whom?" (paper presented at the American Education Research Association, Chicago, April 1991), 12.

42. Julius Rosenwald was the head of Sears, Roebuck and Co. who established a fund to support schooling for African Americans. It began as a school building program and evolved into a general-purpose fund that supported projects such as intergroup education. See James Anderson, *The Education of Blacks in the South, 1860–1935* (Chapel Hill, N.C., 1988), 152–67.

43. Sellers, "Multicultural Education," 12.

44. Graham, *Progressive Education*, 93.

45. *Intercultural Education News* 5, no. 4 (June 1944), 1.

46. William Vickery and Stewart Cole, *Intercultural Education in American Schools* (New York, 1943), xiii.

47. *Intercultural Education News* 3 (1942), nos. 1 and 2; 5 (1944), nos. 3 and 4; 6 (1945), nos. 1, 2 ,3, and 4; 7 (1946), nos. 1, 2, 3, 4. The newsletter, edited by William Van Til, was published by the Bureau for Intercultural Education in New York. Intercultural Education Bureau Archives, Hoover Center for War and Peace Studies, Stanford University, Stanford, Calif.

48. James Pitt, *Adventures in Brotherhood* (New York, 1955), 167; Brady, "Intergroup Education," 15–29.

49. Hilda Taba, Elizabeth Hall Brady, and John T. Robinson, *Intergroup Education in Public Schools* (Washington, D.C., 1952), 16.

50. Hilda Taba and William Van Til, eds., *Democratic Human Relations: Promising Practices in Intergroup and Intercultural Education: Sixteenth Yearbook of the National Council for the Social Studies* (Washington D.C., 1945).

51. Taba, Brady, and Robinson, *Intergroup Education in Public Schools*, 4.

52. Taba, Brady, and Robinson, *Intergroup Education in Public Schools*, 6–7.

53. Taba, Brady, and Robinson, *Intergroup Education in Public Schools*, 52–55.

54. Brady, "Intergroup Education."

55. Elizabeth Brady, interview by author, tape recording, Northridge, California, October 19, 1993.

56. Taba, *Dynamics of Education*, 243.

57. George Shaftel and Fannie Shaftel, *Role Playing the Problem Story* (New York, 1952).

58. Hilda Taba, *With Perspective on Human Relations* (New York, 1955), 101.

59. Taba, Brady, and Robinson, *Intergroup Education in Public Schools*, 63.

60. Taba, Brady, and Robinson, *Intergroup Education in Public Schools*, 23.

61. Taba, Brady, and Robinson, *Intergroup Education in Public Schools*, 38.

62. Taba, Brady, and Robinson, *Intergroup Education in Public Schools*, 229, 230.

63. Taba left the University of Chicago in 1951 for a position at San Francisco State College and a consultancy with Contra Costa Schools' social studies program. Working collaboratively with Mary Durkin and colleagues in the schools and at San Francisco State, she continued to conduct research and write about social studies curriculum. See Norman E. Wallen and Mary C. Durkin, "Hilda Taba's Research on Children's Thinking," in *Jubilee Conference*, 70–87; and Jack Fraenkel, "The Contribution of Hilda Taba to Social Studies Education," in *Jubilee Conference*, 30–49.

10

Alice Miel: Progressive Advocate
of Democratic Social Learning for Children

Elizabeth Anne Yeager

Alice Miel
Photo by Blackstone Studios

Alice Miel, a nationally prominent curriculum development scholar-practitioner at Teachers College, Columbia University, for three decades, frequently has been overlooked in research on the history of social studies and citizenship education, even as attention to women in this field has risen. This chapter specifically examines her contributions to the practice and theory of children's democratic social learning and views her work as historical antecedent to current research on diversity in the social studies and the elementary school classroom in general. Miel's career offers a valuable source for deeper understanding of an important era in American schooling, as well as insight into women's contributions to social education.

Three themes emerge in Miel's work. First, she advocated democratic ideals and the development of democratic behavior as the ultimate goal of schooling. Second, she applied theories of social learning and democratic principles and processes to various aspects of the school curriculum. Third, she applied her ideas about a democratic social learning environment to specific areas of the curriculum, particularly to the social studies, and to the elementary school curriculum as a whole.

One important point must be made about historical interpretation of Miel's work. Above all, Miel's was a scholarship of the reflective, practical, and personal that she sought to make highly relevant and accessible to school practitioners and to her students. However, much of the historical and philosophical context of her scholarship cannot be documented in conventional ways. Miel often did not document in footnotes, memos, journals, and recorded conversations the nature of the context in which she lived, taught, and worked. She was an activist and intellectual who read widely, internalized many of the prominent ideas of her day, reflected these in her teaching and research, and generated practical ideas on how these might apply to elementary schools. The fact that she was not a textual scholar of, for example, John Dewey, George Counts, William Heard Kilpatrick, David Riesman, or Gunnar Myrdal and did not always explicitly reference their work is not evidence that she was unaware of their impact, nor is it evidence that she did not understand their major points. Indeed, she extended some of these ideas into the classroom in highly accessible language. However, it must be acknowledged that she did not footnote extensively in many of her published articles. One must simply infer from reading her work and through knowledge of the context of her career at Teachers College, her professional relationships, and her activism in education that she knew a great deal both inside and outside the world of education. When possible, in this chapter, I will refer to contextual issues that likely influenced her thinking.

Biographical Sketch

The progressive movement in education emerges as the strong undercurrent in Miel's story. After completing normal school and graduating from the University of Michigan, Miel taught social studies and Latin in Michigan public schools from 1924 through 1936. In Ann Arbor, Miel collaborated with her principal, G. Robert Koopman, and other colleagues on several curriculum projects. One of these projects yielded a junior high social studies curriculum guide that reflected the awakening concern of Koopman, Miel, and their colleagues about the effects of the Great Depression on society and the schools, as well as their emerging belief that "the breakdown in our social, economic, and political structure has brought into serious question the objectives and purposes which have dominated public education during the past quarter century."[1] Incorporating the ideas of John Dewey, as well as those of leading Progressive Era educators such as Harold Rugg, Ann Shumaker, and William Heard Kilpatrick, Miel and her colleagues demonstrated their conviction that the school curriculum must be modified to emphasize the study of contemporary social problems.[2] Another landmark experience for Miel was a 1936 session at Ohio State University with Laura Zirbes, a prominent figure in the field of elementary education. Miel left with a commitment to understanding children, not just content, and to providing for their individual differences.

Indeed, "child-centered" progressive education during the late 1930s, according to Cremin, had become the conventional wisdom in American educational thought and practice.[3] Miel moved into this company in the early years of her career in education. A 1938 *Time* cover story perhaps overstated its conclusion that no American school had completely escaped the progressive influence; clearly, not all American educators embraced these ideas.[4] By the 1940s, both internal divisions and external attacks led to a fracturing of the progressive movement.[5]

At this time of transition for the progressive education movement, the locus of Miel's story began to shift to Teachers College, where it would remain for the next three decades. Miel became more deeply involved in progressive ideas, even as the movement itself began to wane. She began as the doctoral student of Hollis L. Caswell then served as professor from

1944 through 1971; she later chaired the Department of Curriculum and Teaching at Teachers College from 1960 through 1967.

Miel's career at Teachers College spanned the later years of the college's preeminence as the "intellectual crossroads" of the progressive education movement.[6] Her tenure there also spanned the movement's alleged decline and disarray in the 1950s as the main target of conservatives who attacked progressive philosophy and demanded a return to the "basics" of schooling. In the 1960s, Miel's last decade at Teachers College, the national mood shifted again as Charles Silberman and other humanist educators decried conformity and rigidity in school curricula and wanted to return the focus of education to the needs of individual learners.

When Miel joined the faculty, the postwar era had brought turmoil to the world of education in general, and to Teachers College in particular, through conservative attacks on progressive education led by such critics as Arthur Bestor, Admiral Hyman Rickover, and Mortimer Smith, who advocated a return to "traditional" academic content in the schools.[7] During the late 1940s and 1950s, Teachers College also experienced a number of internal struggles as the progressive movement splintered. Miel's work does not seem to have been directly attacked by conservatives, and from all appearances, Miel maintained her strong convictions and continued on the same scholarly path. Later, she acknowledged problems within the progressive movement and criticized its lack of a unified base of support, as well as its lack of new ideas.[8] Although she acknowledged that Dewey's ideas had been distorted by some—for example, in some educators' "overemphasis on the individual" and in "activities just for activity's sake"—Miel argued that most of progressive education was constructive.

Beginning in the 1950s, the Red scare affected Teachers College. Communist hunters looked askance at this institution in particular, regarding it as the de facto headquarters of left-wing subversive educators.[9] Miel had personal experiences with the Red scare on several occasions and was subjected to vague accusations of Communist affiliation.

In general, though, she remained largely insulated from the more extreme manifestations of anti-Communist activity throughout the nation. Her career did not suffer; in fact, Miel was promoted to full professor in 1952, a time when slightly more than one-third of the college faculty were women. In an era when women often found promotion difficult in academia, Teachers College was a pioneer in this regard.[10] Miel recalled the large number of female professors and students who were "treated as equals," and she never felt that she was either "punished or promoted" because of her gender.[11]

In looking at some of Miel's research accomplishments, two of her studies during her tenure at Teachers College merit particular attention. From 1958 to1962, she directed the Study of Schools in Changing Communities. From this project, she developed her 1967 book with Edwin Kiester, *The Shortchanged Children of Suburbia.* This research study has been characterized as a "groundbreaker" in its emphasis on what suburban schools were failing to teach about human differences and cultural diversity.[12] Also, in 1966 Miel worked with A. Harry Passow on a study of the Washington, D.C., public elementary schools.

In terms of other accomplishments, Miel was one of the early presidents of the Association for Supervision and Curriculum Development (1953–54). In the 1970s, she became a guiding influence in the founding of the World Council on Curriculum and Instruction (WCCI). The establishment of the WCCI was a natural outgrowth of her interest in improved curricula for all children and her work with doctoral students from all over the world. She also played an active part in the Association for Childhood Education, International (ACEI) for several years. One of the distinguishing features of her career was her advocacy of global understanding through cooperation in international educational activities. Through these activities, and through her supervision of more than 140 doctoral dissertations, Miel's influence was indeed widespread.

Miel, Democracy, and Democratic Social Learning: Contexts and Meanings

Meanings, manifestations, and enactments of democracy were at the center of Miel's career, although she never adhered dogmatically to a precise definition of democracy. She believed that, although certain fundamental ideas were embedded in the term, its meaning must be continually developed and nurtured by people who professed it. Like Dewey, she conceived of democracy as more than a system of government; it was a unique way of being, thinking, and living with others.[13]

Miel's interpretation of democracy was developed in the context of the era of Franklin and Eleanor Roosevelt, whom she greatly admired. John Dewey's ideas in *Democracy and Education* especially informed Miel's beliefs. In particular, Dewey argued that as long as the structure of schools remained undemocratic and repelled intellectual initiative and inventiveness, all efforts toward reform would be compromised and their fruition postponed indefinitely.[14]

In terms of Miel's understanding of democracy in practice, especially her own opportunities for democratic participation in educational settings, she benefited from her experiences in the Ann Arbor public schools. There, Miel worked with and observed democratic leaders who created settings in which teachers and students could practice democracy. As a doctoral student at Teachers College, Miel developed her ideas in the context of the Teachers College democratic mission that the faculty had articulated during World War II.[15] Also important in her Teachers College experience was Miel's study with Hollis L. Caswell, whose work in curriculum development influenced her belief that schools should play an active role in helping to mold a democratic social order.[16]

Miel believed that the school was democracy's proving ground because it had a large share of the responsibility for socializing the nation's young people into participation in civic life.[17] While some critics may have demurred that democratic lessons could be gained from an institution that mandated participation, Miel viewed the school as society in microcosm, where people from many backgrounds learned about freedom and responsibility, individuality and cooperation—all with an eye toward democratic citizenship.

Furthermore, throughout her life Miel continued to develop a keen sense of the historical context of social problems that, for her, raised acute concerns for the future of a democratic society: postwar reconstruction, the Cold War and Red scare, the social tensions between "haves" and "have nots," and the Watergate scandal. In particular, she was deeply affected by the state of race relations and civil rights in American society. Miel often taught African American students in her classes, and she had several formative experiences that brought racial issues into increasingly sharp focus for her as she learned about and sometimes witnessed her own students' experiences with prejudice and discrimination.[18] Miel sought to move beyond the outmoded notion of racial tolerance, which, for her, connoted "putting up" with people who were different, to a more active, broader notion of intercultural understanding and appreciation.[19]

Miel also sought to refute the claims of back-to-basics school reformers who were, in the 1970s, enjoying their moment in the spotlight. She argued that the "basics" also extended to the "moral-ethical-social realm" and that they should be given a prominent place in the school curriculum. Miel was convinced that students' understanding of freedom and responsibility should be high on the agenda of every school in the United States. She returned to these themes in 1986 in the context of the "educational excellence" movement, manifested in reports such as *A Nation at Risk*, which called for higher achievement in the schools in order to ensure American competitiveness in the global economy.[20] Miel criticized "remedies [that] give little consideration to the individual. . . . Young people are being put under enormous pressure to perform for their society's sake. . . . It is distressing that those claiming our nation is at risk do not see how risky it is to overlook the power of a populace informed about, committed to, and competent in the ways of democracy."[21] For Miel, the overarching responsibility in democracy was to know how democracy worked and how to maintain it through changing conditions.

With all of these influences in mind, Miel focused her work on fundamental ideas about what she considered to be appropriate democratic social learnings for children. Furthermore, she connected these ideas to her interest in democracy by focusing on the development of social behaviors that would best serve a democratic society. Her writing featured a number of recurring themes, particularly in her 1957 book with Peggy Brogan, *More than Social Studies*.[22]

In these writings, Miel said that, first, a democratically socialized person saw democracy as an ideal arrangement for keeping individual and group considerations, freedom and responsibility, in balance. Such a person had respect for the individual, as well as for group intelligence, welfare, and cooperation. In a democracy, Miel argued, especially in critical times, students needed a better grasp of the tools of learning than under any other circumstances in order to safeguard against irrational thought and behavior. Miel conceived of these skills in terms of social learnings for which the schools should share responsibility with the family and community and specified that such learnings included bearing a friendly feeling; having concern for all mankind; valuing difference; being a contributing member of a group; seeing the necessity of a cooperative search for conditions guaranteeing maximum freedom for all; taking responsibility for a share of a common enterprise; problem solving and working for consensus; evaluating and cooperating with authority; refining constantly one's conception of the "good society"; and learning effective communication.

Throughout her work on children's social learning and how this learning contributed to democracy, Miel consistently emphasized the idea of the cooperative person. Given her typical awareness of contemporary intellectual currents, it is likely that she was influenced partly by David Riesman's landmark 1950 book, *The Lonely Crowd: A Study of the Changing American Character*. Riesman discussed the changing nature of work in America and the gradual, necessary shift away from the highly individualistic work orientation towards that of what he called the "other directed" person, characterized by cooperation, teamwork, and concern for others.[23]

Miel discussed this notion of cooperation and "other directedness" within the context of life in a democratic society not just in the workplace. She reiterated the theme of cooperative learning to build good relationships—what she called the "fourth R"—in schools and specifically focused on getting along with people and the development of "friendly feelings" as essential components of democratic social learning. Miel recommended three approaches that teachers could use to help children improve human relationships: creating a friendly, respectful atmosphere in the classroom, teaching ways of managing group endeavors, and teaching about peoples' commonalities and differences. Miel also focused on social learning opportunities for world understanding, and she criticized "culture units" commonly taught in the elementary schools for encouraging unhealthy stereotypes of cultural and ethnic groups.

Miel argued that the elementary school was in a unique position because it presented opportunities throughout the school day for practicing democracy through discussion, problem solving, consensus building, and learning "world citizenship." Miel's illustrations of these concepts in her writing were selected to show the practical possibilities of educative experiences centered around problems as children themselves met them, many of which arose in school living or in the community. Most important, elementary school teachers could model democratic behavior and help children learn from those in society who exemplified the highest values.

Furthermore, Miel strongly believed that no single school subject, including the social studies, could be expected to carry the full load of children's social education.[24] However, in terms of the unique contribution of the social studies to children's learning experiences and to their democratic socialization, Miel and Brogan's *More than Social Studies* pointed to the field's capacity to place social learning at the center of the curriculum. Teachers could provide experiences designed to develop children's interpersonal and intergroup relationships through solving problems of daily living; satisfy children's curiosities about the world; to solve problems of understanding and community action; and build positive attitudes toward others through organized individual and group studies. Most important, they could help children develop socially useful concepts, generalizations, and skills so that they could organize their experiences.

In fact, in bringing social learning to the forefront of the social studies curriculum, Miel and Brogan criticized traditional approaches to the organization of the social studies based upon compartmentalized subjects and separate textbooks. Also, Miel and Brogan asserted that children reaped no benefits of social learning when they were simply taken through the motions of choice and discovery. If, as the authors believed, the fundamental goal of social studies derived from its social learning function, then any approach that overrelied on a preplanned scope and sequence could not help but fail. Myriad learning opportunities were embedded in the concept of "social" studies, but these would be wasted if social studies were "divorced from living [and] looked upon merely as a new way to cover subject matter" instead of as a way to learn lessons "needed by people in a democracy."[25]

This analysis notwithstanding, Miel's other publications rarely focused on the role of specific social studies subject matter in a social learning context. She suggested how the social studies could "make much more difference in the lives of individual children and in the society educating them."[26] However, her suggestions usually were quite general and did not delve into disciplinary perspectives. She sought instead to discourage teachers from merely "conveying bits of information."[27] Rather, teachers could help children to "clarify, organize, and extend information . . . to see how facts are interrelated, and to draw useful generalizations."[28] Miel stated that social studies on the elementary level, although not always well developed, contained opportunities for thoughtful study of people, current events, societal movements, and global problems that required children to investigate, cooperate, and become better informed about their world.

Nonetheless, Miel recalled that her view of social studies was less than warmly received in some circles. She believed that social studies content in the traditional sense was important and was "well covered" by other scholars, but she argued that the field had "stopped with merely providing an information base. . . . [T]here was no understanding of relationships, let alone caring and action."[29] Her social studies focus, centered on problem areas and cutting across different disciplines, was different and not confined to the area of the curriculum labeled "social studies."[30]

Perhaps the most concise, illuminating example of Miel's perspective on the social studies came in 1981, when she offered ideas for the development of sociopolitical "giftedness" towards useful social ends. Miel adeptly characterized talent in this area as uniquely and totally "group linked. . . . It cannot be developed or demonstrated except in a social context."[31] This feature, she claimed, placed a special burden on the social studies to help students understand themselves and others and to participate constructively in societal and global affairs. In a cogent statement of the mission of the social studies curriculum, Miel argued that social studies must be designed for *understanding* of the world, *caring* for others, and *action* on community problems with which students had a reasonable chance for success. Influenced by Dewey's books *The Child and the Curriculum* (1902) and *Experience and Education* (1938), Miel averred that with such a well-rounded, interdisciplinary and interdimensional approach to the social studies, students would "see how the information they are gaining relates to existing bodies of knowledge."[32] Moreover, teachers could help them "to organize their learnings and fill in gaps so that they are constantly building a more systematic view of the world."[33] If social studies content were selected to facilitate observation, generalization, evaluation, and application of learnings to new situations, students would become "lifelong social learners."[34] According to Miel, there could be no better equipment for leaders and all participants in democracy than knowing ways of gaining understanding, extending feelings of caring, and acting on convictions.

In some ways, Miel's ideas about caring anticipate the work of Nel Noddings in this area. However, Noddings elevated this concept to major public attention largely on the basis of feminist theory. Miel never characterized herself as a feminist scholar, but one may discern similarities to Noddings in her exploration of different types of caring that can be encouraged in children. Space does not permit a detailed exploration of Miel's thoughts on caring, but she elaborates on this topic in *More than Social Studies* and again in the 1981 book *Strategies for Educational Change: Recognizing the Gifts and Talents of All Children.* Also, Miel's 1960 speech to the Association for Childhood Education, International, influenced by the 1959 United Nations Declaration of the Rights of the Child, illuminated her view of how education could contribute to children's rights to growth and to the development of their abilities, judgment, values, and human relationships.

Miel identified three dimensions of the development of an educated person that schools must emphasize in order to guarantee those rights for children. First, *learning to care* meant caring about oneself, then caring about others, then caring about moral and social responsibility. Also, caring about oneself and others related to caring about ideas and their verbal and nonverbal expression. Second, *learning to make informed judgments,* one of the bases of becoming a useful member of society, supplied children with pertinent information and skills necessary for caring about ideas and responsibilities. Miel argued that the school can develop power in the children to go on learning under their own direction for the rest of their lives and that such power consists in part of knowing sources of information and useful methods of learning from each in order to solve problems, test solutions, and evaluate consequences. Furthermore, the elementary school must reinforce children's trust in themselves as independent decision makers. Third, a child must *learn to take an active role* in his or her world, using problem solving and relational skills to translate concerns and judgments into socially useful action. She said that the elementary school must help children to go the complete circle—caring about unrealized human potential all over the world, deciding what will improve conditions, and taking useful steps (with others) in creating better conditions. The elementary school's role, therefore, was to provide an education that made sense to every individual, that left a "useful residue in the form of attitudes, knowledge, and skills that make it possible and likely that the individual will continue to be a self-directed learner," and that helped each individual to be able to lead a dignified and useful life.

An Assessment of Miel's Views on Social Learning and Social Studies

Several factors likely limited the acceptance of Miel's conception of social learning. First, Miel believed that social learning should be taught throughout the school day and not compartmentalized into one particular academic subject area, and especially that it should not be the exclusive domain of the social studies. This view posed problems for teachers and curriculum workers, who, even at the elementary level, increasingly tended to think in terms of discrete subjects, whether they were integrating these subjects or teaching them in traditional organizational forms. "Social learning throughout the day" was probably too nebulous a concept to fit into such a structure, especially one with a predetermined, written course of study. Moreover, teachers may have shied away from explicit attention to the complexities of moral development and social action as components of social learning, preferring instead to inculcate certain proper behaviors in their students, and social studies teachers may have felt no unique responsibility for these components in their curriculum.

Second, the circulation of Miel's ideas was restricted by the publication of *More than Social Studies* during the conservative educational reform movements of the late 1950s. In this era, Cold War–inspired fear of, and competition with, the Soviet Union, especially after the launch of the Soviet satellite *Sputnik,* placed the American educational system on the defensive and generated widespread criticism of schools for letting the Soviets gain the upper hand in science and technology. Experts from traditional academic disciplines were called upon to improve schools; educational reform emphasized the disciplines at the expense of students' individual and social needs. The publication of Miel's book coincided with increasing criticism of American schooling and demands that math and science, especially, receive priority in education. The *Sputnik*-inspired National Defense Education Act, linking federal support for schools with national policy objectives, ensured that social studies would be deemphasized and that traditional academic history likely would prevail in new federal guidelines for education. Miel's notions of social learning throughout the curriculum simply found no place in antiprogressive times and perhaps were viewed with deep suspicion by some conservatives, who favored "traditional" American individualism, as advancing a socialist or communist agenda.

Third, Miel lacked affiliation with subject matter experts in the social studies, and she did not consider herself to be a specialist in any of the social studies content areas. These factors likely limited her role in this area of the school curriculum. Somewhat ironically, considering her criticism of overly prescriptive written courses of study, Miel considered herself a weak teacher of history at the junior high school level, mainly because she had taken so few history courses at normal school and had to rely heavily on the textbook to supplement her background knowledge.[35] In all likelihood, her nontraditional views of the social studies, as well as her lack of academic history credentials, also precluded her involvement in the National Council for the Social Studies, of which she was never a member.

Significantly, too, the social studies became increasingly dominated by subject matter experts—mostly male—in academia who viewed and shaped this field through the lens of their particular disciplines. Miel did not have the academic credentials or teaching background to be considered an "expert" in any of these academic circles. For example, in the 1960s, the research of Jerome Bruner, Philip Phenix, Joseph Schwab, and others on the "structure of the disciplines" was in vogue in the curriculum reform discourse.[36] Bruner, for example, suggested that each discipline had an inherent structure and that curriculum content should be presented in a form that helps students to comprehend this structure. Phenix argued that the curriculum should consist entirely of knowledge that comes from the disciplines, because the disciplines revealed knowledge in its teachable forms. Moreover, advocates of discipline-centered views claimed that curriculum developers should rely on the "expert interpretations of subject matter specialists who reveal the logical patterns that give shape to their discipline and imply the order in which its elements should be learned."[37]

Miel's work did not focus on inherent structures in particular realms of knowledge and the feasibility of "expert" agreement on the dimensions of that structure. Rather, much of her work revealed a strong belief in a focus on other variables that influenced learning, especially those that related to social context. In fact, partly because of her concern that "problems of a modern society cannot be solved by specialists in any one discipline," she produced at least one brilliant critique of the "structure of the disciplines" approach.[38] She cautioned that no general agreement existed on what a discipline was or on what the structure of particular fields should be. Moreover, structure was not a thing, unchanging and unchanged, to be packaged and handed over "ready-made and full-blown."[39] Furthermore, Miel criticized Bruner's neglect of the "interrelationships among disciplines . . . [and of] the question of the structure of the curriculum as a whole within which the fields of knowledge are to find their place."[40] Miel was largely preoccupied with a "disciplined way of dealing with social policy questions, where values must be applied and strategies worked out."[41]

Another highly fashionable social studies "movement" in which Miel did not become involved was the "new social studies" movement of the 1960s, particularly because this often resulted in written courses of study that she eschewed. For example, Miel traveled to Harvard University to hear about the new curriculum, "Man: A Course of Study," which she believed to be too narrow in its focus because it lacked emphasis on "modern man and his problems."[42] Her interpretation of the role and function of the social studies in the school curriculum still diverged from the "conventional wisdom" that social studies meant the study of discrete subjects at particular grade levels.

A confluence of factors, then, circumscribed Miel's contributions to the social studies discourse and contributed to her remaining a lesser-known figure in this field. These included, certainly, the historical context of the school curriculum and her emphasis on social learning at the expense of deliberate attention to—and even criticism of—the common social studies disciplines. Although many of Miel's ideas and criticisms were well founded and well stated, her voice sounded one of only a few discordant notes in the increasingly loud chorus of approval for a more traditional academic, subject-centered curriculum.

Diversity Issues in Miel's Research

One of the issues that most concerned Miel as she explored meanings of American democracy and democratic citizenship was the diversity of

American society. In particular, she focused on problems of children who experienced intellectual, economic, or cultural deprivation because of their ethnicity and/or socioeconomic background. She viewed the solving of such problems as central to the mission of American democracy, and she saw the schools as a place where these children could have, among other things, positive social learning experiences. As a Michigan junior high school teacher, Miel worked in the Ann Arbor schools, which were, in many ways, a model setting.[43] The Donovan School at which Miel became a teaching principal was in a low-income neighborhood. She retained strong impressions of the life experiences of the children with whom she had worked and of their particular social learning needs. These impressions later figured prominently in her career at Teachers College as she taught and wrote about the importance of children's cooperation, understanding, respect, and relationships.

Concern for diversity and equity issues surfaced early in Miel's work. For example, Gunnar Myrdal's *American Dilemma* (1944) took American socioeconomic, cultural, and class issues in a profound new direction and seems to have influenced Miel, who cited Myrdal in her 1946 book, *Changing the Curriculum: A Social Process.* Myrdal focused on the disadvantages suffered by African Americans, criticizing in particular the inferiority of vocational training programs offered to African American youth and, consequently, the discrimination and lack of opportunity they faced in the job market. More broadly, Myrdal excoriated the United States as a backward nation for its failure to provide appropriate educational opportunities and employment to its youth and for maintaining a socioeconomic underclass. Myrdal viewed education as the "great hope" for both individuals and society, as the foundation for equality of opportunity for the individual, and as an outlet for individual ability.

Nonetheless, Miel's concern about diversity and equity issues did not fully manifest itself until some of her later work, most likely after these issues were brought into sharp focus for her by her experiences in the late 1950s and 1960s, as she heard about and witnessed her African American students' struggles with racism and discrimination.[44] After years of a general emphasis in her work on social and democratic learning, Miel became deeply involved in several major research studies, especially case studies, that related to diversity and equity issues in schools. First, Miel worked with A. Harry Passow in the mid-1960s on a comprehensive curriculum study of the Washington, D.C., public schools. Miel studied the elementary schools in the District. She in turn facilitated contacts and correspondence between her students at Teachers College and approximately eighty classroom teachers. Miel and her students set out to examine several aspects of the Washington, D.C., elementary program: the social-emotional climate; learning objectives; the utilization of time, space, and human and material resources; organization and types of subject matter; and opportunities for learning the skills of information processing and democratic living. When their task got under way, they discovered a sterile physical and intellectual environment that emphasized efficiency at the expense of children's active participation in their own learning. The researchers concluded that most learning activities appeared to be designed to promote order, silence, passive conformity, rigid adherence to a time schedule, and uniform instruction of children. Challenging subject matter and intellectual stimulation were scarce, as were basic instructional materials. The report also stated that teachers seemed to expect little progress from the children and that there appeared to be no joy in the learning process. From the perspective of Miel and her students, the Washington, D.C., elementary schools were failing to meet either the intellectual or the social-emotional needs of the children. Data on the children's academic performance and teachers' impressions that the children were not learning confirmed their observations.

Foremost among Miel's recommendations from this study was the suggestion that the District's elementary schools provide children with opportunities to develop a "social personality," characterized by individuality, autonomy, independence, respect, and a sense of well-being.[45] Their creativity, decision making, and participation in classroom activities must be encouraged and affirmed. Miel and her students also advised that instruction in these schools become more flexible and individualized, taking into account the special needs of various children. Finally, they emphasized that none of these recommendations could be fully implemented unless changes were made in teachers' self-concept and professional status. Miel and her students also recommended changes in the schools' subject matter. They criticized the curriculum for disregarding "actual events and problems in today's world" and suggested that the curriculum be more relevant to the students' lives.[46]

Miel's concern for "relevance" was particularly significant because the Passow study directly addressed the large African American population in the Washington schools. Years before the multicultural-curriculum debate moved to the forefront of the educational discourse, Miel and her students helped to draw attention to the educational needs of minority children. In a foreshadowing of the debate to come, Miel and her students advocated a culturally inclusive curriculum that went beyond "the introduction of a little Negro history into the social studies curriculum"[47] and instead featured the contributions of African Americans from all walks of life to American society and placed their stories and experiences in appropriate historical perspective. The "desirable direction" they recommended was for teachers to begin with the experiences of the children in their homes and communities. Teachers and students would then work toward a general understanding of minority-group concerns, an examination of the contributions and interactions of different cultural and ethnic groups in society and around the world, and an analysis of "the way society makes decisions and solves problems."[48]

Miel's concerns for intercultural relations and the problems of minority groups as key issues in American democracy can be discerned throughout her career. Miel advocated a "broadened" view that went beyond mere "tolerance" and "understanding" to actual improvement in relationships among all groups—not only those groups based on race, culture, and religion but also those based on gender, occupation, educational level, age, and regional identity.[49] She criticized teaching approaches that emphasized only the strangeness or quaintness of other cultures. Miel believed that intercultural education, when properly conceived, had two primary, mutually reinforcing goals: "helping children discover how much like other people we are" and "helping children to understand why differences in cultures have arisen and to value differences as a way to enrich us all."[50]

Miel's concern for young people's cultural awareness and valuing of cultural difference eventually led her to a concern about the nature of suburbia in the United States. Certainly, the homogeneity and conformity that seemed so pervasive in suburban life was not a new topic; for example, Helen and Robert Lynd addressed it in 1929 in the book *Middletown*. This classic study emphasized the orderliness, routinization, and rote learning typical of schools in Muncie, Indiana. Later, James B. Conant's book *Slums and Suburbs* (1961) seems to have had a powerful impact on Miel's thinking. Conant provided a striking contrast between affluent, spacious, well-staffed suburban schools and run-down, understaffed, overcrowded inner-city schools. He argued strongly that the American public must address these disparities or face the "social dynamite" of social disorganization, alarming dropout rates, and unemployment, all of which would largely harm minorities who lived in American slums.

Miel first broached the incipient concept of suburbia and the "postwar rush to the country" in 1964.[51] Although a city dweller and resident of the Morningside Heights neighborhood near Teachers College in New York City until her retirement, she nonetheless viewed with increasing dismay the suburban growth phenomenon on, for example, Long Island and other new developments near the city. Her central question was whether suburban children, raised and educated in homogeneous environments, were being deprived of important social learnings about similarities and differences among people. The article, based upon the results of her five-year Study of Schools in Changing Communities, surveyed the attitudes of several hundred rural, urban, and suburban children toward themselves, their families, and their neighborhoods. Miel determined that, significantly, the "dominant middle-class cultural values" of the time—for example, order and conformity of dress and behavior—were being transmitted on an unprecedented scale throughout school and society.[52] Moreover, these values were being inculcated in all types of children, without regard for their cultural backgrounds, frames of reference, and experiences. She viewed this as problematic because "a whole constellation of educative media" worked to standardize young children's opinions and attitudes, and the school itself "contributed its share in the achievement of such homogeneity."[53] Furthermore, she strongly believed that "in a world with new problems, the full development of *individual* potential," creativity, and resourcefulness should take priority over fostering alikeness.[54]

These concerns emerged fully in Miel's book with journalist Edwin Kiester, *The Shortchanged Children of Suburbia* (1967), an outgrowth of her Study of Schools in Changing Communities from 1958 to 1962. This research project, conducted in suburban schools and funded primarily by the American Jewish Committee, was developed in the context of the social unrest and civil rights struggles of the 1960s. Indeed, the book's publication coincided with the onset of great civil disorder in American inner cities. It focused on "how the public schools prepare children for a world peopled by men and women of many different nations, races, religions, and economic backgrounds" when misunderstandings about human differences "are precisely what the chief problems of our time are about."[55]

Miel believed that this book best represented her research efforts. In fact, she received the National Education Association's Human Rights Award in 1968 as a result of this publication. Like the Washington, D.C., study, *The Shortchanged Children of Suburbia* was prescriptive in a general sense. That is, Miel herself recommended an "action program" for teachers to broaden social learning opportunities for their suburban pupils. Passow described this project as a "groundbreaking" study of what suburban schools were failing to teach about human differences and cultural diversity.[56] Fred Hechinger, education editor of the *New York Times,* described the book as an analysis of problems in enclaves of affluent homogeneity, where status quo was a virtue and where children's horizons were artificially limited. Hechinger further criticized what he saw as the "self-satisfaction," "overwhelming preoccupation with material possessions," and "the distortion of values" of the children of suburbia.[57] Moreover, he argued, in this atmosphere teachers often appeared more anxious to avoid than to answer troublesome questions and to pretend that controversial issues and inequities did not exist in American society and throughout the world.

In this major study, Miel and several doctoral students from Teachers College extensively researched the pseudonymous, ostensibly representative suburb of "New Village." They collected information on the community, administered questionnaires, and interviewed sixty teachers, fifty parents, over one hundred elementary children, and over one hundred community members.[58] They concentrated on the role of the elementary school as the "chief training ground for American children" and on the opportunities that children had in their schools and communities for social learning about life in a multicultural, pluralistic democracy.[59]

Miel and her colleagues reached conclusions that troubled them. First, they found that "extraordinary effort was required to bring about any encounter between a child of the suburbs and persons different from himself."[60] The suburban child's world remained highly circumscribed and insulated. Second, the children in their study reflected only a superficial "tolerance" of differences. Beneath the surface, prejudices toward people of different races and religions, especially toward African Americans, already were deeply ingrained in the children. Third, although New Village parents and teachers seemed eager to address religious differences, they were much more likely to ignore or avoid racial ones, especially those relating to poverty and economic inequalities. The children in this study did not know about—nor did they want to know about—people of different races or socioeconomic status. Furthermore, the children's strong preference for conformity and for a single norm of appropriate behavior underlay all of their attitudes. Finally, Miel found that parents and teachers in New Village placed much higher value on skill acquisition and factual learning than on social learning. Teachers found it unrewarding to address social attitudes because this had little to do with "getting into the right colleges."[61]

For these reasons, Miel determined that suburban children were being "shortchanged" in their social learning, and, despite the "many enviable features" of their environment, they were educationally "underprivileged."[62] The "action program" that she suggested for suburban schools and their communities emphasized greater attention to the development of "higher thought processes," to children's value systems, and to a more "realistic picture" of their own community in relation to others.[63] She also made numerous specific recommendations for the study of race, religion, and socioeconomic status—all aimed at dismantling stereotypes, avoiding facile generalizations, studying different groups in their appropriate cultural and historical contexts, and understanding the concerns and struggles faced by particular groups in American society.

Within the New Village scenario, then, Miel was able to reassert her conviction that human diversity was a proper subject for the school curriculum in a democratic society. Indeed, she argued that there was "no more urgent business in the schools of America."[64] She firmly believed that "children must be educated to deal fairly and realistically with questions of social justice, civil rights, national unity, and international peace."[65]

Miel's ever present concern for international peace deepened after World War II, when she traveled to Japan in 1951 as a curriculum consultant. She spent much of her time in Hiroshima, where she witnessed the city's painful rebuilding process, visited schools and orphanages, and participated in the reconstruction of the educational system. Upon her return to the United States, she wrote and lectured about life in postwar Japan and tried to correct possible American misconceptions about Japanese views of education and democracy.[66] Miel's travels in Japan profoundly affected her and served as a formative experience in her increasing interest in global issues.[67]

Although she was not involved in the global education movement per se, international peace moved to the forefront of Miel's interests in the 1960s and 1970s, perhaps out of a growing disillusionment with the American political and educational climate. Miel's leadership in the late 1960s and early 1970s in founding the World Council on Curriculum and Instruction was particularly noteworthy. The WCCI emphasized dialogue and action among educators from around the world to improve all aspects of education and contribute to a more peaceful world. The members, whose ranks eventually grew to about seven hundred throughout fifty countries by 1990, continued to promote and participate in international conferences, exchange teaching, study abroad, cross-national research on common problems, and development of curricula that encouraged international understanding, cultural sensitivity, and the reduction of prejudice within and across national boundaries. The WCCI was Miel's primary outlet for her international interests; however, throughout the 1950s, 1960s, and 1970s she often visited other countries, including Uganda, Tanzania, and Afghanistan, as a curriculum development consultant, continuing to focus on democracy and democratic social learning for children.

Miel, Schools, and Democracy: Final Assessments

Because of the nature of the societal concerns she addressed in her work, Alice Miel in many ways embraced and encouraged what Parker has referred to as "advanced" ideas about democracy and democratic citizenship education.[68] That is, she raised issues related to human social and cultural diversity and saw these as central to the ongoing development and "deepening" of American democracy. She also viewed democracy as a way of life that citizens undertake together through deliberation, reflection, and civic action.[69] For Miel, democratic citizenship education must necessarily begin early in school, where children would learn what Goodman termed a "connectionist orientation"—that is, a sense of altruism, responsibility, civic responsibility, community, and connection to other living beings—as an essential characteristic of democratic citizenship.[70]

Miel did not view the school merely as a reactive institution or only as the target of social-change efforts. Her conceptualization of the school's role in a democratic society was an active, albeit indirect, one. She claimed that the educational process—and the curriculum itself—should be "the beginning of helping children to understand social problems and to feel a responsibility for helping to solve them."[71] Addressing social problems was a natural outgrowth of the development of relationships between school and community.

One of the foremost legacies of progressive education was its emphasis on the process of change, deliberation, and continuous renewal.[72] Later historical evaluations of progressive education were somewhat more circumspect than those of Bestor, Smith, Rickover, and other strident critics of the 1950s. Still, they agreed that the progressive education movement ultimately collapsed for similar reasons: professional infighting, ideological fragmentation, removal from the public discourse, overuse of slogans and clichés, inertia, and obsolescence in the face of the continuing transformation of postwar American society.[73] Zilversmit emphasized that progressive education, ostensibly a philosophy of change, had become a fixed set of methods and rhetoric for teachers to learn.[74] Furthermore, the idea of a role for the schools in the advocacy of social change aroused increasing public hostility, especially as the Cold War intensified. But more important, teachers' involvement in social transformation was simply unrealistic, given the reality of power relationships, the authoritarianism under which most teachers worked, and the capacity of schools merely to reflect and reproduce community values and patterns of social organization.[75] Perhaps an overarching reason for the demise of progressive education in the 1950s was the inability of progressive educators to respond forcefully and concertedly to calls for reassessment of the movement.

The apparent lack of sustained attention to Miel's work and ideas may have been a matter of the timing of her life and career within this context. Her work in academia began as progressive education was not only on the decline but under deliberate, if exaggerated, attack from conservatives. Her explicitly stated beliefs regarding democratic socialization and the value of diversity for schoolchildren were not among the favored educational ideas of the 1950s and early 1960s. Moreover, the liberal sociopolitical perspective that Miel openly espoused became unfashionable throughout those years. To a number of Americans during that time, it was even unpatriotic. Unfortunately, because she was at Teachers College during a particular era, Miel also may have been unfairly associated with some of the more irresponsible manifestations of progressive education that came under fire in schools. Even though these manifestations had little to do with the work of Teachers College faculty, they may have played a role in causing her work to be ignored later by academic traditionalists anxious to distance themselves from that movement. Later in the 1950s and 1960s, the "structure of the disciplines" movement elevated the importance of subject matter expertise, which Miel never claimed to possess.

Three other points must be made about how Miel's work should—and should not—be characterized. First, a logical question that arises from an examination of her work is whether she was simply a follower of trends and of other people's ideas—a disciple of others rather than a leader in her own right. A fair assessment of her work, in my view, is that she practiced an effective model of professional development and practical scholarship. That is, she read numerous philosophical and theoretical works that others had written, internalized the ideas that held the greatest meaning for her, and then took a strong leadership role in determining how these ideas could be made real and meaningful in schools. Her views on children's social learning, diversity, cultural awareness, and democracy all were in some sense derivative, but her creative, thoughtful, and democratic leadership style helped these ideas make sense to her students and to practitioners.

Second, much of Miel's work did not observe the traditional academic conventions of statistical, "objective" research. Much of it indeed appears to be based mainly upon a combination of Miel's firm convictions and her own sense of professional ethics, along with extensive observations and conversations in schools. Third, Miel was never an activist in the sense of high-profile political involvement in the issues about which she wrote. Her "activism," as it were, expressed itself through her teaching, research, and service to the profession through the Association for Supervision and Curriculum Development, the WCCI, and ACEI. After her retirement, she lived a quiet life in Florida, occasionally speaking or writing when invited, mainly in order to reemphasize the ideas about democracy that she had advocated all of her professional life. Underlying all of these ideas was a deep concern for the intellectual growth and well-roundedness of all students, and her work revealed attention to a number of variables that influenced learning, especially those deriving from the social context of schooling.

Still, there remained a "timelessness about many of the problems the progressives raised and the solutions they proposed. . . . [They had] an authentic vision [that] remained strangely pertinent to the problems of mid-century America."[76] Poor slum schools still existed. So did wretched rural schools, outmoded and harmful teaching practices that ignored the unique needs of students, glaring social inequities, and dehumanized approaches to knowledge. Clearly, Miel's work consistently illustrated her capacity to call attention to some of the nation's enduring educational and social problems.

Writings of Alice Miel

Alice Miel and Peggy Brogan, *More Than Social Studies: A View of Social Learning in the Elementary School* (Englewood Cliffs, N.J., 1957), 5–6.

Every society must conceive a certain relationship between the individual and the group. Totalitarianism has a relatively simple answer to the question of what the relationship should be: the State is supreme and the individual is subordinate to the group.

Democracy's way is more complicated. Our type of society cannot simply reverse the principle and make the individual supreme over the group. Nor can we, in the name of freedom, leave the individual without the support of positive group association. Either would be quite as coercive as the totalitarian way.

The process of democratic socialization means learning more and more responsible membership in a society whose discipline requires that the individual maintain his integrity and discover his uniqueness within the context of a group which supports him but which he also supports and enriches. In other words, democratic socialization embodies the interwoven processes of individuation and socialization.

Alice Miel, "Social Studies for Understanding, Caring, Acting," in *Strategies for Educational Change: Recognizing the Gifts and Talents of All Children,* ed. W. L. Marks and R. O. Nystrand (New York, 1981), 257–58.

Members of a society who have a grasp of order, loyalty, justice, and consensus appropriate for a democracy are equipped with concepts basic to such a society. They can understand that democracy rests on certain fundamental beliefs— belief in the worth and dignity of the individual, in shared decisions and cooperative problem solving, in reason and persuasion instead of force and violence, in the ability of human beings to govern themselves if they have the necessary information, and belief that cultural gains . . . should be widely diffused among the masses. . . .

Young people need such patience and care in developing meanings for words like democracy, freedom, and justice. These concepts are not learned at one time but continue to take on fuller meaning as a person grows older. They also are concepts that must be enlarged and changed as the world changes around the individual. . . .

When social studies programs feature many rounded, in-depth experiences with multiple learnings cutting across familiar disciplines, students will need opportunities to see how the information they are gaining relates to existing bodies of knowledge. . . . If students are also helped to observe, analyze, and evaluate the processes they are using in their learning, they will have more control over use of such processes throughout their lifetime. There could be no better equipment for political leaders and all participants in our democracy than knowing ways of gaining understanding, ways of extending feelings of caring, and ways of acting on convictions. Content for social studies should be chosen with this in mind.

Alice Miel, "Education and Democracy in a New World," in *Reflections: Personal Essays by Thirty-three Distinguished Educators,* ed. Derek L. Burleson (Bloomington, Ind., 1991), 268–78.

[In democracy] both difference and likeness must be valued in achieving respect for persons. Differences that are enriching, not destructive, and likenesses that bind people together while not thwarting creation of something new are the important elements in developing respect for persons. The design of a democratic society requires the individual to see his own private welfare as intimately bound up with provisions made for the public welfare, and thus we arrive at the

democratic concept of common welfare. . . . Approaches teachers might use in developing democratic concepts include:

1. *Helping students feel good about themselves and others by providing opportunities to create those important feelings and to send and receive such feelings.*

2. *Helping students extend their life space through understanding and feeling compassion for more people in more places on the globe, thus giving them an early start on attaining a world view.*

3. *Helping students increase competence in problem solving through opportunities for short-term problem solving, group enterprises, group studies centered on problems of understanding, and group studies centered on problems of action.*

4. *Helping students build socially useful meanings by adding to meanings that are only partially formed, changing meanings that are undemocratic, and building new meanings when needed.*

The overarching responsibility in a democratic society is to know how democracy works, how it was won, and what it takes to maintain it as people and conditions change. Specific types of responsibility to be learned by all include being true to oneself; exercising one's rights but also respecting the rights of others; sharing the work, the wealth, the good ideas; being alert to problems and needs of self and fellow human beings on this planet; and being skillful in making decisions, carrying out those decisions, evaluating consequences, and making corrections.

In a democracy responsibility is a matter of free and intelligent choice, including willing acceptance of one's share in maintaining and enhancing a free society. To develop a sense of responsibility, teachers can guide students in assessing a situation and discovering what should be done. . . . Helping students develop the attitudes, understandings, and skills relating to freedom and responsibility should be a priority on the agenda of every school.

Notes

This research was made possible by a Spencer Foundation/American Educational Research Foundation Doctoral Research Fellowship. The author is most grateful for this support.

1. G. Robert Koopman et al., *Helping Children Experience the Realities of the*

Social Order: Social Studies in the Public Schools of Ann Arbor, Michigan (Junior High School) (Ann Arbor, Mich., 1933), iii.

2. Rugg, Shumaker, and Kilpatrick were leading Progressive Era advocates of "child-centered" education, in which teachers and students worked together to determine what was worthwhile to learn and how to learn it. *Helping Children Experience the Realities of the Social Order* drew upon several prominent strains of progressive educational thought. One stressed the Deweyan notion, from Dewey's 1902 book *The Child and the Curriculum,* of education as experience and of the child and the curriculum as two limits that define a single process. Education was the continuous re-creation of the individual through experience, curriculum was the organization of experience, and the school was society's agency for furnishing a selected environment in which directed growth could take place more effectively during certain periods of a child's life. Another aspect of *Helping Children Experience the Realities of the Social Order* propounded Boyd Bode's concern for a new social order whose primary focus was the development of the capacity of personality. Third, the guide also drew from ideas of Kilpatrick ("The Project Method" in the 1918 *Teachers College Record*) and Rugg and Shumaker's *Child-Centered School* (1928) about how the teacher's role could be reconceptualized in order to promote the concepts of freedom, individuality, and initiative in a child-centered classroom.

3. L. A. Cremin, *The Transformation of the School: Progressivism in American Education, 1876–1957* (New York, 1961).

4. Larry Cuban, *How Teachers Taught: Constancy and Change in American Classrooms, 1890–1980* (New York, 1984); O. L. Davis Jr., "Epilogue: Invitation to Curriculum History," in *Perspectives on Curriculum Development, 1776–1976,* ed. O. L. Davis Jr. (Washington, D.C., 1976), 257–59.

5. Boyd H. Bode, *Progressive Education at the Crossroads* (New York, 1938).

6. Cremin, *Transformation of the School,* 175.

7. Arthur Bestor, *Educational Wastelands: The Retreat from Learning in Our Public Schools* (Chicago, 1953); H. G. Rickover, *Education and Freedom* (New York, 1959); Mortimer Smith, *And Madly Teach: A Layman Looks at Public School Education* (Chicago, 1949).

8. Alice Miel, interview by author, tape recording, 11–13 October 1994, Gainesville, Fla.

9. David Caute, *The Great Fear: The Anti-Communist Purge under Truman and Eisenhower* (New York, 1978).

10. L. A. Cremin, D. A. Shannon, and M. E. Townsend, *A History of Teachers College, Columbia University* (New York, 1954).

11. Miel, interview.

12. A. Harry Passow, telephone interviews by author, 4–6 January 1995.

13. John Dewey, *Democracy and Education* (New York, 1916); John Dewey, *The Public and Its Problems* (Chicago, 1927).

14. Dewey, *Democracy and Education.*

15. Cremin, Shannon, and Townsend, *History of Teachers College.*

16. Hollis L. Caswell and D. S. Campbell, *Curriculum Development* (New York, 1935).

17. Alice Miel, "Teaching for a Democracy," *Educational Forum* 50 (1986): 319–23.

18. Miel, interview.

19. Alice Miel, "Living in a Modern World," in *Toward a New Curriculum: Yearbook of the Department of Supervision and Curriculum Development, National Education Association*, ed. Gordon Mackenzie (Washington, D.C., 1944), 11–21.

20. Commission on Excellence in Education, *A Nation at Risk* (Washington, D.C., 1983).

21. Miel, "Teaching for a Democracy," 322.

22. Alice Miel and Peggy Brogan, *More than Social Studies: A View of Social Learning in the Elementary School* (Englewood Cliffs, N.J., 1957).

23. David Riesman, with Nathan Glazer and Reuel Denney, *The Lonely Crowd: A Study of the Changing American Character* (New Haven, Conn., 1950).

24. Alice Miel, "Toward Democratic Socialization," *Childhood Education* 26 (1949): 50–51.

25. Miel and Brogan, *More than Social Studies*, 120.

26. Alice Miel, "Social Studies with a Difference," *Education Digest* 22 (1962): 45.

27. Miel, "Social Studies with a Difference," 45.

28. Miel, "Social Studies with a Difference," 45.

29. Miel, interview.

30. Miel, interview.

31. Alice Miel, "Social Studies for Understanding, Caring, Acting," in *Strategies for Educational Change: Recognizing the Gifts and Talents of All Children*, ed. W. L. Marks and R. O. Nystrand (New York, 1981), 257.

32. Miel, *Strategies for Educational Change*, 268.

33. Miel, *Strategies for Educational Change*, 268.

34. Miel, *Strategies for Educational Change*, 268.

35. Miel, interview.

36. See Jerome S. Bruner, *The Process of Education* (New York, 1960). Philip Phenix, "The Use of the Disciplines as Curriculum Content," *Educational Forum* 26 (1961): 273–80; Philip Phenix, *Realms of Meaning: A Philosophy of the Curriculum for General Education* (New York, 1964); Joseph Schwab and P. E. Brandwein, *The Teaching of Science* (Cambridge, Mass., 1962). George L. Mehaffy, "Symbolic and Occupational Functions of Curriculum Discourse: An Exploration of Curriculum Theory During the Disciplines Era" (Ph.D. diss., University of Texas at Austin, 1979).

37. William H. Schubert, *Curriculum: Perspective, Paradigm, and Possibility* (New York, 1986), 238.

38. Alice Miel, "Knowledge and the Curriculum," in *New Insights and the Curriculum: Yearbook of the Association for Supervision and Curriculum Development*, ed. Alexander Frazier (Washington, D.C., 1963), 79–87.

39. Miel, "Knowledge and the Curriculum," 80–82.

40. Miel, "Knowledge and the Curriculum," 86.

41. Miel, "Knowledge and the Curriculum," 84.

42. Miel, interview.

43. Miel, interview.

44. Miel, interview.

45. Alice Miel et al., "Study of the Washington, D.C. Schools Elementary Program: A Report of the Task Force on the Elementary School Program, 1967" (final draft). From the Alice Miel Collection, Museum of Education, University of South Carolina.

46. Miel et al., "Washington D.C. Schools," 28.

47. Miel et al., "Washington D.C. Schools," 28.

48. Miel et al., "Washington D.C. Schools," 28.

49. Miel et al., "Washington D.C. Schools," 16.

50. Miel et al., "Washington D.C. Schools," 16.

51. Betty Psaltis and Alice Miel, "Are Children in the Suburbs Different?" *Educational Leadership* 21 (1964): 436–40.

52. Psaltis and Miel, "Children in the Suburbs," 440.

53. Psaltis and Miel, "Children in the Suburbs," 440.

54. Psaltis and Miel, "Children in the Suburbs," 440.

55. Alice Miel and Edwin Kiester, *The Shortchanged Children of Suburbia* (New York, 1967), 8, 10.

56. Passow, interview.

57. Miel and Kiester, *Shortchanged Children of Suburbia*, 6–7.

58. Miel and Kiester, *Shortchanged Children of Suburbia*, 9.

59. Miel and Kiester, *Shortchanged Children of Suburbia*, 12.

60. Miel and Kiester, *Shortchanged Children of Suburbia*, 13.

61. Miel and Kiester, *Shortchanged Children of Suburbia*, 55.

62. Miel and Kiester, *Shortchanged Children of Suburbia*, 14.

63. Miel and Kiester, *Shortchanged Children of Suburbia*, 57–59.

64. Miel and Kiester, *Shortchanged Children of Suburbia*, 68.

65. Miel and Kiester, *Shortchanged Children of Suburbia*, 68.

66. Alice Miel, "Education's Part in Democratizing Japan," *Teachers College Record* 55 (1953): 10–19.

67. Miel, interview.

68. Walter C. Parker, "'Advanced' Ideas about Democracy: Toward a Pluralist Conception of Citizenship Education," *Teachers College Record* 98 (1996): 104–25.

69. John Dewey, *The Public and Its Problems* (New York, 1927); Walter Parker, "'Advanced' Ideas about Democracy."

70. Jesse Goodman, *Elementary Schooling for Critical Democracy* (Albany, N.Y., 1992).

71. Miel, interview.

72. Arthur Zilversmit, *Changing Schools: Progressive Education Theory and Practice, 1930–1960* (Chicago, 1993).

73. Cremin, *Transformation of the School*, 348–51.

74. Zilversmit, *Changing Schools*, 193.

75. Zilversmit, *Changing Schools*, 176–77.

76. Cremin, *Transformation of the School*, 352–53.

11

The Search for a Coherent Curriculum Vision: Hazel Whitman Hertzberg

Andrew Mullen

Hazel Whitman Hertzberg
Special Collections, Milbank Memorial Library,
Teachers College, Columbia University
December 1976

Sometimes when I look coldly at the subjects in which I am deeply interested," Hazel Hertzberg reflected midcareer, "they seem to be wildly eclectic." The examples she proceeded to furnish clearly supported her self-assessment. Among other interests, Hertzberg listed modern American Indian reform movements, the culture of contemporary American adolescents, population-control education, and the history of the social studies curriculum in American schools. Her publication record to date demonstrated further the range of her interests. Writing and speaking for both popular and scholarly audiences, Hertzberg had addressed topics as diverse as the pre-Columbian Iroquois, the United Nations, competency-based teacher education, and anthropology in the secondary school curriculum. "Wildly eclectic," in Hertzberg's case, was possibly an understatement.[1]

A "Fragmented" Career

Hertzberg spoke frequently, often despairingly, of the "fragmentation" of the social studies curriculum in American schools of her own time. Social studies educators seemed to be experiencing even greater difficulty than usual in, as she put it, "deciding whether to teach 'this and not that.'" She spoke in retrospect of the "kaleidoscopic quality" of curriculum reform in the 1970s, the "advocacy of a whirling series of particular topics and procedures, some of which had considerable merit," but all of which failed to add up to any sort of coherent program. Hertzberg knew whereof she spoke. Her own far-from-linear career clearly mirrored the social studies curriculum of the period in which she was professionally engaged and in fact merits study partly on that basis. In the topics she studied and promoted, one may even detect something of the faddism, the cult of contemporaneity, that she at times disparaged.

Between 1957 and 1988, Hertzberg was a student, professor, and eventually chair of the venerable social studies department at Teachers College, Columbia University. As a professor at Teachers College her primary responsibility was preparing future secondary teachers and future teacher-educators in the field of social studies. At the same time, she was called upon regularly to assist in shaping the social studies curriculum at the local, state, and eventually the national levels. Hertzberg was keenly aware of the role her departmental predecessors at Teachers College had played in curriculum policy making at the national level, and she herself aspired to play a similar role. Early in her career she enjoyed modest successes in introducing anthropology and a more scholarly approach to thestudy of Native Americans into the social studies curriculum in her home state of New York. An invitation in 1970 to join the federally funded Social Science Education Consortium, a de facto national academy of social studies theorists, soon provided her regular opportunities to speak and write for national audiences.

Her early success in promoting particular social studies components and her own career notwithstanding, Hertzberg increasingly recognized that she and her contemporaries were failing to articulate any comprehensive vision for the curriculum as a whole. And this was no mere theoretical problem. As one of Hertzberg's colleagues observed in 1977, the absence of any shared professional vision had been manifested in the schools as "a generalized kind of confusion, a sense that neither pupils nor public would care very much if social studies disappeared from the curriculum altogether."

Much of Hertzberg's thirty-year career in social studies education can be characterized as a quest for some coherent and comprehensive vision that could address the apparent confusion and indifference in the field. If Hertzberg never fully arrived at such a vision, she remains of interest for her self-conscious efforts to deal with so many knotty questions along the way, questions and issues that remain pertinent to citizenship education today. Some of the theoretical issues and questions that Hertzberg confronted are considered below in the context of her professional story. First of all, and of particular professional interest early in her career, was the appropriate relationship of history and the nonhistorical social sciences in the social studies curriculum. A second set of issues that Hertzberg struggled with, increasingly topical in the years since her death, was the proper response of social studies educators to the nation's growing cultural diversity. What sorts of national and subnational loyalties and identities were the schools supposed to cultivate? The perennial question of what history is good for represents a third set of issues to which Hertzberg responded. A fourth issue, particularly insistent during Hertzberg's final years, concerned the relationship of "history" to "social studies." To what extent did one have to choose between a commitment to teaching rigorous, academically respectable history in the schools and a commitment to educating for the development of citizen-activists? A final question with which Hertzberg struggled throughout her life was what it meant to educate for citizenship. Was the goal of developing an informed and competent citizenry best approached directly or indirectly? What was the relationship of history and social studies education to education for citizenship?

From Social Gospel and Socialism to Social Studies

Hertzberg was nearly forty before she demonstrated any direct professional interest in the teaching of history or social studies in American schools. The self-described "two semi-independent but related careers" she went on to build in social studies education and American Indian history actually followed what may be seen as a third career as a social activist—not to mention her ongoing work as wife and mother.

Hazel Whitman was born in 1918 to upper-middle-class parents in Brooklyn, New York. Her father, a civil engineer, died when Hazel was young. Her mother was primarily a homemaker but had been a musician and an active suffragist in her youth. Hertzberg's grandmothers had both been engaged in nondomestic employment throughout their lives, one as a teacher and the other as a practical nurse. Given the number of strong women in her immediate and extended family, it never occurred to her, she observed later, to think that women were in some way inferior to men. The heroines she listed in a school exercise as an eleven-year-old—Molly Pitcher and Joan of Arc—suggested that she had from early on some sense of a woman's potential for active participation in public life. Next to her family, Hertzberg considered the local Congregational church the chief formative influence in her early years. Although Hazel would later marry outside the Protestant faith, she continued to associate her social conscience with her Congregationalist and social-gospel roots.[2]

Hertzberg attended a public elementary school, transferring to the Berkeley Institute, an independent school for girls, at the age of twelve. She entered Middlebury College in 1935. Disliking the sorority-dominated social life and wanting a stronger program in economics to respond more intelligently to the nation's current woes, Hertzberg transferred after two years to the University of Chicago. That same year she traveled to Mississippi to work on an interracial Quaker farm for dispossessed tenant farmers and to Memphis to volunteer with the Southern Tenant Farmers Union. At the University of Chicago Hertzberg was active in the American Student Union, a left-leaning national collegiate organization, and served as national chairman of the Young People's Socialist League, affiliated with the American Socialist Party. She also returned to Mississippi a second summer with her fiancé, equipped with a grand plan to unite tenants and landlords in a common commitment to principles of nonviolence.

After leaving the University of Chicago in 1939, Hertzberg worked on behalf of a succession of pacifist, humanitarian, and socialist organizations. Returning to New York in 1941, she married journalist and fellow activist Sidney Hertzberg. In addition to mothering two children, she edited a monthly publication supporting independence for India, administered an Indian famine-relief agency organized by her husband, and coordinated publicity and fund-raising for a domestic relief agency providing aid to sharecroppers. In 1949 the Hertzberg family moved to suburban Rockland County, New York, where their activism was channeled into more conventional directions. Hertzberg organized a chapter of the League of Women Voters and—abandoning the Socialist ticket—cochaired the county campaign in 1956 for Democratic presidential candidate Adlai Stevenson. A local journalist suggested in this latter context something not only of her campaign style but also of her permanent character when he christened her, after a 1954 storm of that name, "Hurricane Hazel."

In the educational-watershed year of 1957—just one month before the launching of *Sputnik*—Hertzberg accepted a position teaching seventh-grade English and social studies in suburban New York. The state of family finances appears to have been the immediate stimulus for this initiative, but it was compatible with a long-standing commitment to social betterment. The position also allowed her to participate in the world of her children, now twelve and fourteen. Simultaneous with her entry into teaching, Hertzberg began taking graduate classes at Teachers College, initiating a relationship that would culminate in 1968 with the awarding of a doctorate and the offer of a full-time faculty position at her home institution. Teachers College would remain her professional base.

Anthropology, Indians, and New York State History

Even before accepting full-time responsibilities at Teachers College, Hertzberg had begun to engage the kind of questions that would interest her for the duration of her career. One of these was the appropriate pedagogical relationship of history to the nonhistorical social sciences. In the immediate post-*Sputnik* years there was much discussion as to how to incorporate more of the latter into the precollegiate curriculum, as well as speculation as to how much history would or should be sacrificed in the process. A related question concerned the degree to which the various social studies fields were to be unified for instructional purposes— whether, in effect, educators could agree now that "social studies is," as opposed to the more traditional "the social studies are." The model Hertzberg developed for her seventh-grade social studies class represented one very concrete response to a set of dilemmas typically discussed only in the most abstract terms.

When Hertzberg began teaching in the fall of 1957, her primary concern was more existential than the proper relationship of history to the social sciences. It was to make seventh-grade social studies something more than what her son, from his own experience of the subject, would later call "Canajoharie-makes-chewing-gum history." The compilation of disconnected facts about New York State history and geography that constituted the existing official state syllabus appeared to hold little potential meaning for her students. Hertzberg developed, between 1957 and 1963, a model for teaching the state's history in terms of three distinct cultural eras. In contrast to conventional historical arrangements, she organized the year's work so as to hold time relatively still. Students immersed themselves for several months in the culture of the Iroquois, skipped to what she referred to as the "age of homespun," and then skipped again to the "emerging city" of the period 1890–1914. In each of the three units, she chose to slight political and formal economic content in favor of social history. Activities and investigation were all to be built around categories of analysis with which students had firsthand experience: the roles of men and women, of children and adults; the organization of time, including the rhythms of day, week, and season; and topics such as education, religion, and health care. In each of the three cultural eras, the methods of one or more scholarly disciplines were to be emphasized—archaeology and anthropology, for instance in the case of the Iroquois unit; sociology in the context of the turn-of-the-century city. An anthropological emphasis actually pervaded the entire year, as students were encouraged to see each epoch in the state's history as a cultural whole.

In her teaching, Hertzberg thus implicitly argued that history and the nonhistorical social sciences need not be seen as rivals. History, appropriately taught, incorporated the other social sciences. One could actively embrace these fields without sacrificing chronology and historical context. Hertzberg's model for teaching New York State history was eventually adopted by the state department of education and published for statewide use. Some indication of the success of her efforts is suggested by the letter of a disaffected Albany official who complained in 1968 that teachers across the state were referring to the "Hertzberg program" for social studies.

Hertzberg's program for New York's seventh-graders led indirectly to a lifelong involvement in Native American history. At the same time, it led to her involvement in a second set of issues concerning the proper treatment in precollegiate history of minority groups in general. In 1962, while visiting American Indian reservations and rummaging through museum collections for her seventh-grade curriculum materials,

Hertzberg discovered a topic for her doctoral dissertation. Beginning with the work of an early-twentieth-century Iroquois leader, Arthur Parker, her study eventually extended to a whole network of Progressive Era Native Americans—individuals who attempted to build a "pan-Indian" identity among diverse peoples who had heretofore perceived themselves chiefly in terms of membership in a particular tribe.

In the process of establishing herself as a historian of American Indians, Hertzberg became increasingly aware of the political implications of the history of marginalized groups. Such history clearly had the potential to change the way minorities and the mainstream culture defined themselves and their relationship to one another. Bringing the history of various out-groups into the precollegiate curriculum was coming into fashion just as Hertzberg completed her doctoral work. The federal Ethnic Studies Heritage Act (1972) and a National Council for the Social Studies yearbook on ethnic groups (1973) testified to, and served to extend, this incipient interest. Hertzberg initially exploited this trend in the interest of her own career. She taught for many years a course in American Indian history at Teachers College. At the same time, she had deep concerns about treating American Indian history or the history of any other group as separate from the history of the whole society. Compartmentalized histories, she believed, ultimately contributed to compartmentalized societies.

As early as 1963, in reference to tensions between groups of students at Harvard, Hertzberg had written to her son of her concern to maintain as cohesive a society as possible. If the reasoning of her son's peers were carried to its logical conclusion, she suggested, "this country would be a series of little ethnic Balkans": a country "reduced to a series of special interest groups looking at the world only from their perspective, unable to rise above it." It was this fear that informed the advice she later gave to history teachers.

As the guest editor in 1972 for an issue of *Social Education* on teaching about American Indians, Hertzberg spoke approvingly of the greater attention being given to ethnic studies. But she also warned of what she perceived as the dangers. Educators should give serious thought, she said, "to the possible consequences . . . of a primary commitment to ethnicity without a sufficiently strong compensating commitment to national goals and ideals which can unite us. . . . The price societies pay for warring ethnicities can be soberingly high." Moreover, as she wrote on a later occasion, efforts to overcompensate for past marginalization could themselves foster "an unrecognized and therefore unexamined and uncombated form of prejudice and bigotry." Traditionally, "public education [had] been viewed as one of the chief builders of an American identity more encompassing than particular ethnicities." As to what degree, and in what manner, that mission should continue into the future, Hertzberg did not offer any definitive statement. Throughout her career, however, she continued to raise the question.

An "Academic Backwater"

To the extent that Hertzberg ever established an academic or professional focus, she did so in the field of curriculum history. One of only a great number of interests early in her career, the historical development of the social studies curriculum and the professional communities that had created and sustained it became, during the 1970s and 1980s, a consuming passion. Although Hertzberg died before completing her proposed history, she published a preliminary version of her work in 1981 (*Social Studies Reform, 1880–1980*), and it remains the standard work on the topic. Not surprisingly, it is for her work in this area that she is best known today. At the same time, it is initially difficult to understand the attraction of this topic for a person of Hertzberg's activist temperament and ideals. Certainly it was difficult for her family to understand at the time why her interests shifted in that direction. To her son, it seemed that Hertzberg was getting stuck in an "academic backwater."

If it appeared to others to be an arid academic exercise, Hertzberg's study of her own professional predecessors was in fact an ongoing act of professional renewal and an eloquent personal demonstration of the value of studying history in general. By the mid-1970s, Hertzberg clearly needed renewing.

More than ever, as she confessed to one correspondent, she was feeling "scattered," uncertain of her professional identity and priorities. Her demoralized state was symptomatic of a larger sense of crisis in the field of social studies, a crisis Hertzberg attributed to curriculum movements initiated in the previous decade. She believed that such movements had undermined any existing consensus or shared sense of purpose in the field without providing any alternative foundations. Dwindling enrollments, fiscal crises, and fierce intradepartmental conflicts in Hertzberg's home institution had further demoralized her and exacerbated a need for a clearer sense of what she was about.

It was under these circumstances, then, that Hertzberg began to immerse herself more deeply in her professional roots, attempting not only to understand how the current situation had developed but also, in her words, to seek guidance and to draw strength from the past. Over the course of her remaining years, Hertzberg continued to receive sustenance from this "usable past."

In two discoveries she found particular inspiration. She found, first of all, appealing professional role models, men and women who were attracted both to historical scholarship and to employing history in the fashioning of critical, engaged citizens. She seemed especially attracted to individuals of the Progressive Era: Frederick Jackson Turner, Albert Bushnell Hart, and Lucy Salmon, among others. Their vision for history instruction in the schools became Hertzberg's vision, and for the rest of her life she quoted such individuals liberally in her speaking and writing. The use of Turner's words in the Foundations department Hertzberg initiated in *Social Education* in 1987 is one example of the way she chose to speak through the words of her professional predecessors.

A second discovery from which Hertzberg drew considerable inspiration was the degree of interaction in the past among three groups that had much less contact in her own time. Records of professional meetings from the early years of the century revealed that historians, schoolteachers, and educationists had routinely come together to discuss matters of common interest and had in fact perceived themselves as engaged in a common enterprise. The gradual segregation of that earlier community into isolated enclaves had had unfortunate results, Hertzberg believed, for all three groups, producing historians with little commitment to speak to larger questions of public identities and public values, and teachers and educationists with little commitment or ability to appropriate the rich resources of the past.

What began for Hertzberg as a quest for personal renewal became fuel for a campaign in her final years to reunite divided professional communities. In writing about her discoveries, Hertzberg hoped to remind both historians and those concerned more directly with schools of their connections in the past and potentially symbiotic relations in the future. Perhaps, she wrote in 1981, "the single most effective way to re-interest the historical profession in the schools (which I think is essential for the health of both) is to produce a lively and significant body of historical work." Such an effort was "obviously not sufficient," she acknowledged, but it seemed a prerequisite. In justifying her history of the curriculum in these terms, Hertzberg implicitly provided a rationale for history in general. History, in reminding us of past connections, had the potential to bring divided communities together. Moreover, she believed that the kind of professional inspiration she had experienced herself was potentially available for others. She billed the graduate course she taught for many years on the history of the social studies curriculum as "history that speaks to the present." Students would finish the course, she hoped, with a clearer understanding of "visions realized and visions lost," not to mention a clearer understanding of their own vision for the field.

"History" versus "Social Studies"

In 1977 Hertzberg's home institution sponsored a conference entitled "Restoration of School History." Believing that the teaching of history was in some indefinite way on the decline in American schools, Hertzberg and her colleagues met with New York City–area teachers to attempt to understand the current situation and plot strategies for addressing the problem. This conference was only one sign of what became a national outpouring of concern over the condition of precollegiate history in the 1980s. Such concern helped to fuel the movement for national standards and eventually prompted at least two major efforts to redefine the curriculum in social studies: the National Commission on Social Studies in the Schools (NCSSS) and the Bradley Commission on History in the Schools. Hertzberg played an active role on both commissions and in fact was one of only two individuals to serve on both.

For many voices in the effort to "restore" history in the schools—Diane Ravitch, Chester Finn, and Lynne Cheney, among others—supporting "history" meant castigating "social studies." On the other side, a number of less familiar voices seemed willing to frame the debate in similar terms. Throughout the 1980s, advocates of history and advocates of social studies traded recriminations in professional publications and the popular press. The ambiguity of both terms, inconsistencies in usage, and a tendency to confuse professional rhetoric with practices in the schools made it difficult to sort out the underlying issues. If "history" and "social studies" were not the clearest terms in which to frame it, the debate did in fact represent a deep underlying polarization of opinion in the field. For one camp the highest priority was a rigorous grounding for students in academic history. Others expressed a primary commitment to developing citizen-activists.

In her work on the two commissions, as in other capacities, Hertzberg might well have been expected to fit cozily into the "pro-history" camp. As early as 1969 she had confessed to being "disturbed by the anti-historicality" of many voices in contemporary society. In the early 1980s Hertzberg became deeply concerned by proposed revisions to the social studies curriculum in New York State, and she lobbied at great length against a plan that one prominent educator called "the most serious threat yet to history." An editorial piece left unpublished at Hertzberg's death began by warning, "History is in trouble in our schools." With respect to her fellow social studies educators, moreover, Hertzberg could be as caustic as any. There was, she acknowledged, "a great deal of nonsense in the social studies among some of its theoreticians and specialists." Such individuals often "had no real roots in either a discipline or the realities of the classroom."

In the end, however, Hertzberg avoided partisanship in the history-versus-social-studies debate of the 1980s, choosing to be both pro history and pro social studies. The superficial debate over the name, first of all, she believed was of marginal importance. "I know how distasteful the term is to those who think of it as a synonym for mush." The solution was "to get rid of the mush, not of the name." Secondly, however committed she was to history, she thought it would be "folly . . . to ignore the influence and importance of the social sciences," fields that, as we noted previously, she believed were complementary rather than antagonistic to history. Finally, and most important, Hertzberg refused to believe that underlying commitments to the study of history and the development of citizen-activists were incompatible. After all, as she expressed it in notes she prepared for a talk in 1986, properly taught,

> history is a study that . . . teaches skepticism, inquiry, and critical thinking. At its best the study of history allows students to become witnesses to the great achievements and tragedies of humankind, permits them to participate in the great controversies of the past, invites them to explore the ways of living and working of people in other times and places of history can be profoundly liberating, as students of women's history and black history have so dramatically demonstrated. History teaches us to ask both "why?" and "why not?" In so doing, it frees us from the apparent inevitability of the status quo.

For Hertzberg, then, far from existing in opposition to civic activism, history provided the skills and habits of mind, the vicarious experience, and the raised consciousness upon which such activism depended.

The Education of Citizens

Hertzberg had high hopes for the two commissions on which she served in the late 1980s. She anticipated that the National Commission on Social Studies in the Schools, in particular, would take its place in history next to the major turn-of-the-century curriculum commissions, articulating a clear vision and influencing curriculum and instruction for generations to come. Whether or not such hopes were ever realistic, Hertzberg herself was not able to participate fully in the attempt to fulfill them. In 1988 while attending an international conference on citizenship education, Hertzberg died unexpectedly in Rome. And while the final report of the NCSSS, published in 1989 as *Charting a Course: Social Studies for the Twenty-first Century,* was posthumously dedicated to Hertzberg, it is not clear to what degree she would have approved the commission's recommendations. Certainly the report did not offer the kind of compelling, comprehensive, and definitive vision that Hertzberg had originally aspired to offer.

At the same time, a preliminary memorandum she completed for the NCSSS in 1986 offers one of Hertzberg's clearest statements on a subject in which she had been involved, directly and indirectly, for the previous thirty years: the education of citizens. Although much of Hertzberg's speaking and writing might well be classified under citizenship education, she herself did not normally address the topic directly or in those exact terms. In this case, she had no choice, since "Education of the Citizen" had originally been part of the NCSSS's title.

As a banner under which to offer curriculum advice, the notion of citizenship education seemed to Hertzberg ironically "both too narrowly and too diffusely focused." In practice, at least, "citizenship education" was an inherently fuzzy category that "can and often has become a catchall for curricula advocated by particular interest groups." However much one might wish otherwise, the goal of developing effective citizens was not "linked to a specific and developing body of knowledge with its own conventions of inclusion, verification and ethics." Of equal danger, citizenship education was (again, in practice) all too often construed too narrowly, becoming mere indoctrination or a meaninglessly abstract study of governmental functions, or an exclusive or primary focus on current events.

And yet if citizenship in and of itself did not constitute a legitimate area of the curriculum in Hertzberg's view, she affirmed certain goals sometimes associated with the notion of citizenship. In particular she believed that students needed to develop—one of her favorite expressions—a sense of the "public good." But a sense of the public good and a commitment thereto required first of all an ability and predisposition to identify with something larger than self. Such an ability and such a habit of mind had traditionally been cultivated through the study of history—through encountering "the whole of the experience of human beings." The goals of history and of preparing for effective citizenship were thus potentially overlapping if not quite identical. It so happened that the former could be taught directly, the latter indirectly. If effective citizenship was the desired end, the study of history was potentially the most effective means to it.

"I'll Be Damned If I Go In for Female Chauvinism"

It remains to be considered how—throughout her professional life—Hertzberg's words and deeds were affected by gender. Out of respect for Hertzberg, one almost hesitates to raise the question. She herself rarely called public attention to her sex, choosing to ground her professional identity in her roles as historian, teacher educator, teacher, and citizen. She fits in certain respects the profile of the generation described by Columbia English professor Marjorie Nicolson. In contrast to the first wave of feminists, Nicolson spoke of her peers as coming "late enough to escape the self-consciousness and belligerence of the pioneers, to take education and training for granted." Moreover, in contrast to a later generation, Hertzberg observed that she had also come early enough that she likewise "escaped . . . the engulfing domesticity of the 50s." She was, according to her son, always chiding her husband for alleged male chauvinism. But in fact he had always fully supported her career, and that as much as anything may explain why "she didn't have as much patience with feminism as she might have had" or choose to make her sex a public issue.

If she did not choose to call attention to her sex in public, however, Hertzberg's private correspondence reveals some willingness to acknowledge challenges associated with being a woman. Early in her position at Teachers College she confided to a female mentor and former Columbia professor that it was "a bit complicated to be the only female" in a sizable department of established males. Although she perceived herself as "no militant feminist," she was determined not to be the "shrinking violet type" either. On a number of occasions she revealed that she felt torn by the demands of "combining a commitment to excellence in one's job with a deep commitment to one's family." Her decision to have children in the first place meant that she was approaching forty before she launched a full-time, nondomestic career—a circumstance with obvious implications for her scholarly output.

Hertzberg's career may have been shaped by her gender, moreover, in ways that she herself was not aware of. If the contemporary literature of "difference" feminism is to be trusted, the fact that Hertzberg was female may help to explain, first of all, her routine references to building consensus and community and her concomitant disapproval of hierarchical relationships. The latter was a particular theme in Hertzberg's professional life, equality being at the heart of her understanding of democracy. In the planning stages of both the national curriculum commissions on which she served, Hertzberg called for the full and equal participation of classroom teachers along with educationists and professional historians. Too many times in the past, she believed, historians had handed down their thoughts to teachers "like Thanksgiving baskets left at the doors of the deserving poor." The fact that Hertzberg was a woman may be related, second, to her difficulty in compartmentalizing her personal and scholarly lives. Hertzberg did not limit her involvement with Native Americans, for instance, to conventional scholarly activity. Among other things, she served on the board of an Indian school, wrote of reservation life for the *New Republic* (edited at the time by her son), and routinely served as an advocate for Native American friends in education and government. Finally, Hertzberg's tendency to frame issues in concrete and personal—rather than abstract and impersonal—terms may be a reflection of gender. At the end of a disquisition on the need to preserve the democratic process and the role of educators in doing so, for instance, Hertzberg testified to thinking "of my little grandson and [wondering] what sort of future is in store for him."

If, as I have argued, gender was an important factor in shaping the course and character of Hertzberg's career, it is much more difficult to demonstrate how gender was expressed in Hertzberg's vision for the education of citizens. Hertzberg did not, for instance, to my knowledge, ever call explicitly for more attention to women in history texts for American schools. This in itself, however, is not insignificant, especially considering that Hertzberg was familiar with much of the emerging scholarship of women's history and interacted fairly regularly with historians who were women at Columbia and in the American Historical Association's Committee of Women Historians. If others around her were calling for, and working towards, a more inclusive curriculum, why did Hertzberg not join in, or express more enthusiasm for, their cause?

Although Hertzberg wrote relatively little on this subject, scattered comments may be pieced together to suggest two related responses. First of all, Hertzberg was cautious about promoting the study of any kind of "fragmented" history. As noted already in reference to the study of Native Americans, Hertzberg believed that the manner in which history was studied affected the way members of a society defined themselves in the present. Attention to the stories of particular social subgroups apart from an understanding of the larger social fabric represented, for Hertzberg, a potentially diminished ability to maintain any kind of collective social vision for the future. To the extent that women were portrayed in history as part of an organic cultural whole, as, for instance, in the curriculum she published for New York State history in the 1960s, Hertzberg obviously supported "inclusion." But all too often, Hertzberg believed, politicized efforts to include more attention to previously ignored groups led to material simply being "tacked on." "Women and minorities . . . make hasty entrances and exits and seem to be coming from another play." For Hertzberg it was less important, metaphorically speaking, that we all received equal speaking parts than that we remembered we were all part of the same play.

Hertzberg's failure to push harder for greater attention to women in the curriculum may also be explained in terms of her commitment to universal ideals. To the extent that one can separate the two, Hertzberg was more concerned for advancing human justice than for specifically redressing the grievances of women. "I think the women are greatly discriminated against," she wrote in 1963, "but I'll be damned if I go in for female chauvinism." For Hertzberg, the essential fact was not that she or any other member of her sex was a woman so much as they were members of the human race. It was this essential fact that led Hertzberg to state that while she wished to be a role model for her women students, she also wanted to be a model for her students who happened to be men. The "public good" that Hertzberg referred to throughout her life was not segmented into what was good for men and what was good for women, any more than it was divided into what was good for whites and what was good for blacks. For Hertzberg, at least, educating students to seek the public good involved, among other things, educating them to participate in a society where gender was not an issue.

◆

Several years after his mother's death, Hendrik Hertzberg tried to make sense of her life and career as a whole. He was initially stuck for an explanation of why his mother had traded an early life of direct social action for an apparently less socially relevant career in curriculum and instruction. Perhaps, he said, "she figured if she couldn't save the world, she could at least save the social studies." Whether Hazel Hertzberg ever literally attempted either, she obviously cared deeply about both. The words and deeds she left behind serve as one reminder that the two goals are not necessarily unrelated.

Writings of Hazel Whitman Hertzberg

Hazel Hertzberg, "The Challenge of Ethnic Studies," *Social Education*
36, no. 5 (May 1972): 469–70.

*The position of ethnic groups in our society is a matter of overriding national
concern and the public school is one of the major areas in which this concern is
expressed. The historical role of the school in furthering the development of a
democratic society and in creating a sense of national identity makes such a focus
on education appropriate and inevitable. No subject is more sensitive to these
roles than the social studies which deals with them most directly. The price we
have paid for the denigration or neglect of particular ethnicities has been high and
corrective measures are both necessary and welcome. We hope that this issue of*
Social Education *will help carry this salutary process further. Introducing the
study of new ethnic groups affords both an opportunity and a responsibility to
rethink the place of ethnicity in the social studies. For the gains we have made in
our concern with ethnicity have also brought problems. These the social studies
should help clarify rather than compound.*

*One source of confusion is the fact that the meaning of "ethnicity" is frequent-
ly unclear. It is part of a shifting group of related terms whose specific referents
change. For example, our society is often spoken of as "pluralistic," by which is
meant that it includes a wide variety of groups whose varying characteristics and
interests should be respected. Not so long ago, pluralism usually involved affirming mutual respect among religious communities: Protestants, Catholics and Jews.
Catholics, Jews and Negroes, as well as some other groups, were then considered
"minorities," by which was meant, in part, that they suffered from disabilities in
relation to the rest of the population. Today the term "minorities" has shifted
meaning and refers to non-whites almost exclusively. At the same time, pluralism
has acquired less a connotation of mutual respect and more a connotation of the
need for majority respect for minorities and for improving minority self images. In
addition, "ethnics"—whose forebears came primarily from southern and eastern
Europe and who were once classified as belonging to "minority" groups—have
recently been assigned to "Middle America," a term which when it surfaced two
years ago seemed to refer largely to people inhabiting Midwestern prairies and
small towns. . . . Women are not thought of as either ethnics or an ethnic group
but are quite often designated as a "minority." Thus, the focus of pluralism moves
around, highlighting some groups and shifting away from others.*

*What seems to remain fairly constant is an identification of those within its
range as having been hitherto unfairly dealt with, largely ignored, or poorly
understood, both in the schools and in society as a whole. As a consequence,
including such groups in the social studies curriculum is almost always thought*

of as compensatory. While the critique of the past curricular treatment of the group is usually sound, the tendency to overcompensate for past errors of omission and commission is not. The problems associated with this tendency deserve our earnest consideration.

First, it is widely but erroneously assumed that because people have been and are discriminated against that they are thereby free of prejudices of their own. Ethnic groups, like other associations of modern men, harbor prejudices, often directed against other ethnic groups and often with deep historic roots. If we emphasize the positive values of ethnicity without discussing its negative aspects, we not only render a considerable part of history quite incomprehensible but we leave our students unprepared to deal with group antagonisms. As we add ethnic groups to the curriculum, this problem will become more acute.

Second, ethnic groups are often portrayed as much more monolithic than they actually are. Class, locality, region, sex, occupation, age, education, and many other factors operate to create considerable differentiation within groups. To treat them as monoliths is not only unfair to their variety but may help to reinforce the dominance of one element by identifying the whole with one of its parts and assuming deviations therefrom as somehow heretical.

Third, ethnic groups are often presented as virtually time-free, unchanging entities which came into being in ages immemorial and have remained the same ever since. In point of fact, some are of quite recent invention, as when people whose primary loyalty was to a local community began to think of themselves as belonging to a "nationality" group because they were so regarded by the rest of society. . . .

Fourth, it is often implicitly assumed that an individual must belong to a particular ethnic group. Not only does this view ignore the tremendous amount of mixing that has taken place which may make it quite difficult for a person to choose among his varied ancestry even if he wants to, but it may reinforce the insecurities of individuals marginal to a group which often turn out to be most vociferously hostile to outsiders. . . .

The young are particularly vulnerable to these boiling hatreds and have in many cases played an active role in giving vent to them. As educators we should give serious thought to the possible consequences for our own society of a primary commitment to ethnicity without a sufficiently strong compensating commitment to national goals and ideals which can unite us. This is probably the most fateful question we will face in the coming decade and one to which we can, and must, find answers both more humane and viable than our present ones.

Notes

1. Detailed documentation for material throughout this essay is provided in the author's dissertation, "Clio's Uncertain Guardians: History Education at

Teachers College, Columbia University, 1906–1988" (Ph.D. diss., Columbia University, 1996).

2. Biographical material on Hertzberg is based primarily on Hazel Hertzberg Papers, Teachers College, Columbia University; and Hendrik Hertzberg, interviews by author, tape recordings, 24 August and 7 September 1994, New York, N.Y.

12

Courage, Conviction, and Social Education

Andra Makler

Where do ordinary people, steeped in lifelong experiences of humiliation, barred from acquisition of basic skills of citizenship—from running meetings to speaking in public—gain the courage, the self-confidence, and above all the hope to take action in their own behalf? What
are the structures of support, the resources, and the experiences that
generate the capacity and the inspiration to challenge "the way things
are" and imagine a different world?
                                    —Sara M. Evans and Harry C. Boyte,
          Free Spaces: The Sources of Democratic Change in America

Stories that lives tell to others do not always match the experience of
those who lived them: the life, the teller, and the tale are all instructive.
The civic and educational contributions of the women included in this
book, whose influence was felt, discussed, and widely acknowledged by
many of their contemporaries, are barely mentioned in standard historical accounts and sometimes are not visible at all. As social studies educators and curriculum theorists, we should be disturbed by this constructed marginalization, for it distorts the record and weakens the
narrative we present to our students. Recounting these women's contributions reminds us of the power in our voluntary association to pursue
shared interests. Though blocked from membership in lawmaking bodies, women joined with other women to effect social change and influence public policy on a wide swath of issues. These issues—franchise
reform, acculturation of immigrant families, cessation of discriminatory
practices, support for the validity of alternative viewpoints, and provi-
sion of a forum for voices silenced in more traditional meeting places—
represented responses to the complex social, political, economic, and ethical dilemmas associated with building an inclusive democratic society.
As these chapters show, women used voluntary associations (suffrage

253

groups, settlement houses, professional associations, committees) to fight for societal reforms, including affirmation of the political and civic rights of women.

This book is positioned alongside—I almost said in opposition to—the dominant discourse on citizenship education, which has emphasized participation through voting and teaching students the skills of public deliberation. To verify the historical and contemporary dominance of this discourse, we need only skim the chapters in Walter Parker's reader, *Educating the Democratic Mind*, or Ronald Evans and David Saxe's primer on issues-centered teaching.[1] For me, however, participation is not a skill. It is a way of being in the world, a way of seeing, of defining one's self in relation to others. For each woman discussed in these chapters, the choice to be herself in the public world was a deliberate moral choice, an ethical stance taken and held despite personal hardship, pain, and, frequently, public scorn.

Our Declaration of Independence notwithstanding, rights are not inalienable; they are socially constructed—especially the right to have our concerns taken into account legally and publicly—and only become meaningful when the political structure enforces sanctions for their abuse or withholding. Thus I see these chapters as raising some profound and rather troublesome questions about gendered identity formation and definitions of citizenship education that place learning to debate public issues and vote at the apex of social studies curriculum.

Perhaps, as the lives of these women trumpet, the central issue in education for democratic citizenship is the development of agency. This book asks us to consider how persons not welcome in the power structure, and females in particular, come to construct a sense of self that enables them to act as change agents in the public arena, given all the attendant consequences for their personal lives.

Civic Women and a Sense of Agency

In *Free Spaces*, Evans and Boyte ask, "What are the environments, the public spaces, in which ordinary people become participants . . . in governance rather than spectators or complainers, victims or accomplices?"[2] The women in this book provide significant answers to this question. Although they came from rather traditional family backgrounds and education, they persisted in following their own values. They achieved a stunning level of higher education. They sustained atypical marital relationships, chose other women for their lifelong companions, or remained unwed. Acting as females in the public arena, they did not mimic male values and often opposed male standards of behavior. At times, however, their resistance to gender norms flagged; like Bessie Pierce, all accommodated to certain conventions.

Each woman profiled here had sufficient imagination to fashion "public spaces in the community" where she was able to learn and display a "new self-respect, a deeper and more assertive group identity, public skills and values of cooperation and civic virtue."[3] I say they fashioned these free spaces because a settlement house kitchen, a college or elementary classroom, a walk around the neighborhood with four-year-olds, a dinner meeting, a small community focus group, the doorway of a caseworker's client, a national commission, were the venues in which these women worked. It required both imagination and skill to see these places as spaces of "relatively open and participatory character" that would support the "norms of egalitarian exchange, debate, dissent and openness" characteristic of free spaces.

As Boyte and Evans make clear, a free space exists first in a person's mind; that is, a person must first see a possibility to use a particular place or experience—such as a meeting with others—as an opportunity to further more participatory aims. In acquiring their own education the women in this book used school as such a free space. In their teaching, in classrooms and other settings, they connected a community of learners with the greater society outside.

Through community studies and social science research, Salmon, Addams, Taba, Wright, Beard, Hertzberg, Miel, and Pierce each worked to include the experience of excluded others as part of the curriculum, in order to gain insight and understanding and to extend participants' notion of the community to which all belonged.[4] Rachel DuBois reinvented the school assembly as an opportunity to bridge the social segregation of residence patterns and inform students about the cultural heritage and contributions of American citizens usually excluded from the school's curriculum. Although only DuBois and Taba explicitly named this educative work "intergroup relations," many of the women organized mutual learning through the egalitarian medium of face-to-face conversation rather than the hierarchical structure of formal parliamentary-style meetings or classroom lectures.

These women all exhibited significant leadership and management skills: Barnes in promoting and developing innovative materials and teaching approaches across the nation; Pierce as vice president and president of the National Council for the Social Studies (NCSS) and member of several national commissions; Beard in her efforts to establish a center for women's history; Addams in organizing and running Hull House, not to mention her efforts in the women's international peace movement; Miel and Hertzberg as chairs of university departments; DuBois as chair of the Intercultural Relations Board; Salmon in her suffrage organizing; Mitchell in starting and running Bank Street School; Miel, Taba, and Pierce in conducting large-scale evaluations or historical studies; Wright in her research for the legal brief that became *Brown,* her social work, and her development of Howard University's guidance department; Hertzberg in her state-level curriculum organization and participation in several national commissions.

Although the norm for women was to "be seen and not heard," they framed alternative choices and exercised them. Despite vestiges of a "cult of domesticity" that assigned the public sphere of commerce and politics to men and the private sphere of home to women, these women enacted the role of public intellectual. One thing we learn from the life histories of the sample of women included here is that women's roles over the last 150 years are not yet well enough understood to give a fully nuanced picture of how U.S. society worked across many social levels. For example, Marion Thompson Wright's life is a testament to her willpower and the support of her family system. A mother at sixteen, Wright returned to high school to complete her degree, a difficult achievement even today. She had to conceal her marriage, and her children, in order to remain a student at Howard University and then to retain her faculty post there; the awful nature of her choices is stunning. What promoted her sense of agency?

Addams, Beard, Taba, Salmon, Wright, and Miel pioneered new forms of research, asking new questions about segments of the community not studied by their colleagues. Addams and Wright used techniques of social service casework as a research methodology. This required creativity and daring, for as both Thomas Kuhn and Peter Novick have documented, the academic community is typically skeptical, even hostile, when old paradigms are challenged.[5]

These lives show us that although socialization to gender and class norms is undeniably salient, adults are not prisoners of their class and family circumstances. These women exercised free will; they acted on their convictions. By neglecting their work and their stories, we shortchange our sons and daughters by foreclosing their opportunities to wrestle with the complexities of the relationship between gender norms and the development of feelings of agency and competence for both sexes. One of the most potent promises of the American dream has been that here individuals can shape their own destinies. Historically that was not the reality for women as a group, nor has it been the experience for visible minorities as groups. However, perhaps it is the case that despite undeniable cruelty and hardship, our social system (if not our politics) has been relatively open to individuals equipped by temperament (and what else—training? the support of a key individual? religious faith?) to withstand terrible social pressures and personal pain.

Norms, Gender, and the Citizen Role

Expectations for fulfilling the role of citizen have always been differentiated by gender. In an essay on the history of citizenship, Chantal Mouffe exposes the inherent contradiction in the schoolbook notion that all adult citizens are equally citizens.[6] Western political theory in effect proposes a fiction: that all who participate in the category of citizen (and women were so regarded from the founding of our Republic) are "full and equal members of a democratic political community." The rub is in the second part of the definition—that is, that "their identity is shaped by the rights and obligations that define that community"—because the rights and obligations of female identity were not, and never have been, identical to those of male identity. Like Jefferson's claim that all men are created equal, this view of citizenship is hard to square with the historical record of discrimination.

Originally, the role of citizen was a secular role, giving a person a status beyond that of subject; it acknowledged the distinction between the military obligation and rights of a soldier and those of an ordinary citizen. This distinction clearly ignores women. Citizenship was a valued right because membership in a city or state carried specific protections not available to those classified as nonmembers or stateless.[7]

In her essay, Mouffe locates the roots of contemporary Western ideas about citizenship in the classical Greco-Roman concept of the self-governing political community where "to be a citizen was to be capable of governing and being governed"; citizenship, however, was restricted to the free native born (and rights and responsibilities were differentiated according to gender).[8] During the Roman Empire, citizenship categories were broadened to include members of the lower classes and some conquered foreigners, concurrent with a shift away from emphasis on "active participation in making and implementing law" to the idea of "equal protection under the law" as the core value of citizenship. In sixteenth-century Italy, Machiavelli's idea of civic humanism, which held that "human potential can be realized only if you are a citizen of a free and self-governing community," heightened the importance of being recognized as a citizen rather than just a resident of a country. In his social contract theory, Rousseau enhanced the concept of citizenship by linking self-governance to consent as the constituting basis of democratic society. That Rousseau's ideal citizen was a free, autonomous male is obvious, for citizens participated "in making decisions that all [were] required to obey," and, during this period, women were rarely allowed to make such decisions.

In their exploration of the history of democracy in the United States, Evans and Boyte note that through the seventeenth century, the term *citizenship* suggested "decision-making in religious congregations or the discussion of local affairs in voluntary groups."[9] Citizens joined together in the "arena of democracy" to form a government. Political engagement was seen as an expression of the values and activities of community life, not as an end in itself.

In nineteenth-century England and the United States, this image of persons linked by their common identity as citizens, with both conflicting and mutual interests in a shared community, gradually eroded. A new image, of private individuals with conflicting interests, emerged as the dominant model of the political community, with a concomitant emphasis on representative rather than direct democracy. Political scientist C. B. Macpherson likens the political system of the United States to a marketplace where "individuals choose among representatives based on their consumer promises."[10]

As the preceding chapters document, women had to express their citizenship and participate in civic life via alternate routes—and so they did. Their approaches were inclusive and valued face-to-face interaction. They worked to promote peace, to improve living conditions for immigrant families, to reduce prejudice, to affirm the important contributions to American life made by groups barred from the mainstream.

Carol Gilligan has made a strong case that including the perspectives of women introduces a heightened sense of moral responsibility, grounded not "on the primacy and universality of individual rights" but instead rooted in "a very strong sense of being responsible to the world."[11] The civic women in this book show a sense of responsibility to the world; each lived her own version of how to be a responsible citizen.

As with most normative social roles, our understanding of how to fulfill the role of citizen depends heavily upon who we are—our race, class, gender, age (and sometimes our religion), where we are, and what custom dictates. Role models can help us to find our way through, and sometimes around, the thicket of norms and expectations. The women in this book are such models. Each forged a path for herself. However, as Margaret Smith Crocco notes in the introductory chapter, these women are not presented as ideal types; there are significant differences of priority, perspective, and civic participation among them. Rather, their stories are presented to stimulate a broader and perhaps deeper understanding of the role of citizen, grounded in the contributions made by these women. Their lives provide alternative models of how to practice democratic living and education, while their work demonstrates a valuing of different forms of experience, participation, and leadership, of how to relate to others.

Their presence as figures who made an important contribution both to social life and social education would have made a difference to me when I was teaching high school social studies. Learning about their contributions has changed the way I teach others to teach social studies.

Gender and Discrimination

According to William Chafe, the history of women in the twentieth century is one of paradox and change.[12] Chafe's thesis is that attaining the franchise did not transform power relations or end sexism. Despite the rhetoric that by voting a citizen influences national policy and participates in (self-)governance, women more effectively achieved policy goals and substantive socioeconomic change through their work in voluntary associations. Civic women actively involved in sociopolitical reform and academic life during the Progressive Era and the period of the Cold War often experienced discrimination and prejudice because of their sex or race. (For the women in this book, class prejudice was muted because of their level of education and their relatively privileged family backgrounds. Wright and Taba are the notable exceptions here, and Wright's race and Taba's heavy accent were more salient markers than class.)

Given the active involvement in public life of the women included here, it is worth asking: What role did sexism and other forms of prejudice play in their life choices? How did these educated women, who also chose to be educators, reconcile their concerns for citizenship and the health of their society with their undeniably limited access to positions of power? We can discern something about their choices from their actions, but paradoxes remain. Beard and Salmon actively worked against gender discrimination; Pierce and Miel did not. Beard and Hertzberg publicly rejected the label "'feminist." As a black woman, Wright surely felt some pressure to "uplift the race" and improve the socioeconomic as well as the political status of her people; how did this influence her life choices? She worked with black female leaders like Mary McLeod Bethune and Lucy Diggs Slowe, but not with white feminists. Was white racism a factor in this choice? Each was a woman "teaching for change." How did the questions Kathleen Weiler poses in her book of that name play out in their lives?[13] How salient for them were the questions I have posed?

Taba first came to the United States from Eastern Europe between the two world wars. Bernard-Powers believes that although she had studied under both Dewey and Kilpatrick and held a Ph.D. from a prestigious American university, Taba clearly was denied a faculty appointment in her home country of Estonia because she was a woman. In this country, Taba was the point person for several large evaluation studies, and—like Alice Miel and Bessie Pierce, who engaged in similar research—she saw her male associates receive national recognition for this work without corresponding acknowledgment for her role as principal investigator. Perhaps because of her immigrant status, Taba was among the first (joining Addams, Wright, and DuBois) to recognize the significance of the conflicts that students experienced when the culture of the school was antagonistic to their home culture; it appears that her ideas were as important to the development of Tyler's famous "rationale" as Addams's views on the character of educational experience were to Dewey.

Although the women in this book were well educated, none—even those who earned Ph.D. degrees—was fully accepted into the academy. Their male colleagues did not enthusiastically support, nor even discuss, these women's academic contributions in their interactions with wider publics or in their own writings. Charles Beard is a notable exception; his difficulty in getting his wife's name listed next to his own as coauthor of their history books exemplifies the deep-rooted aversion to acknowledging the intellectual capabilities of women.

Subjectivity, Commitment, and Action

The emerging public recognition of a gendered citizenship education calls into question our continuing support of an idea of civic participation focused mainly on individual rights, public deliberation, and voting. Surely many male and female students find value in those civic activities (traditionally ascribed to women's sphere) that provide care, recognition, and support to the vulnerable and disadvantaged members of our communities.

The educational activities at Addams's Hull House sound shockingly like the reforms being touted in my state of Oregon as brand-new and "twenty-first century." They include recognition of the connections between education and life; encouraging real-world applications of academic, school-based knowledge; valuing the varied knowledge and skills brought into the community by immigrant families; and encouraging community service as part of the school curriculum. In some ways Addams's vision, and the vision of the civic women discussed in this book, is more radical than current reforms. Several of these women were vocal pacifists even while the United States was waging war. All worked against increasing centralization of power and knowledge. They supported forms of instruction and curriculum that were more inclusive than the mainstream of their times; indeed, Salmon, Barnes, Beard, Miel, DuBois, Wright, Taba, and Hertzberg developed materials that challenged dominant disciplinary and methodological paradigms. DuBois worked to reduce prejudice by affirming the positive value of diversity and the benefits of sustaining cultural differences among Americans. She maintained this focus at the cost of her job with the Intercultural Relations Board in New York; then as now policymakers feared that strong immigrant and minority cultures threaten social cohesion.

When Mary Sheldon Barnes developed her "object lessons," when Lucy Salmon engaged Vassar women in "doing" history, when Lucy Sprague Mitchell organized neighborhood walks for her preschool charges, when Marion Thompson Wright and Alice Miel investigated the impact of school segregation on children, the U.S. educational system, from preschool through graduate school, was less integrated and less diverse than it is today. Scholars working in the field of literacy education have clearly articulated the main challenge facing educators on the cusp of the twenty-first century:

> The question of difference has become a main one that we must now address as educators. And although numerous theories and practices have been developed as possible responses at the moment there seems to be particular anxiety about how to proceed.[14]

The women educators discussed in this book recognized this challenge as their own, but without the overlay of anxiety so characteristic of our response to diversity today. Further, their work, individually and collectively, offers models for us as we strive to convince students from all kinds of family backgrounds to value education even if their diplomas are no longer tightly coupled to economic and social advancement.

The vision of social education supported in this book is perspectival and is grounded in teaching practices that do not require students—or citizens—"to erase or leave behind different subjectivities."[15] This kind of social education is inclusive, values difference, and pushes beyond shallow empathy for those less favored by the structure of our economic system.

Reformers or Disrupters?

The line between reform and revolution is often blurred. Historian of education Herbert Kliebard characterizes the progressive movement as social meliorism aimed at improving the system rather than radically altering it.[16] It is worth considering the extent to which this categorization accurately depicts the behavior of the civic women in this book. Let us remember that nineteenth-century women were deemed biologically incapable of serious rational thought and critical thinking. They were socialized to defer to fathers, husbands, and older brothers; religious norms, social custom, law, and the education system prevented most from being independent and self-supporting. For a woman to assert herself publicly on a matter of politics, to question or criticize established policy, to depart from traditional teaching methods, or to challenge received academic certainties was a radical action that challenged the structure of social organization in far-reaching ways. It is true that of this group only Addams and Beard actively denounced capitalism or labeled U.S. policy as antidemocratic. However, the values supported by these women and their public and educational activities were more than meliorist; they disrupted cherished assumptions of male superiority and long-established social norms, professional conventions, and accepted practice in several spheres.

Realizing, as philosopher Jane Roland Martin says, that educated women were "bearers of disorder" helps us to understand the ire that provoked Vassar's president to label Salmon's work for woman suffrage "unsuitable behavior" for a Vassar professor.[17] Lucy Salmon circumvented college policy to organize the equivalent of a street demonstration for woman suffrage in the cemetery bordering Vassar College grounds. She also disrupted the norms of academe by investigating the history of domestic science and by using the daily newspaper as a source of credible historical and sociological information, in effect pioneering the field of social history well before its acceptance as an academic field.

Naming the educative and civic actions of these women as disruptive of the social order helps us to see the audacity of Addams's inclusion of immigrant women as equal partners in conversations at Hull House with prominent intellectuals like John Dewey; to recognize the intellectual daring Marion Thompson Wright displayed in using her case experience as a social worker as a model for her academic dissertation research; and to understand why Alice Miel's focus on small-group work to support the active construction of meaning among all students was not a viable political alternative to the academic elitism of the National Defense Education Act as a response to *Sputnik*.

The approaches of Rachel Davis DuBois and Hilda Taba to intercultural relations rejected the ideological framework that national solidarity during the Cold War required schools to downplay differences in order to assimilate members of disparate culture groups into a homogeneous whole. DuBois insisted that the curriculum should include study of immigrant and minority cultures because they were worth knowing about. She seems to have understood that a healthy pluralism was a necessary counterweight to increasing centralization of political power.

Hilda Taba recognized the importance of including minority groups and perspectives in the curriculum. Like Barnes, Salmon, Beard, Pierce, and Hertzberg, Taba believed that all students were capable of learning to think critically. She supported teaching students to distinguish fact from opinion and propaganda as a means to reduce prejudice; there is some evidence that Bessie Pierce also grounded her practice in this rationale. Rather than concentrating on the deficiencies in members of minority groups, Taba developed materials to address and change majority-group attitudes towards marginalized individuals and groups. She maintained that it was necessary to construct experiences for participants that engaged them emotionally as well as cognitively, prefiguring by several decades Banks's value-inquiry model.[18]

Although Banks's volume *Multicultural Education: Transformative Knowledge and Action* includes a chapter by Cherry McGee Banks on the contribution of the intercultural relations movement, his texts on teaching strategies, published between 1975 and 1997, do not note similarities between his model and Taba's.[19] Hilda Taba was most active in developing teaching materials in the 1950s and 1960s; the elementary school social studies textbooks that bear her name were published posthumously by collaborators.

In their models of social studies education, Banks and Taba focus on the importance of teaching students to make valid generalizations. Both strongly caution teachers that students' attitudes and beliefs must be examined as part of social studies curriculum. Certainly, Banks's work goes beyond Taba's; he speaks forcefully about the weakness of "developing empathy" for oppressed or marginalized individuals and groups and argues that recognition of oppression must be coupled with opportunities for students to take action to change unjust practices and situations. But Taba's broad definition of curriculum as "the total set of experiences into which schools direct pupils" provides a rationale for linking classroom learning to action in the greater community.[20] James Beane argues that we all stand "on the shoulders of giants."[21] The absence of attention to the writings and work of women educators impoverishes our sense of possibility and perpetuates the fiction that all giants are male.

The Personal and the Social in Education

Some scholars assert that women educators are relational and particular-istic in their approach to education. Jane Roland Martin writes that pro-fessional women face a special challenge: "to refuse to distance them-selves from the interests and needs of their students, patients, and clients" and to find ways "to link impersonal knowledge to action and abstract theory to concrete practice."[22] Independent thinkers themselves, these women instigated new teaching practices that show respect for, and trust in, their students' capacities and a valuing of personal, practical hands-on experience as educative.

Addams insisted that Hull House was a place for reciprocal exchange, not a place where immigrant women were shorn of their cultural heritage and shamed into modernizing and Americanizing. Although Barnes's source method was heavily laden with ethnocentric assumptions, it was innovative in its use of dialogue, open-ended questions, and the expecta-tion that (women) students could use primary sources to construct their own historical accounts. Years before the federally funded "new social studies" inquiry curricula of the 1960s, Salmon and Mitchell engaged their pupils in study of the social and economic world that was familiar to them as one way to become invested participants in their communities. Miel's ideas about the importance of gaining the social skills of coopera-tive learning prefigured much of the business community's current con-cern that students learn life skills as team players for the workplace.

Through her emphasis on guidance and counseling at Howard, Wright acknowledged the importance of educating the whole person. She also examined the quality of New Jersey's education from the perspective of black students and teachers within that system and worked with the Association for the Study of Negro Life and History to introduce black history into the schools. These endeavors recognized the special difficul-ties black women and black children faced in establishing a sense of self-worth and constructing a sense of confidence and competence in a domi-nant white culture that ignored their existence and their history in school curricula, mainstream advertising, and public policy.

Hazel Hertzberg also worked for inclusion of excluded groups in the curriculum, believing that a more inclusive story provided a more complete picture of our identity as a people and a nation. To assume that we could learn from Indians was radical for its time. Instead of idealizing Native Americans as noble savages, Hertzberg developed curriculum from an anthropological perspective that valued the traditional practices and worldview of New York's indigenous peoples. In treating Indian history and culture as subjects worthy of academic inquiry, Hertzberg's materials displaced traditional stereotypes with accurate information and presented students with an alternative vision of a meaningful life.

Of those included here, Barnes and Pierce exhibited attitudes towards inclusion that do not resonate well with current sensibilities. We all are products of our time. Barnes's acceptance of the view that immigrants required Americanizing to cleanse them of values and habits potentially dangerous to the health of the Republic certainly reflects the dominant perspective of her day. Pierce seems to have advocated for the professional objectivity she learned as a doctoral candidate in history in the high school classroom, maintaining that young people could be trusted to see for themselves that doctrines espoused by groups like the KKK were inimical to American values. Although Pierce's neutrality about such groups is puzzling and her lack of commentary about the difference in platform between, for example, the NAACP and the KKK is frustrating, her inclusion of a broad range of voluntary associations in her book—and her publication of the Lusk Laws in their entirety—shows that she was a strong advocate for freedom of expression, independent judgment, and the freedom to read perspectives that diverged from the mainstream.

For Dewey, society was a living dynamic; as the best form of associated living, democracy was an existential and ongoing project. Because Dewey believed in progress, he believed that education would enhance our individual capacities to improve the social life of the group and thereby also enhance our own quality of life. The women in this book lived these principles as their own.

Using Women's Lives as Sites for Theorizing

If the line between preaching and teaching often is thin, so is the line between hagiography and biography. Obviously, none of these chapters is a full-fledged biography. In my introduction I noted that life, teller, and tale are instructive; now I must acknowledge that listener and reader bring their purposes to bear in deriving meaning from life and tale.

In reading these chapters, I am struck by a thread of shared concerns— to include and value the experience of ordinary citizens alongside, not as a replacement for, the more traditional emphasis on military and political leaders, captains of industry, and inventors; and to respect the intellectual and moral capacity of learners. Salmon pioneered the use of newspapers as a source of valid research data, conducted research on devalued women's work, and encouraged her students to research the cultural life of their communities more than a hundred years before Elliot Wigginton conceived of the "foxfire method."[23] Miel's book *The Shortchanged Children of Suburbia* announced the then radical thesis that suburban children were impoverished by their lack of contact with the poor and minority students in the inner cities. Addams, Taba, and DuBois argued strongly that immigrants and persons from minority communities had something to teach mainstream Americans, even as they learned from the dominant culture; surely Wright also recognized this in her concern to affirm the validity of black children's history and culture.

The issue of pluralism and how to address it is part of all their work. All created strategies for recognizing and valuing lived experience, real life. They were realistic, pragmatic, and analytic: each was an innovator with either an implied or an explicit critique of the status quo. They enacted the role of the public intellectual in the face of their male colleagues' denial of their claim to that role. They all seem to have held a Deweyan perspective on the importance of associated living as core to democracy, rather than a focus on institutions and maintaining governance structures. Two threads are key: the recognition that people from every segment of society contributed significantly to the vitality of civic life in the United States, and the understanding that access to this rich variety of experience, through personal association, was a necessary part of everyone's education for democratic living.

The sample of women included here is small and lacks geographic, racial, cultural, and class diversity. These limitations are significant, but it is still worth asking how their work and ideas might make a difference to our conception of citizenship education. First, although gaining and exercising the right to vote may have been personally important to each of these women, this was not their primary focus. Barnes and Pierce excepted, their life histories demonstrate a pattern of concern about the general welfare of community members, not as an average or a statistical concept such as the mean, but in terms of improving the life chances, to use Max Weber's phrase, of particular individuals. In their teaching practices and curriculum materials, all—including Barnes and Pierce—demonstrate a belief that all young people (and by extension all citizens) have the capacity to think critically and make sound independent judgments. They encouraged their students to apply school learnings to the communities in which they lived and to believe that they could effect change. This rejection of reliance on traditional elites as the source of wisdom about matters of public policy is profoundly democratic.

As noted earlier, in their civic and educational roles, this group of women clearly displayed a sense of responsibility to the world and an interest in social change. Salmon, Addams, Beard, Wright, and Hertzberg all worked as community activists for part of their professional lives. A social welfare perspective was more clearly important to some; however, all supported social change (by working for suffrage, for peace, for integration of whites with blacks, for more face-to-face conversation among members of disparate communities, for use of social science research to improve social conditions for the disadvantaged). In fact, the stance of Addams, Miel, and Taba towards the use of research is remarkably similar to Paulo Freire's model of problem-posing to resolve real community problems.[24]

They showed respect for, and a willingness to learn from, those different from themselves and worked to help others achieve a sense of self-worth. Each supported the practical application of school learnings to their students' lives and recognized that "one size fits all" was not a sound basis for pedagogy or curriculum. Despite the call of progressive educators (e.g., Counts and Rugg) for the school to "change the social order," several questioned the reliance on K–12 schooling as the locus of reform and change in isolation from changes in the larger society.[25] They seem to have been committed to the idea that social change begins with an individual working within a local community. As a group, their life-work was issue centered, recognizing the importance of the world outside the school and the importance of education—at different levels—to forge connections across personal life, work, and school.

The ethical stance displayed in their work is not that of the detached, neutral observer, even though their research methodology fulfilled canonical criteria for objectivity and validity. They acted on their values in their occupational roles and infused these values into the curriculum materials they developed and the teaching practices they followed. They all refused to participate in institutional actions they deemed morally wrong. A few examples will suffice: Rachel Davis DuBois remained a pacifist despite school board pressure to support World War I openly, and she left her position on the Intercultural Relations Board rather than betray her conscience. Jane Addams suffered public scorn and opprobrium for her peace work. Mary Beard shunned the platform of a traditional academic career to sustain her critique of the academy's sexism.

Their work was perspectival, answering Michael Apple's curriculum question, Whose knowledge is of most worth? by widening the circle beyond the expected power brokers and the mainstream boundaries of their academic disciplines.[26] Each acted on her conscience. Indeed, Salmon, Addams, Beard, DuBois, Wright, and Miel (who was called to testify before McCarthy's House Committee on Un-American Activities because of her support for cooperative learning) risked public scorn and retribution from powerful critics when they acted on their principles. This strong sense of agency was, however, tempered by the recognition that strategically certain behaviors or public positions would not be effective. Thus, Pierce chose to work behind the scenes to include more women in positions of power at NCSS. There is no record that Marion Wright ever demanded public recognition for her role in *Brown,* although she did call for wider public attention to black women's contributions to civil rights.

Despite social norms meant to inhibit women from assuming visible public roles, each chose such a role for herself, causing us to ponder what enabled each of them to construct a sense of agency resilient enough to withstand and overcome disappointment, lack of public recognition, and discrimination. Gender discrimination was a factor in each of their lives. From my perspective as an outsider viewing the public record of their lives, I see Pierce and Hertzberg, who fiercely maintained that women could think as objectively as men, as seeking a solution to the dilemma of their gender by showing that women could do what men did and on men's terms. Lucy Salmon, Jane Addams, and Mary Beard, arguably the most intellectually gifted in this group, struggled publicly under the weight of this proposition. Marion Wright bore the brunt of both gender and racial discrimination; she foreshortened a distinguished career by taking her own life.

Changing the Focus

Two growing convictions emerged from my reading of this book, along with some questions. My first conviction is that we have a flawed picture of our history—of family systems, education, gender relationships, and women's place and work within our society—in short, of what life was like for large numbers of women (and, by extension, for those men associated with them). My second is that we ought no longer to support the primacy of citizenship education as the purpose of social studies.

How I want to be in relation to others in my personal as well as my communal life is a central question in democratic living. For several years now Nel Noddings and Jane Roland Martin (among others) have asked that we redesign curriculum to be more inclusive of the life trajectories, possibilities, and values of women and of students whose family heritage is other than pan-Protestant and white. Noddings has urged us to refocus social studies around personal and family relationships rather than attending only to the political sphere.[27] In her book *Schoolhome*, Martin explores similar themes; she also suggests that putting "the 3Cs, caring, concern, and connection" into the curriculum, as the goal or end of our teaching, might help to combat the downward slide into an ethic of consumerism, self-centeredness, and cynicism.[28]

George Herbert Mead developed a theory of social life that situates the development of individual identity within the social context of others' responses to ourselves. Mead used the terms "I-self" and "me-self" to discuss the two parts of our personality.[29] Lev Vygotsky's work in language acquisition supports Mead's assertion that the self develops in relationship to and with others, as does Noddings's theory that our moral development depends upon our evolving capacity to be both the one-caring and the one-cared-for.[30]

To reduce all of civic life to politics shortchanges our humanity and deprives young people of seeing the full range of opportunities to participate in community institutions beyond government councils. It breeds cynicism and disconnection instead of encouraging more communal feeling and connections that in turn motivate us to be more altruistic. When the focus on deliberation of public issues is reduced to a debate in which the object is to decimate the opposing side and win points for one's rhetorical skill, we are not teaching young people to listen with open minds and to seek points of agreement. When we present the public arena as a battle zone rather than a meeting place for listening to, and honoring the validity of, differing viewpoints, we create a construct of public life that excludes young women (and young men) whose cultural and family systems teach them not to raise their voices and socialize them to value consensus seeking and compromise for the benefit of the group. What might it be like instead to focus on construction of personal identity and social roles and include in the social studies curriculum more biography of people from all kinds of backgrounds, many cultural models of ways to live together peaceably, and fewer battles?

Dewey was both idealist and pragmatist. It is pragmatic to recognize that democracy requires constant renewal, from generation to generation; this task Dewey assigned to the school. To educate for democratic associated living means providing young people with lots of practice in the myriad tasks required to maintain, sustain, and nurture the continuing development of personally satisfying relationships in community with others.

Whether these tasks should be differentiated according to gender is precisely what requires our attention, along with figuring out how to support a richness of diversity within our social and biological communities.

We need alternatives. Women's biology and our economic system mean that some women will always be unable to participate fully in the public sphere because of their personal family ties and responsibilities. Visibly different minorities do not have access (yet) to resources and power on a scale that permits running and being elected to political office to be a realistic goal for large numbers. Many social ills cannot be fixed by government; they require investment at the local, neighborhood, and personal levels. Mentoring of the next generation, for example, requires a relationship between persons, not a trip to the ballot box. Our population is changing. Our understanding of equity, freedom, fairness, democracy, the public interest, the public good, and the commonweal must change as the social context in which we live changes.

None of my remarks should be construed as a rejection of the importance of voting or as a rejection of men and the public sphere of politics. Rather, they should be construed as a call to be more inclusive; to engage more citizens more fully in a broader range of community life; to prepare young people for participation in multiple forms of associative living—learning communities; voluntary social, occupational, religious, and other groups; as well as the political caucus, the policymaking forum, and the legislature. All types of voluntary associations can be forums for civic participation, including women's clubs and other nongovernmental organizations that serve specific political and social welfare agendas.

A Different Vision of Social Education

In conclusion, I would like to consider how social education might look were we seriously to draw upon the vision and work of the civic women included in this book. The life histories presented here show that these women constructed educational opportunities in many settings. Across the lifespan, from Lucy Sprague Mitchell's work with four-year-olds to Jane Addams's work with adult women immigrants, these educators asked their students to go out into the streets of the community, to explore and to research the way life was conducted. Several invited members of the community—from all walks of life—to engage with students in conversation about issues ranging from the philosophical to the practical.

I suspect that were we to build upon the work of these women as a foundation for social education, our emphasis would be on encouraging face-to-face conversation meaningful to the participants. This shift would require smaller classes. Conversation cannot be conducted with groups of thirty-five; it requires a feeling of personal comfort and intimacy and opportunities for participants to engage in sustained dialogue. In such settings, subjectivity might seem less threatening than moral neutrality. Participants might be more willing to state and explore their differing points of view. If the framing expectation for such conversation were that we could—indeed would—learn from each other, as Jane Addams insisted at Hull House, there would most likely be less pro forma consensus seeking, more arguing, and more agreeing to disagree. There would also be honest discussion of the difficulties of getting along with each other.

The premise on which the educational work of these women rested (in school, community study, and casework) was that of respect for learners or clients and a genuine desire to help them acquire information, skills, dispositions, habits, attitudes, and understandings. Rather than a curriculum organized around school subjects, relationships would provide the organizing focus: personal, social, community, political, economic, and international relationships. Given the life trajectories explored here, the following questions might be used to organize students' inquiry:

- Who am I?

- For whom do I care?

- What do I care about?

- What is life like for me, my family, and others?

- How did it get to be that way?

- What aspects of life seem good to me?

- What aspects of life seem cruel and unjust to me?

- What do I wish to change?

- How can I help to make things better?

- Who and what do I wish to become?

Although I cannot make the case that each of the civic women profiled took an intense personal interest in each of her students, I do find a pattern of caring that students be intellectually and emotionally engaged in studies and an expectation and hope that such study would bring personal satisfaction to the learner. The life histories suggest that they believed that learning and doing were intrinsically rewarding when personally satisfying; students' personal investment in their own learning was a high priority for them.

The object, or focus, of study would be current problems or issues of immediate concern to the participants in the community, with community defined by the participants. Historical research would of course be part of the study, as would realistic cost-benefit analysis and discussion of strategies for change. I suspect that economic, sociological, and cultural questions might move to the foreground, for each of these women well understood the meaning of trade-offs and opportunity costs and the power of norms. Ordinary people from places near and far would be as common in the curriculum as powerful elites. Women, their work, their contributions, their questions would be as visible in the curriculum as men. There would be less pretense that the "rational male actor" so dear to political philosophers and economists ever truly existed and more discussion of the consequences that follow from specific models and typologies.

The power of voluntary associations to achieve valued ends would be part of this study; these women all were critical of the status quo and worked for reform and change on many levels (of educational methods, curriculum, and their society). Several were openly critical of the ethos of competition embedded in capitalism; such critique would be aired. Along with a climate of support for the expression of different viewpoints and values, there would be far more controversy, for curriculum would portray an explicit moral stance. Learners would be expected to examine that stance and discuss it.

In contemporary U.S. society, life chances are still differentiated by class and gender, and there is strong cynicism that civic virtue ever was more than a rhetorical construct. If part of social studies is to educate to build and sustain democratic communities, issues related to resisting the tyranny of the majority are as important as building consensus; to the extent that these women represented minority viewpoints, advocated for unpopular values (e.g., pacifism during wartime), or criticized prevailing assumptions, this issue might move to the foreground.

Although cynicism is a debilitating condition no activist can afford, those who organize for social change must have accurate data about the structure of society and know well the agenda of those who wield power. A social education based on the work of these civic women would acknowledge pain, suffering, birth, joy, hard work, hope, and death as part of everyone's life experience.

A central task of this curriculum in social education would be to examine, construct, and refine a value system. I recognize that this would be controversial, but the lifework of these women proceeded from a moral stance. This is part of any developmental trajectory, and it ought not be ignored by the school. Given that students come from diverse backgrounds, discussion of moral and ethical codes might be intensely engaging to students.

Instead of spending days learning about wars, inquiry into peace would move to the foreground: study of periods of peace, of peacemaking and -keeping, of conflict resolution, and of why peace is so hard to attain and sustain. Several of these women were pacifists. I cannot imagine a curriculum grounded in their work that did not explicitly consider pacifism and the relationship between a person's ethical views, conscience, and actions. Democratic values would be studied, including issues of social justice, equity, inclusion, and the organization of government. There would be deliberate consideration of the consequences of holding particular values for one's choice of action and more discussion of the implications of permitting one's conscience to be one's guide.

Cultivation of voice would receive attention, along with self-expression in a range of forms, written and oral. Students would be outside the school, doing work in their communities to benefit others. They would study the role of voluntary organizations and churches, learn that nongovernmental organizations are powerful forces for change and education in many parts of the world, and ponder the reasons for this. Which conditions lead to the "full and equitable participation" that is prerequisite to continuing democratic association in a civil society would be an open question; students would be encouraged to consider their part in creating "working solutions" to this question as part of their adult responsibility to the world.

Many teachers and scholars have suggested infusing some of these elements into the social studies curriculum, but education for citizenship, rather than for associated democratic living, has remained the central task. This curriculum would have a different focus. It would take the reality of our different subjectivities as a central organizing proposition and engage students in the serious work of developing a sense of purpose in their lives, for as Maxine Greene notes, "Clearly, there is a connection between overcoming the silences and releasing persons—excluded, disqualified persons—to struggle into being, to become, to choose themselves."[31] In choosing to become themselves by struggling into being through education, the women profiled here also sought to bend the future to their will—a future shaped by their own vision of education, democracy, and citizenship.

Notes

1. Walter C. Parker, ed., *Educating the Democratic Mind* (Albany, N.Y., 1996); Ron Evans and David W. Saxe, *Handbook on Teaching Social Issues* (Washington, D.C., 1996).

2. Sara M. Evans and Harry C. Boyte, *Free Spaces: The Sources of Democratic Change in America* (Chicago, 1992), viii.

3. Evans and Boyte, *Free Spaces*, ix.

4. References to the women profiled in this book and their publications are drawn from the preceding chapters unless otherwise noted. These references are not cited because this chapter attempts to generalize across all the life histories here presented. Readers are asked to refer to the chapters specific to each woman.

5. Thomas Kuhn, *The Structure of Scientific Revolutions*, 2d ed. (Chicago, 1970); Peter Novick, *That Noble Dream: The "Objectivity" Question and the American Historical Association* (Cambridge, England, 1988).

6. Chantal Mouffe, "Citizenship," in *The Encyclopedia of Democracy*, ed. Seymour M. Lipset (Washington, D.C., 1995), 217–21, 217.

7. This was Philip Nolan's dilemma in *Man without a Country*. It also has been the historical experience of marginalized groups such as Jews in fifteenth-century Spain and sixteenth-century England, Native Americans from the ratification of the U.S. Constitution until they were granted citizenship in 1924, "displaced persons" from Eastern European countries that became part of the Soviet bloc at the end of World War II, Francophile Vietnamese nationals from the North who migrated to the South after the fall of Dien Bien Phu, and black political exiles from the Republic of South Africa in the 1960s.

8. This quotation and those that follow in this paragraph are from Mouffe, "Citizenship," 218.

9. All quotations in this section are from Evans and Boyte, *Free Spaces*, 11.

10. The quotations from C. B. Macpherson, *The Life and Times of Liberal Democracy* (Oxford, 1977) are drawn from Evans and Boyte, *Free Spaces*, 14.

11. Carol Gilligan, "Woman's Place in Man's Life Cycle," in *The Education Feminism Reader*, ed. Lynda Stone (New York, 1994), 26–41, 35.

12. See William H. Chafe, *The Paradox of Change: American Women in the Twentieth Century* (New York, 1991).

13. Kathleen Weiler, *Women Teaching for Change* (New York, 1988).

14. New London Group, "A Pedagogy of Multiliteracies: Designing Social Futures," *Harvard Educational Review* 66, no. 1 (Spring 1996): 66–73, 61.

15. New London Group, "Pedagogy of Multiliteracies," 72.

16. Herbert M. Kliebard, *The Struggle for the American Curriculum, 1893–1958* (New York, 1992).

17. Jane Roland Martin, "The Contradiction and the Challenge for the Educated Woman," in *Changing the Educational Landscape: Philosophy, Women, and Curriculum* (New York, 1994), 100–119, 108.

18. For a description of the value-inquiry model, see James Banks with Ambrose A. Clegg Jr., *Teaching Strategies for the Social Studies*, 4th ed. (New York, 1990), 435–45.

19. Cherry A. McGee Banks, "The Intergroup Education Movement," in *Multicultural Education, Transformative Knowledge, and Action: Historical and Contemporary Perspectives*, ed. James Banks (New York, 1996), 251–77; James A. Banks, *Teaching Strategies for Ethnic Studies* (Boston, 1997, 1991, 1987, 1984, 1979, 1975).

20. See Hilda Taba, *Curriculum Development: Theory and Practice* (New York, 1962).

21. James Beane, "On the Shoulders of Giants: The Case for Curriculum Integration," *Middle School Journal* 28, no. 1 (September 1996): 6–11.

22. Martin, "Contradiction and Challenge," 114.

23. Eliot Wigginton, *Sometimes a Shining Moment: A Foxfire Experience* (Garden City, N.Y., 1986).

24. For a description of Freire's approach, see Paulo Freire, *Education for Critical Consciousness* (New York, 1973); and Decker F. Walker and Jonas F. Soltis, *Curriculum and Aims*, 2d ed. (New York, 1992), 61–63.

25. George S. Counts sounded a clarion call for reform in *Dare the School Build a New Social Order?* (New York, 1932). Harold O. Rugg's textbooks include *Our Country, Our People: An Introduction to American Civilization* (Boston, 1938); and *An Introduction to Problems of American Culture* (Boston, 1931). See Kliebard, *Struggle for the American Curriculum*, 202–8 for a discussion of the junior high school texts Rugg published; they were critical of the capitalist system and presented history from the perspective of disadvantaged and conquered peoples. The Teachers College Library has a full set of Rugg's textbooks and pamphlets.

26. Michael W. Apple, *Ideology and Curriculum* (Boston, 1981).

27. See, e.g., Nel Noddings, "The Gender Issue," *Educational Leadership* 49, no. 4 (December 1991/January 1992): 65–70; and Nel Noddings, *The Challenge to Care in Schools* (New York, 1992). See also Nel Noddings, *Caring: A Feminine Approach to Ethics and Moral Education* (Berkeley and Los Angeles, 1984).

28. Jane Roland Martin, *The Schoolhome: Rethinking Schools for Changing Families* (Cambridge, Mass., 1992); and Jane Roland Martin, "One Woman's Odyssey: To Philosophy and Back Again," in *Changing the Educational Landscape: Philosophy, Women, and Curriculum* (New York, 1994), 1–32, 25.

29. George Herbert Mead, *Mind, Self, and Society from the Standpoint of a Social Behaviorist* (Chicago, 1934).

30. Lev S. Vygotsky, *Thought and Language* (Cambridge, Mass., 1962).

31. Maxine Greene, "Plurality, Diversity, and the Public Space," in *Can Democracy Be Taught?* ed. Andrew Oldenquist (Bloomington, Ind., 1996), 27–44, 36.

Index

academic freedom, 157

Adams, Charles Kendall, 25

Addams, Jane, 2, 12, 13, 73–88, 256; on citizenship, 86; on citizenship education, 80; and civic participation, 260–61; on class barriers, 82; conflict model of society, 83, 84; cooperative society, 83, 84; cultural feminism of, 84–86; on democracy, 74–75, 86–87; *Democracy and Social Ethics*, 76, 79, 87–88; on democracy education, 86–88; on equality, 80–81, 86; on focus of education, 74; gender issues, 74, 82; Hull House, 13, 74, 77, 83; *Hull House Maps and Papers*, 83; on immigration and immigrant problems, 77–79; and labor unions, 82, 83–84; and Marxism, 82–83; and Mitchell, 128; *Newer Ideals of Peace*, 76; and nonviolence, 82–83, 85; pacifism of, 13, 85; philosophy of social justice, 82; on pluralism, 79, 80–81, 86; relationship of personal and social in education, 264; on rights, 74, 75, 76–77, 86; on social democracy, 74, 85–86; and social order, 262; on social relationships, 75–76, 86; social theories influencing, 82; and suffrage movement, 79–81; theory of education, 13; treatment of, in educational literature, 2, 3; *Twenty Years at Hull House*, 83; on value of life experience in education, 266; and work-ing class, 82–84. *See also* liberal democracy

African American education, 100, 110–11; *The Education of the Negro prior to 1861*, 97; *The Mis-education of the Negro*, 97; Carter G. Woodson, 97; Wright, 109

African American history, 97; ASNLH, 97; Merle Curti, 98, 109–10; DuBois, 170; *The Education of the Negro prior to 1861*, 97; Miel, 221–22; *The Mis-education of the Negro*, 97; Woodson, Carter G., 97

AHA (American Historical Association): Pierce, 153–56, 160–63; Salmon, 51–52, 61; and social studies, 160–62

Americanization: Addams on, 78; and ASNLH, 3, 97, 109; assembly programs, 170, 173, 174, 175–76, 181–82; ideology of, 77–78

Americans All—Immigrants All (DuBois) (national radio project), 177–78

Association for the Study of Negro Life and History. *See* ASNLH

Bank Street College of Education, 2, 14, 126, 139–41; curriculum development, 140; goals of, 140

Bank Street School. *See* Bank Street College of Education

Barnes, Mary Sheldon, 2, 12, 17–41, 255; on American type, 34; biases, 32–33, 34–35, 38–39; career, 26–31; childhood and education, 20–21,

About the Contributors

JANE BERNARD-POWERS is associate professor of elementary education at San Francisco State University. Her writing and work have dealt with social studies education in relation to feminism and gender issues, and women's education history with a special focus on the Progressive Era. Her publications include The "Girl Question": Vocational Education for Young Women in the Progressive Era (1992) and numerous journal articles.

CHARA HAUESSLER BOHAN received her doctorate in curriculum and instruction from the University of Texas at Austin. She earned a B.A. in history from Cornell University and an M.A. in social studies education from Teachers College, Columbia University. She has taught history, government, and geography at the Horace Mann School in New York City and at William B. Travis High School in Austin. Currently, she supervises and instructs secondary student teachers in social studies at the University of Texas at Austin; her dissertation was on Lucy Maynard Salmon.

MARGARET SMITH CROCCO is associate professor of social studies education at Teachers College, Columbia University. She has an A.B. from Georgetown University and an M.A. and a Ph.D. from the University of Pennsylvania. Her research interests include social studies education, diversity, and women's history. She has published Pedagogies of Resistance: Women Educator Activists, 1880–1960 (1999) with Petra Munro and Kathleen Weiler.

O. L. DAVIS JR., professor of curriculum and instruction, University of Texas at Austin, has served as president of the Association for Supervision and Curriculum Development; Kappa Delta Pi, international honor society in education; Society of Curriculum History; and the American Association for Teaching and Curriculum. He received the first Citation for Exemplary Research in Social Studies Education awarded by the National Council for the Social Studies (NCSS), was named a laureate by Kappa Delta Pi, and received the Distinguished Career Research in Social

Studies Education Award from NCSS and the Lifetime Achievement Award for Outstanding Contributions to Curriculum Studies from the American Educational Research Association.

SHERRY L. FIELD is associate professor of social science education at the University of Georgia. She is editor of *Social Studies and the Young Learner*, a member of the Executive Board of the College and University Faculty Assembly, past chair of the American Education Research Association's Research in Social Studies Special Interest Group (SIG) and Text and Textbooks SIG. She is past president of the Society for the Study of Curriculum History and serves on the advisory boards of the Harvard Children's Democracy Project and the American Promise curriculum project. Her research interests include foundations and history of social studies, children's acquisition of social studies concepts, and use and development of curriculum materials.

ANDREW MULLEN, as a Canadian and resident alien in the United States since childhood, has always had a practical interest in citizenship and in what it means to be (or not to be) an American. He studied European history at Houghton College and elementary education at Colorado College. He has taught elementary-age students in a number of settings, including residential environmental education centers in New York and North Carolina, an inner-city public school in Colorado, and an independent school in Kentucky. He received his Ph.D. in 1996 from Columbia University, where he studied social studies curriculum and the history of American education. Currently, he is assistant professor of education at the University of Maine at Machias.

FRANCES E. MONTEVERDE received her bachelor's degree from Indiana University of Pennsylvania and her master's degree from the University of Alabama, Tuscaloosa. She studied Latin American history at the University of New Mexico and taught social studies at an Albuquerque public high school. For more than twenty years she lived in Mexico City, where she served as teacher, social studies department chair, and administrator at the American School Foundation, A.C. She earned her doctorate in curriculum and instruction at the University of Texas at Austin in 1996. She was an assistant professor in the Department of Education at Hanover College, Indiana, from 1996 to 1999. She is now an independent scholar whose research focuses on critical thinking, social studies education, treatment of foreign cultures in U.S. schoolbooks, teacher education, and the life of Mary Sheldon Barnes.

ANDRA MAKLER is an associate professor of education and chair of the Department of Teacher Education at Lewis and Clark College. She is particularly interested in the ways teachers represent their knowledge through curriculum. She has written a life-history curriculum for use in middle and high school U.S. history courses and is working with teachers on a book about the many ways they teach about justice.

PETRA MUNRO is associate professor of education and women's and gender studies at Louisiana State University. Her research interests focus on the narrative analysis of curriculum history, women's life histories, and the discourses of qualitative methodology. She is a coauthor of *Repositioning Feminism and Education: Perspectives on Educating for Social Change* (1995) and author of *Subject to Fiction: Women Teachers' Life History Narratives and the Cultural Politics of Resistance* (1998). At the moment, she is completing her book "Engendering Curriculum History."

MURRY R. NELSON is professor of education and American studies at Pennsylvania State University. He has been a Senior Fulbright Lecturer at the University of Iceland and a Fulbright Roving Scholar of American Studies with Radet for Videregaende Opplaering of the Royal Norwegian Ministry of Church and Education. He is the author of more than 150 scholarly articles and has authored or edited seven books and monographs, including *Children and Social Studies* (1987, 1992, 1998), *The Future of the Social Studies* (1994), and *The Social Studies in Secondary Education, a Reprint of the 1916 Seminal Report with Annotations and Commentary* (1994). He is past president of the Pennsylvania Council for the Social Studies, the Society for the Study of Curriculum History, and the College and University Faculty Assembly of the National Council for the Social Studies, on whose Board of Directors he currently serves.

ELIZABETH ANNE YEAGER is assistant professor of social studies education at the University of Florida. While a doctoral student at the University of Texas at Austin from 1992 to 1995, she completed her dissertation on Alice Miel while holding a doctoral research fellowship from the Spencer Foundation/American Educational Research Association (AERA). She received the Outstanding Dissertation Award in the area of curriculum from the Association of Supervision and Curriculum Development, the AERA (Division B), and the Society for the Study of Curriculum History; she was also a finalist for the National Council for the Social Studies Outstanding Dissertation Award. Her work on Alice Miel has been published in *Theory and Research in Social Education* and the *Journal of Curriculum and Supervision*.